More Praise for

UN-AMERICAN ACTIVITIES

"Witty and tremendous fun to read ... Belfrage turns a skeptical and perceptive eye on both the sunny surface and the ugly underside of the '50s." —Tessa DeCarlo, *San Francisco Chronicle*

"A life so rich in incongruity that it breaks the analytic bonds of conventional autobiography." —Carol Brightman, *The Nation*

"Sally Belfrage's memoir is as radiant as her own self. Aside from being a deeply moving remembrance of a lousy time past, it's a very funny book and goes like a house on fire."

—Studs Terkel

"Moving, often funny, often hair-raising ... fascinating as a memoir of its era." —Brooke Allen, *Wall Street Journal*

"[A] richly drawn memoir...shaped by the political dramas of the 1950s—particularly by the author's childhood embarrassment that the radicals who were being publicly reviled were the friends she had always known and loved—its emotional force lies in the family drama."

—Elinor Langer, *New York Times Book Review*

"Sally Belfrage's memoir of the McCarthy era evokes to perfection the contradictions and oddities of those bizarre witch-hunt years. Daughter of a prominent radical, doomed aspirant to conformity, she recreates her passage from puzzled child to more knowing teenager to mature woman with uncanny vividness and matchless wit. *Un-American Activities* is funny, affecting, and utterly winning." —Jessica Mitford

"The ultimate misfit . . . looks back on it all with caustic amusement and a pitch-perfect ear for the clichés that defined the all-American girl she was striving to become."

—Christopher Lehmann-Haupt, *New York Times*

"Sally Belfrage's beautiful memoir is heart-rending, hilarious, and as roller-coasterish as the decade she has forever captured."

—Victor Navasky

"[An] arresting, unappeased vision . . . Belfrage's partly comic, highly painful and ultimately unreconciled memoir. . . is about something deeper and more destructive than the troubles of a family singled out by McCarthyist oppression. The awfulness was internal." —*Los Angeles Times Book Review*

"*Un-American Activities* reads as though the protagonists of Janet Hobhouse's *The Furies* and Salinger's *The Catcher in the Rye* had parents who were hunted down by the FBI, jailed, left jobless and deported. Belfrage superbly combines the hard facts of the House Un-American Activities Committee with the haunting inner voyage of one special adolescent girl coming of age on her own." —Barbara Probst Solomon

"No one studies a culture with more intensity than someone who has her nose pressed against the glass. . . . Belfrage's take on the conformism of the period is accurate and devastating." —Joyce Johnson, *Washington Post Book World*

"This is a moving and distinctive memoir: a one-of-a-kind life set down against an all-American 'interesting' time and described in a voice that is at once smart, funny, and vivid." —Vivian Gornick

"Fascinating and irresistible. Sally Belfrage has captured the passions of a shameful era, and the figures in her landscape are as entertaining as your own intimates. Her book is enormously moving as well as witty, and those who remember the 1950s will admire her brilliant recreation of the decade, while young readers will be excited to explore territory which has been off limits for so long." —Nora Sayre

"Compelling." —*Vanity Fair*

"In this wry and poignant memoir, Belfrage shows how growing up in the conformist 1950s for her inextricably mixed the personal and the political." —*Publishers Weekly* (starred review)

"A roller coaster memory ride through the McCarthy era." —*Kirkus Reviews*

UN-AMERICAN ACTIVITIES

A MEMOIR OF THE FIFTIES

SALLY BELFRAGE

HarperPerennial

A Division of HarperCollins*Publishers*

For Nick and Anne

A hardcover edition of this book was published in 1994 by HarperCollins Publishers.

UN-AMERICAN ACTIVITIES. Copyright © 1994 by Sally Belfrage. All rights reserved. Printed in the United States of America. No part of this book may be used or reproduced in any manner whatsoever without written permission except in the case of brief quotations embodied in critical articles and reviews. For information address HarperCollins Publishers, Inc., 10 East 53rd Street, New York, NY 10022.

HarperCollins books may be purchased for educational, business, or sales promotional use. For information please write: Special Markets Department, HarperCollins Publishers, Inc., 10 East 53rd Street, New York, NY 10022.

First HarperPerennial edition published 1995.

The Library of Congress has catalogued the hardcover edition as follows:

Belfrage, Sally.
    Un-American activities / Sally Belfrage.
        p.   cm.
    ISBN 0-06-019000-0
    1. Anti-Communist movements—United States—History—20th century. 2. Radicalism—United States—History—20th century.
    3. Belfrage, Sally. 1936– —Childhood and youth. 4. New York (N.Y.)
    —Biography. I. Title.
    E743.5.B363   1994
    974.7´043—dc20   93-45827

ISBN 0-06-092626-0 (pbk.)

95 96 97 98 99 ❖/RRD 10 9 8 7 6 5 4 3 2 1

Contents

She looked as if she were telling the truth, though with women, especially blue-eyed women, that doesn't always mean anything.

—DASHIELL HAMMETT

PROLOGUE

I'd put it this way: happy memories are all alike—they fade into a pleasant blur; miserable memories stay distinct forever. Maybe that's why so many people claim to have had an awful childhood, while the actual children that you see look generally content enough . . . yet all the while, they are collecting evidence for what will turn into their *bitter past*, gathering recollections that will cling to them like burrs.

When I was a child I wanted to be famous; by adolescence I yearned to be invisible. In the fifties it was every American's duty to lie low and blend in, but other people seemed to have so much less trouble at it. Wherever I looked for cover there were minefields and boobytraps. My parents were foreigners and got married a lot, they went in for weird food and funny clothes, they were always moving. My mother was a mere English eccentric, but my father was a Red and so in trouble all the time, if not in jail. The phone was tapped from the minute I could talk on it, and the FBI had been at the door since I was tall enough to turn the knob. Our name was unique and unmistakable, therefore everybody knew. And even in white Anglo-Saxon Protestant America, wherever we went we were just about the only white Protestants, and atheists to boot.

Worst of all, my parents didn't care what other people thought of them. They were indifferent to the insult their behavior represented to *real* Americans. Their style of life was almost deliberately provocative. For a while I went to school with the offspring of immigrant Italian railroad workers—try telling them my father was running interference for them and their economic rights. They hated everything he stood for. Anyway, their economics were in a lot better shape than ours. My father was so foreign he didn't even know what "running interference" meant. What's more, he didn't give a damn. He despised the popular enthusiasms almost as much as he despised money. He dared to prefer ideas over things at a time when the whole country was rising up against ideas and the worst insult that was still considered polite was "egghead."

The "McCarthy era," misnamed for a senator from Wisconsin, made havoc for its victims: people lost their jobs, friends, homes, lives. My family lost our country. To a child growing up at the wrong end of it all—being taught at school the marvelous platitudes of American custom and constitution, and then going home to the realities of police power, living among people who were constantly afraid that this precious day might be their last tranquil one—there were three choices: accept one version, accept the other, or take on both and split in two. Schizophrenia can be kid stuff if you learn it as a kid.

"McCarthyism" didn't begin or end with the senator; he was only, in the early fifties, its loudest mouth. That particular time also corresponds with the time when the worst trouble hit my family—but why it hit and who we were needs to be explained first.

Once upon a time, when my parents were young in London working for Lord Beaverbrook on the *Daily Express*—he as a film and drama critic, she with her women's page headed "MOLLY CASTLE"—they had been the ones to make the style, so why should they follow anyone else's now? When my father wore a soft collar to a first night, Noel Coward confronted him in the interval to say, "You are a cad, sir!" But soon everybody was wearing soft collars. My mother was First Woman of Fleet Street, telling other women what to see and hear and think. Even her name was a construct— Molly a nickname for Mary, Castle her first husband's surname, so much nicer than her own Pigott. Her beautiful image was displayed from this end of Britain to that, her example as independent working woman a model for many. What did she care two decades later if some railroad workers' kids thought she was cracked?

As if they owed it to their public, my parents celebrated their feelings for each other time and again, he in two autobiographies and she in four novels—one about finding him, one about catching him, two about losing him. In *This Is Where We Came In,* she describes their wedding night:

It was midnight. In the distance Big Ben tolled out twelve booming strokes. Down all the streets the newsboys came running with their extras. Their voices sounded near or far, but they all had the same refrain:

death of the king
DEATH OF THE KING
Death of the King
DEATH OF THE KING
DEATH death Death death DEATH!

[She] presently fell asleep to the sound of this strange, repetitive chant: a macabre wedding march.

It was her idea that they would never part. Often in her novels, the two of them are to be found talking like this: "Darling, something tells me that we were meant to grow old together, a funny old couple from whom our children have long ago turned to their own future." In another

novel, written thirty years later, he is still her main concern:
"Without [him], and the feeling of infinity that I've invested
in him, life simply means nothing to me."

As for him, "To express how certain I now was about
her," he wrote in *Away from It All,* "I could say that there
had never before been any certainty of anything in my life."
In *They All Hold Swords,* he amplified:

> She was English, and of precisely my own class background;
> and I had long since rejected the possibility of anything
> worth while turning up in that quarter. It occurred to me
> once with something of a shock, when we were spending a
> Sunday together in the country, that she was exactly the
> kind of girl my parents would approve of my marrying: an
> extraordinary fact suggesting that they were really wiser
> than I had given them credit for being.

At the end of their public romance, which enchanted the
millions, they sailed off into the sunrise—for they traveled
east—on a global honeymoon. It included a visit to the
Soviet Union. That did it. Together they saw selected bits of
the future that worked. Enthusiasm swept him away; she
followed happily after.

My mother was in truth rather less concerned with systems and ideologies than with her own internal affairs, for
she was pregnant with me. "They had crossed the 180th
parallel," she wrote, "which brought them suddenly from
the extreme right of the map to the extreme left. That will
make a difference to the date on which Fred is born, maybe
[she thought]." "Fred" was me, named for a victim of one
of Hilaire Belloc's *Cautionary Tales:* "When Help arrived,
among the dead/Were Cousin Mary, Little Fred."

Their journey, chronicled in his articles and her column
and then later in their separate books, ended in Los Angeles
when I was born on the corner of Hollywood and Vine.
Even this event was presented to the public in two versions:
hers in the column, his in a book. He was allowed to attend

the labor and birth—unheard of at the time—and *What Happened to Fred* was published widely and later anthologized in volumes such as *The Best of Fun in Bed*. They appointed Myrna Loy godmother. There were no ceremonies, but she gave me an engraved spoon and pusher, in a basket with six bottles of champagne.

A quarter of the world's people in a quarter of the world's land were still ruled from London; my father wanted no part of his imperial inheritance. In the two months following Fred's birth, Franco became chief of state of reactionary Spain. In Britain, there was far more fuss about Edward VIII's affair with Mrs. Simpson than over Oswald Mosley's first anti-Jewish march in the East End of London, or the siege of Madrid, or the new German-Japanese Anti-Comintern Pact. But to my father, everything was a portent of a cataclysm that would lead to the last throes of capitalism. He decided to stay in the sun.

Molly and Cedric loved each other, agreed on the state of the world and what they desired for it, and joined the Communist Party to bring it about. They quit after three months, but kept their radical friends and collected money for the Spanish Loyalists in the fight against Franco and fascism. On the proceeds of my father's first book, they built an art deco house off Laurel Canyon in a spot so remote they were able to think up their own address: 7777 Firenze Avenue. All around in the hilly wilderness there was not another structure to be seen. They made an English garden with flowers and fruit trees and me, naked in the sunshine with puppies and kittens in a "playpen carpeted with grass, shaded with mimosa," as my mother wrote. A maid I called Yaya looked after me and the house while Mummy and Daddy typed their books upstairs. Yaya even visited England with us. Pushing my pram in her white uniform, she drew crowds; my cousins, stunned by the sight, hid under the tea-table and examined her sheets the next morning to see if the blackness of her skin rubbed off. (The world was larger then, or more composed of strangers. In her memoirs,

Patricia Cockburn describes how at around the same time a group of pygmies in Central Africa came from miles around to see her brush her waist-length hair.)

Something terrible was boiling up in Europe. Fascists were bombing civilians in Spain; my parents heard there were plans to evacuate London schoolchildren to the countryside. But we returned to paradise, sun, and singing. Photos show that the fruit trees in the garden had spread their spindly branches as high as the house by then, and the lawn was positively English. Those who came to tea included movie stars and at least five of the future Hollywood Ten. I went to Shirley Temple's birthday party. She was much older than I, but the studio lied about her age. At least I knew who she was, a lot more than I knew about the other big names who brought presents and always seemed to come accompanied by flash bulbs. My parents took me on their walks up and down the green deserted hills, which stretched in all directions from our house; I rode on Daddy's shoulders. We were perfectly happy.

Then came my brother and the Second World War. Nicky made noise and got everyone to feed him all the time, but he had a few nice points. The war had nothing to recommend it. It broke childhood into millions of pieces. But for a child, the war was life; there was no life without the war. And this war was tailor-made for all my father's weak spots: it was up to him to do something about it. He joined up to be a British agent. We were on the move.

We were not only always moving but always in a hurry. You couldn't say good-bye or take things with you. They put the furniture in storage and we caught the train. The Atchison, Topeka and the Santa Fe to Chicago, the Twentieth Century Limited to New York. We had traipsed across the continent in those trains before, but at least we'd come back. Not this time. Daddy went to work from 9 to 5 in the spy office at Rockefeller Center, behind the Atlas man holding the world on his shoulders. We lived in a cramped apartment in Riverdale with no outdoors, and no money. He didn't care and she had to put up with it. Yaya went to

work in a munitions factory. Mummy tried to get jobs on
magazines. She was employed for a while doing publicity
for Gertrude Lawrence, but I gave Mummy chicken pox
and Mummy gave it to Gertrude. Mummy was fired.

She stayed home, mad with boredom. "Somehow she
had got sidetracked into a woman's world, a housewife's
world, and she hated it," she wrote in her third novel about
her life with my father. "Nobody who led a full, stimulating, working kind of life could imagine how hateful and
drab it was." It was the first time she had ever been without
a servant. Arguing with her fictional husband, who is com-
plaining about commuting, she says: "It isn't much fun
doing all the housework either, and carrying home the mar-
keting and taking [Nicky] in that hellish playground with
all those dreary women." Asking herself, "And what have
you been doing these last two years?" her character
answers:

"Well, aside from a little light war work I've pushed a lot of
swings and I've swept a lot of dust under sofas, and run up
some nifty little numbers on my sewing machine, carried
home many string bags full of food because they don't
deliver these days, and I've kept a careful budget which
never balanced, and almost always burned the string beans,
and sometimes I've tried taking a book out in the playground but some other mother would always remark 'Reading a *book*, Mrs. Harrigan?' and then go on to tell me all
about her junior's teething problems."

And, summing up the effect of it all:

"It's been a charming experience and I've hated every second
of it, especially all the seconds I've wasted telling myself
how happy I was, how much in love with my husband, what
a success I was making of being a wife. It's been the most
horrible two years of my life but I wish they could go on,
without changing, for ever and ever. I'm so scared to
change."

I was sent across the street to P.S. 81, which was a terrible comedown from life in the sun. They kept skipping me ahead, which was supposed to be a good idea, but it meant always barging in on people who already knew what they were doing and what to believe. Apparently my father was the only one who had any fun. Years later, when he was made to register under the Internal Security Act of 1950 for being a "Person having Knowledge of or Trained in Espionage or Related Activities," as a former employee of "the New York office of His Britannic Majesty's Government British Security Co-Ordination," he answered questions for J. Edgar Hoover (at any rate the answers were sent to Hoover) about his training and duties:

> Co-ordination of intelligence reports from British field agents in the Americas, from mail censorship in Bermuda and Trinidad, from O.S.S. and F.B.I. standard security procedures. Methods of mail censorship. Liaison (2-way information exchange) with U.S. intelligence agencies. Gathering of political intelligence. Surveillance and precautions against it. Codes; Unarmed warfare; Methods of building an intelligence organization in a foreign country; Demolitions; Use of revolver; Bribery.

But this was not enough for him; he thought he ought to do more, head for the action overseas. He left for Europe in 1943 to work as a British civilian attached to the U.S. Army, and after a period in London and Paris in the Psychological Warfare Division he ended up in occupied Germany recruiting anti-Nazi journalists to staff the newspapers in the American zone.

Other people's fathers were coming home; we didn't see ours for two years. We were parked upstate at Croton-on-Hudson on a prerevolutionary farm. There, my mother had beautiful scenery for consolation, and a maid again, Dilsey Lee, for the drudgery she hated so much. There was less money than ever, though she managed to earn our keep working for magazines and radio shows in the city.

So much moving ends up fracturing memory into space more than time. Everything that happened in one place seems later to have become both telescoped and blurred, in no special order. What you remember is where, not when: the places fix the events. How do people who stay put have memories? What do they attach them to?

Horace Greeley had lived on Finney Farm, it was said, and Mabel Dodge Luhan; Eric Knight wrote *Lassie* in our house; John Reed wrote *Ten Days That Shook the World* about a mile across the fields. The farm's centerpiece was the shell of a concrete barn—burnt out a century earlier and covered with trumpet vines, its windows ingrown with old trees—where Isadora Duncan once danced and now hummingbirds hovered. The current residents tried to live up to these ghosts by creating an ambience that was bohemian and unconventional: they spoke languages, lined their mildewed walls with books, and showed films on a sheet in the big barn. One family lived in the converted ice house, others in the former chicken coop, the pigsty, the hay barn, the stable. We got the cow barn.

I was seven, Nicky three and a half, and we lived there for seven years. There were other girls who, on grounds of common age, were supposed to be my friends. We had a huge, weedy freshwater swimming pool to plunge into all summer, a quarter-mile driveway for sledding in the snow, a spectacular view of the Hudson, and wild woods all around for exploring. Though constantly reminded of how fortunate we were to live in such a perfect place, we shared—we confessed years later when we met again haphazardly—a profound despair covered up by a fraudulent happy-go-luckiness whose manufacture was the last worst torture. Everyone was miserable for a different reason. I wasn't even sure what mine was, until it was over: missing Daddy but not allowed to show it because he was doing the most important thing in the world, fighting fascism.

Nothing very farmlike occurred on Finney Farm, though each family cultivated a V-garden—"V" for Victory—during the war, and over the years the grown-ups took stabs at raising animals. First there were chickens; apart from a mix-up in the food chain (the chickens got fed war-surplus chicken soup), the standard end awaited: execution by axe and a lot of headless running around. A more black-magical fate befell the other animals. Bambi the goat slipped his tether, wandered off, and starved to death with his head stuck in a bucket. Bessie the pig died from eating apples sprayed with DDT. Alice the sheep drowned in the duck pond, leaving Jonas the sheep so sad (or so his bleats were interpreted) that he was made into lamb chops. The horse fell over on the ice and broke a leg, so the police were called in to shoot him; the children weren't allowed to watch but heard the bang, and afterwards the snow was shocking with blood. Normal ducks fly south in the winter; our ducks were found frozen under the ice of their pond. Only the turkeys met a commonplace doom: they were eaten by a fox.

Our dog Frankie (full name Franklyn Delano Claude Clifton Clarence Aloysius Archibald Augustus Heinz Yogi Sylvester Simon Seymour Euriah Montague Belfrage), a mottled mutt from the Bide-a-Wee Home, survived a suspended sentence of death (renewable) meted out for biting the landlord and screwing the landlady's pedigree toy spaniel, Cookie. The two of them got stuck together in the act, howling eight-legged all over the farm, parted finally with brooms and water buckets. This meant that she was ruined, said the landlady, and would never now have purebred puppies. It was hard to grasp the genetics of this, but the power of one's argument when one is the landlady is clear enough. Frankie and my brother Nicky roamed the farm with Nicky's friend Bibi (a son of Rasputin's biographer) and Bibi's dog Jerry. Nicky loved his life. Bibi died of leukemia a few years later, still a child. The landlady died too. Only our cat Callie proliferated: her kittens came along so fast I could hardly keep up with making out their birth certificates.

The children walked Indian file along paths through

woods and fields to Hessian Hills, a progressive school. We called the teachers by their first names, were unoppressed by structure, marks, or tests, and were encouraged to be free and instinctive. The other children seemed to be able to handle this, but I wished somebody, anybody, would tell me something, anything, rather than merely hint or suggest. Instead of textbook geography we made huge papier-mâché maps of the Hudson Valley in 3-D, shaping the land's contours with our fingers, learning them as the blind might, or God. Instead of gym we had "rhythms," wearing Grecian tunics and small suede-soled slippers, expressing ourselves as inspiration suggested to the tunes of an improvising pianist. We listened to "Ballad for Americans" and sang "The House I Live In" in many parts. We never had to learn anything; occasionally we did anyway.

There came a time when instinct told us to destroy the place. It seemed to start in my class. Ruth,* our teacher, turned up one day right after the end of the war with shining, purposeful eyes and a fully formed plan for all of us to visit the occupation forces in Germany. We thought that was a swell idea, me especially: Daddy was there starting up newspapers in Frankfurt and Aachen. Ruth was kind of greenish pale, like the blackboard (green, good for the children's eyes) on which she scrawled enormously, from one end of the room to the other, the names of the financiers of our tour:

RUBIN AND LUBIN WILL PAY

Rubin and Lubin were Croton's richest men. It all made perfect sense. But Ruth was gone the next day. They said she'd been sent to a rest home in Hawaii. We never made it to Europe.

Our class, keenly disappointed, took revenge on the substitute teachers of Westchester County. We saw them all off in less than half a day apiece, generally in tears. At the

* Name changed, as signified by asterisks here and throughout.

same time, the school itself began physically to diminish. Most noticeably, parts of the "apparatus"—not for us the humdrum swing and slide but a huge construction of pipes, ladders, rings, and trapezes to crawl and dangle in creatively, uncompetitively—disappeared daily. Sold off as scrap, someone said. It didn't take long after that. Nobody really told us anything, but one day it was back to public school.

Here I go again, intruding on the set piece. The other kids in the fifth grade all knew what to do, whom to be. Mainly first generation, they were on track to become true Americans, and they did a terrific impression of your regular guy. I was irregular. Nature had unfairly arranged for me to be larger and paler than any contemporary—in school photographs I am twice as tall and wide as the nearest boy, and ghostly white. When my friends went swimming they got brown; I got a second-degree burn. I couldn't play their games and didn't know their songs. They had lots of outfits, and I had one skirt and sweater that didn't match. They had lunch boxes with Velveeta sandwiches wrapped in waxed paper and home-made cupcakes, and I had cafeteria chow mein. They got allowances for candy and movies, and I baby-sat. They had family vacations in the summer, I had camp, then jobs to pay my way. It wasn't that we entirely lacked funds, but my parents spent it on funny things—tickets, books, and later on bailing themselves out. They refused to get interested in the most important thing in American life: appearances.

The other kids went to Sunday school, we had English Sunday lunches: roast beef and Yorkshire pudding, guests with accents, discussions about the world situation, and afterwards the country walk, heading nowhere and back, to admire "the view" or "the leaves." The other kids went to the ballgame with Dad or even camping or fishing; they talked about what kind of new car to get or who would win the Series, not about politics. My friends had to be back home by six, or eight, or ten; nobody told me to come home at all. Not that seeing friends was easy: they mostly lived near each other and the school, which was a daily two-mile trek from our exotic farm. So I played with Callie, midwifing her kittens and photographing them, or listened to the serials on the radio, doodling. Every serial was brought to you by a different cereal; one was for filling the empty spirit, the other for the hole in your insides, and it didn't matter which was which.

Fifth grade, sixth grade. The really vital thing was to be good at hitting balls around. What if you preferred reading books? Everybody went in for extracurricular activities. What if you were covertly engrossed in curricular ones? What if, above all, you had this set-up at home that not only contradicted the plain and obvious route mapped out by the multitudes but was organized by an enemy of the people? An entire generation was listening to "The FBI in Peace and War" on Thursday nights, each God-fearing American heart responding to the righteous thunder that announced the latest episode in the relentless struggle against Public Enemy Number One. Who but us had the FBI following them around?

APRIL 4 1946

FEDERAL BUREAU OF INVESTIGATION

U.S. DEPARTMENT OF JUSTICE

COMMUNICATIONS SECTION

WASH 22 WASH FIELD 2

DIRECTOR AND SAC URGENT

CONFIDENTIAL SOURCE ADVISED YESTERDAY THAT ONE JIM ARONSON/PHONETIC/ CONTACTED RESIDENCE OF CEDRIC BEL-FRAGE. IN BELFRAGES ABSENCE ARONSON TALKED TO THE DAUGHTER. ARONSON SAID HE HAD BEEN IN GERMANY WITH BELFRAGE. THE DAUGHTER ADVISED ARONSON THAT BELFRAGE WAS EXPECTED BACK FROM DETROIT FRIDAY OR SATURDAY.

Daddy came home from the war in 1945, bearing souvenirs (a beautifully bound copy of *Mein Kampf;* a sheaf of orange Nazi Party cards, their dated membership stamps all abruptly terminating on the day when people threw them out the window into the street, where he found them; for Nicky, a sword and dagger; for me, a Bible given him by the man he had installed as editor of the *Frankfurter Rundschau*). Everybody else's war had long been over; the euphoria of Allied victory had receded. But our real war was only just starting. My father was under suspicion. He had even had to enter the country again as an alien, and to prove he would not become a charge on the United States, because while he had been abroad—albeit working under General Eisenhower—his U.S. citizenship waiting period had expired. Was he a foreign agent? He was saying all the wrong things, certainly, still preaching antifascism but now to a landscape of deaf ears. He was certainly writing the wrong things—to begin with, a book about resurgent fascism in postwar Germany, expressing views so unpopular that the book didn't find a publisher for years.

All this tied in with the government's "case" against him. Since his brief in Germany had been to find anti-Nazis to staff the newly reopening newspapers, he had employed among them some communists and socialists. This seemed quite logical to him: hardly anyone but communists and socialists had been anti-Nazi. But to J. Edgar Hoover and others in Washington it was deeply incriminating. Above us settled a cloud of menace. Where it would all end, except in bad trouble, was not known for sure, though occasionally the word *deportation* figured in my father's talk—often enough for us to realize that we were unwanted here, that *they* would be sloughing us off like so much rejected tissue. When? And what would happen between then and now?

In just the same way, Daddy seemed to be sloughing off Mummy. He had come home, but he never really seemed at home. He went to the city more and more and started staying away overnight. And then when he came there were big fights. My mother simply couldn't comprehend how politics could be more important to him than personal love and happiness. She didn't like the risks he was taking for a cause she no longer believed in. But how could he stay with her if she didn't believe in his cause? He *was* his cause. Why else would he risk everything for it?

The FBI had certain difficulties in keeping an eye on Daddy. As a memo to Hoover revealed, "A survey in the vicinity of Finney Farm, Croton-on-Hudson, has established that it would be impossible to maintain a physical surveillance due to the sparsely settled surroundings." Maybe the "survey" had included the day the FBI visited me at home. It wasn't the first time, just the first time nobody else was there. If any of our neighbors on the farm saw the two close-shaven short-haired gents in suits and fedoras, this weird get-up—meant to be so conventional as to render them totally inconspicuous—would have left no doubt who they were. Even I knew. At a glance, I hated them. But the jig was really up because they'd come to the *front door* of our cow barn. Nobody ever came to the front door; it was the kitchen or nothing, as was obvious from the way the grass was worn toward the kitchen door. Not to these two. There was some difficulty, after they had banged the ancient knocker, in opening the heavy, rusty-hinged barn door. There stood a man snapping his wallet open at me like in the movies, revealing his ID, while his eyes scanned the background and he asked, "Your father home, kid?" He must have known Daddy was not at home. "He isn't here," took care of it for then. Alas, no hedges in the yard were tall enough for them to hide behind. Besides, there was Frankie, grr-rring menacingly, to contend with. What to do?

Their problems with Finney Farm were partly overcome when, three days before Christmas, 1946, "a confidential informant was developed," and "through the utilization of the services of the above mentioned informant it has been possible to afford considerable coverage to the activities of subject BELFRAGE." Was one of the neighbors squealing? What else could it mean?

But on the whole, the FBI waited until my father hit the city and tailing him was possible, if seldom rewarding. Of course, in reading through the bushels of material released under the Freedom of Information Act so long afterwards, you don't always know what they knew, because so much has been inked out "for security reasons" (mainly protection of sources). One page of mine had, splayed across the top, nothing but "SALLY MARY CAROLINE BELFRAGE," with the whole of the rest of it smeared black. In Daddy's case there was an entire document revealing only:

> XXXXXXXXXXXXXXX advised that on December 1, 1946, BELFRAGE contacted XXXXXXXXXXXXXXXXXXXXXXXXXXXX XXXXXXXXXXXXXXXXXXXXXXXX and at that time they had a discussion regarding the price of books.

Or another one later on:

> XXXXXXXXXXXX of known reliability, advised on August 1, 1952 that CEDRIC BELFRAGE, National Guardian [the weekly newspaper my father founded in 1948], 17 Murray Street, New York, New York, was a subscriber to the "Honolulu Record" as of July, 1952.

One day they minutely observed him having a drink "with three unknown men at RUDY'S RAIL," and then they watched him buy stamps, board a bus (southbound), visit someone who wasn't home. At the same time, one of the unknowns in the bar with "BELFRAGE" got himself followed to several clothing stores in the vicinity of 57th Street and Broadway, whence he emerged with . . . "packages." Day after day, on and on.

Among all the dross, occasionally they hit on something. Not usually what they wanted to hit on.

> Confidential Informant XXXXXXXXX [our stoolie neighbor?] advised that on January 12, 1946 an unidentified individual contacted BELFRAGE concerning a meeting between the two men. . . . On January 14 this same source advised that BELFRAGE was contacted by a Mr. VEI-TEL (phonetic) and arrangements were made to meet on

Tuesday, January 15th, at 7:00 PM, at TONY'S ITALIAN RESTAURANT, 55th Street between Fifth and Sixth Avenues. According to arrangements made at that time they were to meet for dinner and then proceed to VEITEL's apartment.

In view of this information, arrangements were made to afford the proposed meeting coverage by a physical surveillance. Special Agents John H. Doyle and Frank J. Nolan stationed themselves at 6:00 PM at TONY'S RESTAURANT. . . . At 6:45 an unidentified man entered and said that he was waiting for another party. He used a name which sounded like WIDELL, and, while talking to the Head Waitress, he stated that he was a writer and that he came from Vienna. This man was described as follows:

Age:	About 65
Height:	5'6"
Weight:	170
Hair:	White—shoulder length
Speech:	Speaks with heavy foreign accent

What more could you want in your spy? The hair alone! Open and shut.

At 7:10 PM BELFRAGE entered the restaurant and BELFRAGE and the unidentified individual had dinner and talked at length until, at 10:05 PM, they left together and walked to the Russian Tea Room, located on West 57th Street, between Seventh and Eighth Avenues, New York City. In the Russian Tea Room they stayed drinking and talking until 11:15 PM when the unidentified man left alone. A few minutes later BELFRAGE left the restaurant and he and the man proceeded in different directions. It appeared to the agents on the Surveillance that BELFRAGE and the unidentified man made a conscious attempt not to be observed leaving the restaurant together, or at least that they took precautions along these lines.

Solving the mystery of the unidentified man proved less than formidable, for when they followed him home they saw his name on the mailbox: Berthold Viertel. As a result of spending four hours with my father, Berthold had his own life pawed through. They got his birth in Vienna; his career as a poet and lyricist beginning at age fourteen; his production of plays in Berlin, London, and New York and direction of films in Hollywood; his "association with such outstanding figures in the German Communist parallel of the Comintern as Berthold Brecht and Heinrich Mann"; his split with his wife Salka and how she was broke because of her overgenerosity to German refugees; and their "sons Peter, who was in 1942 a member of the U.S. Army, and Hans, who is reported to be deaf." Considering how far-fetched their investigation was, what a pity to leave out the no less irrelevant but faintly more interesting details, like Berthold's having been the model for the main character in Christopher Isherwood's *Prater Violet,* or that Salka worked on the screenplays of *Queen Christina* and *Anna Karenina* for Garbo and was her closest friend.

So what was it all for? There is something of nagging interest in the idea of two gumshoes forced to stay put at their table in Tony's for three solid hours trying to look plausible, and then another hour in the Russian Tea Room. What did they eat? Did they keep on eating? Drinking? What did they talk about? What *can* they have talked about?

Meanwhile, sinister machinations were going on with "Jim Aronson/phonetic/" that passed them by. Jim was my father's closest friend, encountered on the job in Germany when they worked together as press control officers. The two men thought it liberating as journalists to be doing something they believed in for once. Why not keep it up? Why not start a paper of their own back in America?

And so, in 1948, they did. It was called the *National Guardian,* a "progressive newsweekly" designed as a forum for radicals, a place where the left would refrain from infighting. But you might as well try to stop the rain from falling. These people, these lefties—they weren't rebels for nothing.

Rebellion was not approved of in the fifties. Of course the decade would produce James Dean, he without a cause, and Marlon Brando in *The Wild One* ("What are you rebelling against?" "Whaddaya got?"), but that was more a matter of style than content—your young tear-everything-down anarchic stuff, and you had to wear a leather jacket. In our house we knew about *serious* rebelling. Some people valued the ability to compete successfully; not us. No winners here, winning was too cheap. What we put a premium on was heresy, going against the grain. But for a child, there was no place to rebel that Daddy hadn't been already. He had ages ago picked as targets, as he put it in one of his books, "hypocrisy, jargon, dogmatism, and stuffed shirts," and there he stood, railing against them all, not caring whether he was alone or not, being pure. Isn't that what youth is supposed to do before it sells out and stops noticing the affronts of life? He never stopped noticing. What was left for me to do?

When my teens began, it dawned on me: the only untried, unheard-of, truly original ambition I might pursue was to be *normal*. Let the Reds take on injustice and get persecuted for their pains. Let the Beats in Greenwich Village reinvent Bohemia. Let the bunch of them get seasick on the waves they made. Me, I'd be conventional! I'd be a wife! Not like my mother, who was not the real thing at all, with her glamour and independence. I would be the little woman!

What peace, what magic in finding The Man to blend into, my very own better half, strong and masterful and thrusting and achieving (but caring and tender), with me as helpmeet to inspire and support him on his way up the ladder, rustling up romantic dinners in the frilly apron I'd just whipped together while waiting for the cherry pie to bake. We'd live in a split-level ranch house just like the others on the street, with picture window, sampler on the wall, apple tree in the yard, swing and picket fence. We'd be like those families in the magazines: after work He'd sit reading the paper while the youngsters did their homework and She fussed over dinner and put the finishing touches on the table setting. We'd take the kids for picnics in the country and vacations at the beach, I'd have milk and cookies ready when they came home from school and sit with them while they told me their troubles (what troubles?). The man would make all the important decisions, as befits the Head of the Family. Above all, he would protect us from being conspicuous. I felt as if I'd been born grown up and was now seeking childhood, the safety of being warm and fed and told what to do.

So, how to go about it? Paradoxically, to be invisible in the fifties meant to be successful: everybody was—everybody white and middle-class, anyway—if in an unobtrusive way. The mainstream was a fast-flowing current, and conforming meant getting in the swim, just to keep up. Our economy rushed ahead: climb on board!

But there was a little hitch. When you lived your life with people who mocked all that your fellow citizens held dear, who brandished their ridicule of this great, godly, and free enterprise of American disposable consumer culture and mass-produced conformity, how could you concentrate on taking it seriously yourself? Here you were, trying hard as anything to entertain true sincere religious thoughts about the society, with these people—father, mother, all their friends—hooting their heads off the whole time. After a while it got even worse: you started to get the joke too, you couldn't help it, and then the hooting began in your own head. How were you supposed to keep a straight face? Here's how: If you're learning how to be properly split, your personality wears each side of the mask at once, but only one of them shows at a time.

I was just starting my teens when the fifties began. The very word *teenager* didn't hit the dictionaries till the fifties: it was the big new concept. We rated, we were it. About time, too. For my generation many of the rewards of childhood had been deferred because of the war. "After the war" became interchangeable with "growing up": "After the war we'll have . . ." or "After the war you can be . . ." Not "may," either—"*can*" or "*will*." Therefore the postwar years were the temporal equivalent of the promised land on earth: they were supposed to *deliver*. Here we were, we had arrived, and this was the fifties. *They were delivering*.

As it worked out, there never was an "after the war." There was just a new enemy. But not until much later did people see what a con it all had been.

Of course it's possible to make generalizations about numbered ten-year slots, though they don't much work until after the fact. "We're not in 'the eighties,'" said Abbie Hoffman about a later decade, "we're in a delicatessen in New York City." You could say the fifties were the end of the era when chauvinism was still about countries and a dip was something you did on the dance floor, not stuck your crudités into; before smoking officially killed you and food, air, sex, and water generally didn't; when the drugs in circulation were legal and it was safe to walk alone at night. But such observations have no significance at the time to a person who is simply swamped by the whole thing. When you are growing up in it, it isn't the fifties or the sixties or anything else—it's just a part, your part, of some terrible, vast ocean. You don't give any thought to whether the waves are Atlantic or Pacific; if they're about to drown you, who cares if they started in the Black Sea or the Red, or are saltier or rougher than the Caribbean? In the decade of your youth, the first wave merges with the last, and you know nothing about the time's distinctness: your job is just to keep afloat.

1

Q & A

Here is Edward Bear, coming downstairs now, bump, bump, bump, on the back of his head, behind Christopher Robin. It is, as far as he knows, the only way of coming downstairs, but sometimes he feels that there really is another way, if only he could stop bumping for a moment and think of it.

—A. A. MILNE

My brother and I are conservative about moving. We've been uprooted too often—from Hollywood to New York to Croton—and this new shift to Spuyten Duyvil has only been accomplished through a mean trick on me. In the summer of my fourteenth year, knowing I'd resist if consulted, they sent me to England to visit relatives while shifting our lives out from under us again.

Unfortunately, moving day coincides with my return on the *Liberté*, and so panicked is my mother for the fait to be accompli that she fails to notice, while loading the car, the sudden thinness of Callie, the recently pregnant cat. The kittens get left behind. My father, who has taken the morning off from his newspaper, meets me at the boat and takes me to the new apartment at the exact moment of the convergence of moving van and mother and brother and hysterical cat. Callie has been my best friend for years—they can't kid me she's crying over a car ride. What about all this milk?

It certainly diverts attention from the move. The cat makes so much noise that Mummy lets her out the door and she's gone before I realize it. I knew I'd never see her again. Nightmares: Callie pounding up the West Side Highway toward her failing babes, Callie mashed at Hawthorne Circle by a ten-ton truck, pulped on Route 9A, vaporized beneath the Albany express, lost in the tunnel under Sing Sing.

It isn't a good start. Next morning before the furniture is even arranged, before it has even sunk in that the place is too small for my father *ever to stay with us again*, my mother bundles Nicky out to the nearest P.S. and takes me to a Manhattan aptitude-testing bureau she's heard about. Grieving for my cat, I cry all over the papers and will only answer questions about animals. The agency experts, ignoring the emotional unseemliness, conclude that I ought to be a veterinarian. This suggests *science* to my mother, whose next move, a conversation with the receptionist, reveals the existence of the Bronx High School of Science. "Sounds just the job," says she brightly and Britishly, disregarding my sobs and undiscouraged by the news that admission to Science is by competitive examination, closed to my age group a year earlier, and the fall term a month old anyway. She hails a taxi to the Grand Concourse and in no time is demanding an interview with "the headmaster."

Callie has gone clear out of my mind to make way for the riveting spectacle of Mummy taking on the System. I have never seen her so concentrated and resourceful on my behalf before—all her equipment martialed for, not against me. The principal of Science, the distinguished Dr. Morris Meister, is awestruck. She mows him down. She's so beautiful, to begin with, in such an unusual way. Then there is that accent, that vulnerable imperiousness. What can he do? He agrees to let me take the test. Either I pass or they say I do for fear of my mother. They all seem a little dazed.

*   *   *

Five Hundred Kappock Street, this building we've moved to, is impossibly hard to get to from the school. It's also brand-new and a little weird. Thanks to the latest technology, its seven stories are perched on the edge of a precipice, stealing the view from the four-story apartment house next door, which used to be the swankiest thing around; no doubt we'll lose our edge when the next evolutionary step enables the engineers to cantilever an even taller monster out yonder in midair. All I knew about Spuyten Duyvil before we got here was that it's the next stop after Riverdale, where we used to live, on the New York Central Railway line into town from Croton-on-Hudson, where we also used to live. Its location is still the most important thing about it. Opposite Inwood Park at the head of the Henry Hudson Bridge, bounded on two sides by water—the Hudson and Harlem rivers—and made up of a lot of contrived greenery, glacial rocks, fancy houses, and new apartment blocks, Spuyten Duyvil, like Riverdale, is stuck way off from real life, mine or anybody else's. The site enables its residents to put on airs, as if we're in some pretentious suburb, not part of that low-life borough the *Bronx*. We don't even have to admit it's the Bronx—the address is New York 63, N.Y. I hate the way it sets us apart, for the phony snobbery it supports as well as the other more usual kind of distance that means I will never be able to see friends outside school hours. It's the same old story. At Croton, too, the regular people lived near the school in their unattainable happy norm, with us off being different.

But I really enjoy Bronx Science. A certain determination to be miserable masks this for some time, but gradually the realization is inescapable: I never feel left out here. Feeling left out has always been part of life's package deal, but what I am part of now is a society of left-outs. There is nothing left to be left out of.

Some of my classmates seem pretty unappetizing at first glance: pale, pear-shaped, and lacking a lived-in look. They move as if they aren't used to it, and more than half of them wear glasses, like the brainy-kid caricature in the cartoons.

Later somebody advances the doubtful proposition ("experiments show") that they learned to read too early and damaged their eyes. Is this possible? Anyway, whenever they began, they're sure at it now. Some of them actually do go to bed with encyclopedias. The mental result, if not the physical, confirms this. Some kids can do the homework before we even learn how; some of them were born knowing how, and what they don't know, they ask. You get credit for asking good questions around here! The teachers have a hard time keeping abreast, and the racy atmosphere has everyone worked up with a wild light in their eyes.

I can't believe this place. For years small-town America not only force-marched me a daily two miles to school but force-fed these priorities: be popular, dumb, and sporty, and wear a new outfit every day; conceal good marks or you're a brown nose; faint with fear at exams; snicker at teachers; spend your brains on camouflaging your brains and forget what you wanted to do with them in the first place. Along with making cheerleader, the top girls at Croton-Harmon High aspired to bake cookies with the Junior Debs—"ten girls," as they described themselves in the yearbook, "who meet every two weeks. Four members bake while the remaining knit, sew, or discuss feminine interests."

How shameful to admit you weren't above those things, you just couldn't do them. If only I could do them! Home Ec was not enough. God knows my mother didn't teach me that stuff. She didn't even discuss feminine interests. She only wrote about them, if with a certain condescension. (She has tested her pieces out on me since I was eleven, having taken literally an editor's tip that accompanied the rejection slip: "You want to watch the excess intelligence. Gear your stuff to the average eleven-year-old.")

Gradually it had stopped occurring to me that there was any choice. Even for a long-distance swimmer the sense of pulling against the undertow can get exhausting. And now, talk about choice—it's multiple, it's limitless. Suddenly I can imagine, if not seriously believe, that the craving to be invisible might not be the sole goal in life. Naturally it's still *my* goal, but there are peeks at tolerable alternatives. Never mind the Junior Debs, how about the Automotive Physics Squad? The Protozoan Squad, the Cancer Club, Drosophila Squad? And that's just *after* school.

What's more, at Bronx Science puberty is allowed to happen at puberty! Before that, you can be a child! In my class we are ages thirteen and fourteen: and what we really are is thirteen and fourteen. In Croton, kids were jaded at nine; life was a constant false alarm, a nightmare of destinations without signs, jobs without apprenticeships, parts without scripts. Running and running, can't catch up. Swinging and swinging, never hit the ball. Here, expectations match possibilities. These Science kids are only just starting to pass around *The Amboy Dukes* and *A Stone for Danny Fisher!* In Croton we'd pored over these (increasingly tattered) sex manuals in fifth grade. The first time a copy comes my way in Science I look around for someone to sneer with: They ain't read *that* baby stuff yet, jeez. What do *they* know? Until it comes to me: they know as much as I know, absolutely nothing. We have make-out parties and play Spin the Bottle! In Croton they wouldn't believe it.

All at once, with the pressure gone, klutzes are overnight athletes. Not that our boys will ever beat DeWitt Clinton, and not that we even *have* a football team, the supply of brawn being what it is, but you can see the others are as amazed as I am when, foozling and gawking around, we actually get a basketball in the net. I'm not paralyzed with terror at being chosen last for any team, because it doesn't matter, who needs it? It's just a game.

Of course, there are a few anomalies about the place. I get an unusual set of marks at the end of the term when the teachers have the opportunity to reveal their innermost feelings about my father's politics. A 65 for social studies is almost as ridiculous as a 98 for biology: the reverse of my natural talents. The 65 isn't entirely out of the blue; Mr. X, the social studies teacher, always encouraging us to inform ourselves, reads out the item from the *Times* when my father has been summoned by Senator McCarthy or has pleaded the Fifth Amendment or been arrested again. No comment needed from Mr. X: the way these stories go, you know they are about the enemy. After all, what were we dealing with here? According to Senator Eastland, "a villainous conspiracy to overthrow this government, is it not?" As for that biology mark, never has Mr. Y revealed any political views, although with further scrutiny I note the odd confederate wink—or does he have something in his eye? I don't know how to react to either teacher. Their behavior basically has nothing to do with me. They are scared. Teachers are losing their jobs.

What I'm not, biology marks notwithstanding, is scientific. Although there is something very peaceful and satisfying about the solidity of scientific answers, it's their very certainty that in the end is less interesting than *life*. But I don't know. I like biology, and getting that 98 did no harm. As a matter of fact, maybe I'd just diagnosed myself as unscientific and it's not true. The most interesting mysteries have to do with the organism, as much its cells and bits and pieces as its relationship to others, its political and social arrangements.

We have to choose a specialized science discipline, and I go along to blood and urinalysis, "piss and pus" to its habitués, who are also the class's artier types, the science goof-offs. It is taught by Mr. E, who goes funny colors and reacts to the ups and downs of life by imitating Jack Benny's "Ver-ry funny. Hardy-har-har." Every lesson for half the term we have to prick our fingers; the other half, we bring in jam jars of pee. After a chocolate chip cookie binge one night, mine turns tomato-colored in the diabetes test, and Mr. E's capacity for hardy-hars is sorely tried; surely I'm a goner. Another day, during the boring introductory lecture, one boy is seen unobtrusively sipping at his specimen. Hullabaloo. The jar is empty and Mr. E pretty pale again before the word goes around that it's beer.

I gather that I am something of a behavioral puzzle, but there is a good humor about the teachers' approach that soon knocks most of the impulse out of me. I'm always getting kicked out of French for something or other. There was the day when it seemed impossible to bear another round of preterites and I went so far as to ask my neighbors for the time. Before you knew it they were passing me their watches. Since I couldn't think what else to do with them, I put them on. My arms were bangled wrist to shoulder, and ticking like mad, before this spectacle came to Mrs. Ashrey's attention. Poor, exasperated Mrs. Ashrey. "Go to the office," she said, "and tell them you need to have your head examined."

While they pondered what to do with me, I sat in the hall ticking away and thinking of all the other times outside principals' offices, starting with the first-grade shudders at P.S. 81 with Mrs. Simpson—her austere face, her resolute jaw, her color charts. "Now, little girl, I am going to teach you the difference between red and green." I'd been caught jaywalking. I had jaywalked, it was true. The reason for my offense was that no cars could be seen in the street from horizon to horizon. It is possible that something else, some equally forceful and speedy doom, lay in wait for the small sinner—a Bengal tiger from the Bronx Zoo, maybe, or a derailed runaway roller coaster—but these too were invisible, and besides, why should they have kept to the road? And so I walked. The shame of it lay elsewhere, however: the meekness with which I heard myself answer the questions she asked in the singsong tone reserved for the handicapped and foreign.

"Now, do you know what color this is?"

"Red," I replied.

"And do you know what color *this* is?"

"Green."

"Very *good*! That's *right*!"

The mortification of it! Not to have said "Mauve" or "Burnt umber" or any other of the more interesting shades in my painting kit at home. Then we could have got an educational discussion going. Surely if you allow them to humiliate you at six, you're washed up for life. It's all about power, nothing else. Why did they always assume small equals stupid?

The point about Science is respect—you don't find the adversarial relationship that usually wrecks everything between kids and grown-ups. A corollary: no teacher's pets, no fink kids crossing the line, since there is no line. The one exception to this is the fault of the teacher in charge of discipline, "Black Sam" Levinson, who dishes out detention if we're late or caught absconding, and so provokes us to try to get away with it. Who'd bother if he didn't see us as miscreants in the first place?

It's also a bonus that people have a sense of the ridiculous at Bronx Science when it comes to A-bomb drills. Of course, there's never been much pause in life's long drill routine. Fire drills, air-raid drills—we've been schlepping down to the boiler room since our first institution, and this is just a new twist insofar as Hiroshima changed the rules. Now we have to be prepared for all types of A-bombs. First there are the big, serious, declaration-of-war-type A-bombs that mean filing down to our subterranean pipeland again in a crocodile, two by two. *Sh! Quiet!* One must always observe perfect silence in a bombing. (And if the bough breaks, and if the bomb falls, shall we spend our life here, down among the steam pipes, inside this giant dusty organ, two by two? What will we eat? What will we breathe? Are these the people I want to die with?) Then there are the sneaky, impromptu, unforeseen A-bombs, which come out of the clear blue and mean you have to "duck 'n' cover"—crawl under your desk quick with your arms specially fixed to protect your eyes and brains. Getting the movements right is like mastering a new form of genuflexion to the Almighty.

Hiroshima happened when I was eight. I've assumed ever since that I wouldn't grow up. Who cares about the Big Bad Wolf when the Atomic Rocket is coming to get you? But unlike most problems, at least this one has a solution that's the same for me as for all the other kids: don't think

about it. Too grisly. Whatever you do, do not consider this
bomb or the way it turned the Japanese into their own
shadows.

A "civil defense test edition" of Hearst's *New York
Journal-American* runs the headline "2 A-BOMBS HIT CITY:
KILLED 1,104,814; INJURED 568,393; 1,690,000 HOMELESS."
Americans are building bomb shelters in the backyard and
talking on TV about how the most important piece of
equipment is the gun to ward off the neighbors. It's not
easy to put this together with the stories they've told us
about the world so far, either the ones about how lucky we
are or the others about how nice we are. But there is a diabolical conspiracy to communize America. We have to protect ourselves. We need to have a terrible Bomb to do it. As
the chairman of the Joint Chiefs of Staff says, "The only
language Communists understand is force," and Secretary
of State John Foster Dulles declares that our survival
depends on "demanding that Russia abandon its determination to enslave the world." The trouble is that the enemy
has a terrible Bomb now too. "We pray that He may guide
us to use it in His ways and in His purposes," said our
pious president, Harry Truman, when he dropped it on the
Japs in 1945—but now "it" is in the hands of *atheistic
communists*.

One day, after missing a bus home, I'm walking up the
hill in Spuyten Duyvil to our apartment house when alarms
start hooting all over the place. Testing their bells, I'll bet,
ha-ha!—nothing like as scary-sounding as the ones upstate
for Sing Sing jailbreakers. Now, *those* were bells. For weeks
after they went off you'd cower every time you passed a
phone pole, in case it concealed a skinny axe murderer.

Halfway up the hill, this huge woman is standing squatly
in the road with her hands on her hips. As I approach I think
I hear her say, "Under the tree." I look around. Nobody's
there, so I keep going. "Hey! You! *Under the tree!*" "You"
seems to mean me. Serene and complacent as a cow in long
grass, she is definitely indicating a tree, on which is nailed the
familiar black-and-yellow sign: SHELTER AREA. No shelter is

visible, only the tree. A smile at this gag fails to strike a chord
with her, and she stands on, mutely pointing: she has a job to
do. According to her matching black-and-yellow armband,
she's a warden. It's just me, her, and the tree. (Well, there's the
road, the hill, the view of Manhattan over there, much of the
Bronx in the way, a river in the foreground down below, a lot
of space, a *lot* of space, plenty of scope for a beaut of a bomb
display.) What does the tree make of it? We stand beneath the
leaves until the all-clear.

Like many people at school, my father roars hilariously
at it all. For some reason this laughter is supposed to make
you feel better about dying young. That's nothing, he says,
listen to *this*. He reads aloud from a clipping someone's sent
in to his paper from *Women's Wear Daily*, about a meeting
in Las Vegas of "foremost authorities on atomic weapons."

> Atomic bomb attacks on our cities would place new respon-
> sibilities upon the lingerie industry at every level, it was
> revealed. Strapless and sleeveless designs will have to be
> eliminated as well as designs with tight-fitting front sections.
> At least one scientist thinks slips with loose, made-in panties
> would be needed to afford the fullest protection.

We have a good giggle. I don't bother to mention that I'm
cold to the core. For one thing, I'm not exactly sure why.
The craziness, I think, is even worse than the sudden-death
problem. What kind of a place is it, this planet, where foremost authorities talk that way? It doesn't give you confidence.

The other fear has to be dealt with solo. My father has
tried to prepare me for the future by explaining that any
moment now, without warning, he (we?) can expect to be
deported to England. I tell people, "We might be moving to
England." I don't say why.

It's a while before I can adjust to the fact that at student
lounge on Thursdays after school, when there is dancing to
a jukebox in the gym, nobody will dance with me. Why

not? I stick with the other girls and look nonchalant, but
nothing happens. Even after we've been wising around in a
raisin fight in the bio lab and I happen to *know* the boys
are throwing their raisins at me, they won't dance with me.
A decade later, when I asked Herby Kohl (senior class president, later famous educationalist) how come, he shrugged:
probably it was just he'd never known any blondes before,
he conjectured, and it was somehow intimidating. People to
whom this remark was reported doubted he could possibly
have said it, or if he did, obviously he was joking: never
known a blonde? But I remembered how kids used to ask
me for a lock of hair to show doubters at home, and how
some mothers treated me, like a trunk on a Cunard crossing
labeled for the hold: NOT WANTED ON VOYAGE.

The other thing I'm not, apart from scientific, is Jewish.
At school this makes me a total freak; there are a mere hand-
ful of goyim out of three thousand kids. Not being Jewish at
Science is sort of like running a race with a serious though
not debilitating handicap. Maybe a missing arm. You can still
run, but it's much harder to keep your balance, and you have
to compensate for the lurch in all kinds of ways.

Being Jewish is a serious conundrum. Very few of the
kids are actually religious, but they sure know something I
don't, and they won't tell what it is. Maybe they can't—
since they are not different, they don't even see what makes
me feel that way. Not that they aren't nice to me, but sometimes it feels more like Toleration than Acceptance. Still, it
sure beats the lack of either. So the best thing to do, it seems
to me, is to learn to love my armlessness. A chance to practice comes on Ash Wednesday, when I work up the chutzpa
to go to church at dawn and get my forehead smeared with
black stuff. God is watching: you have to keep your ashes
on, according to the rules, not wipe them off. "Your face is
dirty," people say to me all day. I feel like a real jerk.

I had found God in England. Poor England! Londoners
"making do" in their shabby, coal-blackened city six years
after the war was supposedly over, still nourished by their

stories of the Blitz; holes or rubble where so many houses used to be; those remaining peeling and crumbling, their missing metal railings converted into guns and tanks and not yet replaced; bomb shelters in the parks and gardens; all of London as if underwater in perpetual dingy fog. True, the Festival of Britain was on that summer of 1951—to the natives, a miracle of light and innovation after all the hardship, but pretty bargain-basement next to what Americans could do. And the festival did not affect the weather, the chilly rains of August: my aunt had to take me to Selfridge's for woolen clothes, including a kilt in the Princess Margaret Rose tartan. And the food! Sugar, butter, cheese, and meat were still rationed. The end of the war didn't mean there was anything decent to eat. Spam. In America they told jokes about Spam; here you had to eat it. Nothing but limp lettuce and tiny wizened apples at the "greengrocer's," enormous bluish cubes of whale meat alone and acrawl with flies on the marble slabs outside the "fishmonger's." Trophies of victory.

But my English relatives, the white sheep of the family, were as good as they were happy, and the only explanation I could come up with was their religion. My granny Grace, Daddy's mother, and her respectable offspring lived lives of order and convention. They went out of their way to be *kind* to each other. They preferred being together to the company of others! Who ever heard of such a family? They never sniped or yelled or cried or fought, and they were as considerate to each other as to complete strangers! Do-unto-otherness oozed from them—they rushed to help the less fortunate, or even the more fortunate, and then to say, with heartfelt gratitude, "Thank you *so* much" or "How *very* kind" and "God *bless* you!" for the privilege. If they attributed the way they were to their weekly bouts with the Lord, who was I to look further?

Besides, religion in America has another significance: if you don't have one, you are really out of it. One day of the week, preferably Sunday, you put on your suit, your hat, and your little white gloves, and trot along the road toward the ringing bells. The Church of England in America is called Episcopalian, and the nearest one to us is Christ Church in Riverdale, with Father Barry presiding (suspiciously not a *vicar* but a *priest*). A girl in my building, Debbi Giglio, is going there too, and we team up. The Giglios* live downstairs in a double apartment overlooking the river—new tenants like all the rest, since the building is new. But then, everything about this family is new: they've got the latest gear, and the most all-American aura I have ever seen. They look like they're posing full-time for a FAMILY THAT PRAYS TOGETHER STAYS TOGETHER billboard. I am determined to be just like Debbi.

Religion is as good a place to start as any. Father Barry points us toward his confirmation class, but it turns out you can't be confirmed unless you've been baptized. I'd die before revealing that I never was, even if my godmother was Myrna Loy. I can hardly ask Father B to do it now, with me all of fourteen—I mean, how conspicuous can you get! I tell my father about my problem. Christian at heart though he is, he disapproves of the smells, bells, and dressing-up aspects of religion, but as usual he doesn't directly inflict his views on me. On one of his weekly evening visits to the Spuyten Duyvil apartment he brings along his friend Claude.

The Reverend Claude Williams is an Alabama preacher and the subject of one of my father's books. Trouble comes at him at home nonstop—lynch mobs, the Ku Klux Klan burning crosses on his lawn; he's been jailed, even horsewhipped, for organizing and defending black and white sharecroppers. He's always on top of the situation as far as you can tell, though his accent is so thick it's hard to understand much of what he says. Daddy understands him fine. They have a lifelong project to rewrite the New Testament eliminating the miracles. When Claude comes visiting, they sit around with a bottle of bourbon ("The best way to get the spirit is to drink it internally," says Claude) and figure out about loaves and fishes. This is all in aid of bringing the thing down to earth, where—hey, presto—it is still available, only now it's called communism.

They start out with quite a few toasts, but the favorite is

to Sister Price, the pastor of a little church in North Carolina, who, having heard Claude preach, stood to say, "I know the gospel of grace. I've read of the gospel of the kingdom. And in Revelation we're told that there's an everlasting gospel. But this is the first time I've heard the gospel of *three square meals a day*." That's what their loaves and fishes are about, and Daddy always says that in their pure form, Christianity and communism are the same thing. I'm not sure what his relatives in England, the religious ones who got me going on all this, would make of that idea.

Coming to grips with my dilemma, Claude gets a bowl of water from the kitchen and, drawling this and that, dabs some on my forehead. He does it to Nicky too, while we're at it. Later, in the mail, we get classy-looking Baptismal Certificates with ribbons and embossed lettering. There's one miracle eliminated.

Actually, Reverend Claude's miracle program doesn't go down well with the Chicago Presbytery—who are of the fundamentalist school that holds the Bible to be literally true, including the bits about arks and whales, never mind a few loaves and fishes—so when he is denounced as a heretic a matter of weeks after our baptism, he has no defenders and is out of a job: defrocked. He could get another church up north, Unitarian or something, but being an old-fashioned incantatory preacher, and a distinctly southern-style troublemaker, he isn't interested. I don't bother to tell Debbi or Father Barry about Reverend Claude.

My baptism is not the kind of thing to instill confidence in a new initiate, but I drown my doubts in extra fervor. The height of piety, I wear my straw hat with cherries on it, and every Sunday after praying, I prey on my mother for creating our unholy lives. It's easy to tell that the Christ Church altar rail is the place to be: one sip of communion wine on an empty stomach and the Holy Ghost irradiates the soul. What's more, just over yonder dressed in white is Bob,* a doll, the acolyte. If you ignore the greaseball haircut, he definitely looks like an angel. But not an Angel. Bob is a Knight, and a rival of the Angels. The Knights have cool green jackets with white felt letters spelling out their name in a semicircle on the back. Bob is tall and dark, with this great physique, which looks just as terrific in his red-and-white acolyte's skirts. Somehow he makes me want very badly to be holy, even after he tries to rape me behind a dune on Jones Beach.

Father Barry's idea of how to keep the boys out of mischief is the Episcopal Young People's Fellowship. We gather in the church hall Saturday nights. The girls watch the boys horse around with basketballs and stuff, punching and cuffing each other between dribbles, shouting, "Giddoudaheah yabumya, I swear ta God I'm gonna killya." Then somebody puts on a Teresa Brewer record, and Father Barry smiles from the sidelines as we lindy-hop. The boys' feet are enormous. There aren't too many slow dances in the church's collection, and never more than a couple in a row, because the guys might get smoochy and it could all lead to the ruination of innocent girls. After an hour or two we say good night to Father Barry, and then the evening starts. We drive up the Henry Hudson Parkway for a few chicken runs—who can speed fastest longest up the oncoming lane of the highway without flinching—and end up at Louie's for pizza. I hate alcohol but can just swallow a couple of rye-and-gingers. I have to because I am almost fifteen and it's against the law, so I am proving I am a person. But you have to be real careful about not eating or drinking a single mouthful after midnight if you're taking communion the next morning. That's when the boys drive the girls home and attack them in the back seat.

Pretty soon the demands and contradictions of this religious life begin to get worrying. Where does it say in the New Testament that you have to wear a hat to church, or walk around with soot on your face on Ash Wednesday, or eat nothing after midnight before communion? What does any of that have to do with Christ? What does anything in Christ Church have to do with Christ? Who under its steeple has the slightest relationship to the golden rule beyond an ability to mouth it? Do these questions occur to anyone else?

2

APPEARANCES

*The old eternal triangle. Anthony and Cleopatra and—what on earth
was the wife's name? Nobody ever remembers the wife. Any woman
would rather be cast in the role of Cleopatra. Maybe all women were
basically whores. The great, the repeated tragedy of women was to
be no longer desired.*

—MOLLY CASTLE, NEW WINDS ARE BLOWING

There are memories, increasingly distant, of Daddy nearby
writing a book in some very small room containing a very
large table, a portable Smith-Corona, a glass-brick ashtray
full of used Revelation tobacco, several neat stacks of paper,
a box of soft black editorial pencils, and smoke. Between
spurts of tapping with his two middle fingers came the ding-
ding of the pipe as he emptied its dottle in the ashtray. My
mother was typing too, in another room, and their sounds
together made my favorite harmony.

Love and joint industry: the ingredients of Mummy's
happiness. Successful journalist, beloved wife of Cedric—
those were her chosen roles. Once in a while she'd even take
a stab at playing mother, relaying some useful lore from a
long-gone housemaid about how the strings on bananas
cause tuberculosis or if you make that nasty face the wind

will change and it will stay that way, or, in put-on Cockney, "Don't touch that stick! A dog may have smelt it!" Before Nicky was born she sang to me, and then to him, "My Curly Headed Baby" in a tremulous soprano halfway between love and tears: "So lullalullalullalulla by by/Do you want the moon to play with/Or the stars to run away with . . . "

But now her depression is only equaled by ours, and the jokes are over. In our house everyone is miserable. Nicky wishes we had never left Croton, Mummy wishes she had never left the thirties, and I wish I had never been born. We are not permitted to mention the real problem: that the marriage is over, the family is finished. Not that permission comes into it exactly; it's more that very English concept of Done and Not Done. In their day, D & ND had to do with clothing and table manners, vowel sounds and aspirates, and "an occasional frown or encouraging glance from the parents was usually enough to inculcate them," as my father wrote. In the top drawer, "it was the 'done' thing to read at breakfast or in a train, but not at other meals or in a car," to wear a tie for golf though never for tennis, a belt for all sporting trousers instead of one's daily braces, and never a bowler in the country or a cloth cap in town. One didn't put down the knife with the blade on the edge of the plate, cheat at cards, or get drunk. One was a gentleman.

In our house, reverse snobbery has long ago brought most such strictures into disrepute, to the extent that they are under conscious control; instead, D & ND concern feelings, expression of. It is absolutely ND, for instance, to observe aloud that now we have moved, Daddy doesn't live with us anymore. In Croton he had almost lived with us sometimes, even though he wasn't there much ("because" he was working so hard in the city that he couldn't come back too often), and even though when he did sleep at home it was in his study, not with Mummy. But a silent fiction was maintained that fed hope. Sometimes they still had friends over for jolly meals, and they'd fill the house with music and the sickening smell of frying kippers on Sunday mornings (reading over this meal, if no other) and pursue the obsessive English pastime of going for endless walks to nowhere and back. Even their terrible fights meant it wasn't sealed and signed yet; if what went up must come down, why couldn't what came apart come back together? After the war they'd sort of come back together again, hadn't they? But nobody said anything.

One subject nobody said anything about was Anne Marie, the Frenchwoman who had come to Finney Farm to be our "governess" when my mother sailed to England to visit her parents after the war. Anne Marie was very tall and chic and young, with a collection of tiny teddy bears that I coveted in vain. Although she made token efforts to teach us French with lotto cards, it was pretty obvious that Anne Marie had a lot more than lotto cards going on with Daddy. They'd met in occupied France, and it wasn't hard to figure out that Mummy was being a Good Sport by taking herself out of the way—hoping it would blow over? But nobody said anything.

They didn't even say anything when the child was born, after Mummy came back and Anne Marie had left the premises (and not long afterwards, the country). Somewhere, it seemed, I had a sister. The way I knew was that in Daddy's desk in the back of a drawer I found photos of a sweet dark-haired baby. *Who is this baby?* It gradually began to make sense when the photos turned into a toddler, and later yet a little girl. I remembered Anne Marie's European handwriting, and there it was at one point, on a photo of a four-year-old: "You can already see what I will look like when I grow up."

Nobody ever mentioned the word "divorce," either, but that made the possibility no less real than the sister in the drawer. Too real to write or say: it was D– – – – – –, unspoken, like the Hebrew name for God among Orthodox Jews. The beauty of a lack of solid information is that you can always pretend things are really the way you want them to be. Up until the moment they shipped me to England in June 1951, I'd mounted a fairly successful campaign to ward it off and so sustain the hope—or the hope of a hope—that it might not come true. I'd wish on stars, the breastbones of fowls, dandelion fluff, other people's birthday candles. Like a charm, before sleep at night I'd write minutely in my diary, on the bedpost, on the wall, D– – – – – –, as a way to get in front of it somehow, objectify and sap its power, stop it happening by my magic.

But underneath you always know, because when everything else is fine and you think you have forgotten it, the pain comes. It is a constant and can only be drowned out with noise, laughter, working—even fighting, shouting, crying, anything—because in stillness, in just a piece of a second of aimless drifting, or in an accidental ecstasy when you might permit yourself the fatal observation *I am happy,* you have to face the music: in the echo of the thought, in that tiny instant's reflection, the pain washes in. "Oh, yeah?" it says. "In that case . . . " There seems to be a whole list of things activity disguises, but really the list is only one thing long: pain, amorphous and final, and finally undefined.

The apartment in Spuyten Duyvil is a mess. I hate it there. Clutter, litter, smells. A reflection of the morale, naturally. Nobody ever cleaned up anyway except Daddy or a maid. Now, with Daddy only a weekly visitor, no money for a maid, and my mother's attitude to housework unchanged, the kitchen and bathroom are never mopped and the toilet is stained with gentian violet, which she uses for a fungus infection on her thighs. How am I supposed to get my saddle shoes white in a bathroom like that? Dishes, papers, books. There isn't a single original surface to be seen. When the doorbell rings to announce visitors in the lobby, we have about three minutes, if we're lucky and the elevator isn't waiting for them, until they get to the door. Sometimes I rush out to the hall and summon the elevator up to give us more time. My brother and mother and I ricochet around trying to stuff the mess under the couch, straighten Mummy's bed (the first thing you see when you come in the

door), close the curtains to hide her chaotic study, get the
week-old newspapers and last night's dinner and today's
breakfast and Mummy's latest game of solitaire off the
table, and kick what's left into the room I share with my
brother. Whatever we accomplish never disguises the basic
filth, and the Giglios five floors down have convinced me
that from this sin alone there is no redemption. Most gruesome, the unannounced nightmare visitor is often Father
Barry from Christ Church, and something about his attitude, which combines piety and pity, makes me feel like one
of those "100 Neediest Cases" the *New York Times* writes
up at Christmas.

The apartment is much too small, just a living room,
kitchen, and bedroom, plus a dinette my mother has com-
mandeered to work in. Nicky and I have the bedroom,
which is partitioned. The partition doesn't reach the floor
or the ceiling, so it is an illusion, and it certainly fails to
contain the noise of Nicky's clarinet practice or the fantastic
smell of his feet. After the cow barn's eight rooms, there
isn't anywhere to hide, no doors to slam, no places to put
things away, and it was idiotic to move to a swanky new
building when for the same rent we could have found somewhere big enough.

For my mother, the attraction is the *view*. She gets claus-
trophobic if she can't see space outside the window, even if
there isn't any inside the window. It can't be just any old
space, either. She is very visually susceptible for someone
who is half-blind. In Croton as she sat at the dining table
she discerned some sort of personal monster in the paint-
work of the horse barn opposite, so forever after everybody
had to move to let her sit with her back to it.

Here we have a top-floor view of the whole of the Bronx
over to the VA Hospital, plus a small curve of the moat
between us and upper Manhattan. Down below in the
immediate foreground is an enormous car graveyard. It's the
wrong part of the building: from the other side—the Giglios'
side—you can see the Hudson, two bridges, the Palisades, all
green and water. That's the view she'd had in mind, but it's

too expensive. Besides, you can always go up on the roof and have any view you want. The roof is our extension—the stairs start right outside our door. It's the place to go to brood or sulk or dream, and there is no scene worth the name that ends without someone crashing out to the roof.

Not Nicky, mind you. Nicky has a pacific personality. I try not to think about how nice he is, because it makes me feel rotten that I'm not, and reminds me of the way she loves him. He stays out of it, whatever it is. When he's home, which is as rarely as he can manage, his scrawny body in its torn blue jeans is bent step-shaped on bench and table, skinny behind in the air, elbows propping his chin, holes in the soles of his high-top sneakers: he is reading the comics or boning up on his baseball statistics in the *New York Herald Tribune,* whistling through his teeth, trying to drown us out, jam our station, muffle our madness.

My mother and I have opened frank hostilities. She is in constant, fraught anxiety, and since I'm one of the few tangible causes—not like political fear, exhaustion, imagined poverty, real poverty, the instability of her work, getting older, and the biggie: no man—it often expresses itself on me. I give her plenty of grounds. First, I blame her for losing him: it seems to me she could have kept him, why didn't she keep him, why did she have to cry and fight with him the whole time? Second, I look like him; I remind her of him constantly. Third and worst, I'm the one person he adores unconditionally, and it is beginning to dawn on me that my very existence is a problem to anyone—to his best friend, other women, all kinds of people, not only her—who is competing for his love and attention.

Why should people have to compete for love? Does it come in finite quantities? Are they afraid there isn't enough to go around? Sometimes my mother tells me about her own mother, who was nicknamed Piggy, and who competed with her. Piggy was, she says, very beautiful and vain, and she flirted with her daughter's boyfriends. She made Mummy feel worthless. It's all so corny, you read about this kind of thing all over the place and in detail in Mummy's psychology library, but reading does no good, any more than reading why you eat too much when you're miserable helps you to stop.

There is not a moment's peace. I feel as if I'm being par-boiled for life, heated up in preparation for the big roasting. She doesn't just sear me, though; she makes dramatic raids on my pain. That's not true: we do it to each other. I pro-voke it. Her life is miserable enough without my making it more miserable by insisting how miserable my life is. Every day she has to race to *McCall's* and think up bright new ways for women to look, smell, diet, decorate, cook, and mother, knowing the magazine will give her the push the second she's not cute enough. Her heart is not in it. Then she has to tear home to feed us a meal out of cans and boxes, and what does she get? Complaints. Not too many, though, because all you have to do is go too far or pick the wrong moment and her face is collapsing like a little child's, and by then it's already too late: she is crying. She has cried my whole life, and she's still at it. If only she'd answer back! But if you have a reason for being mad or sad, she has a better reason for being madder and sadder. You can't even get out half a grievance without her rush of tears about five of her own. Even without visible cause she can set herself off, drifting around humming prewar romantic songs in a bleak little Gertie Lawrence warble, and crying.

When she does that, it's as if the world has no bottom. It's like an endless falling dream.

It's easy to remember when the crying started, because I started it. Daddy was working at his spy office in Rocke-feller Center and he would come home on the train, just like a normal commuter, every evening at 7:00 in time for din-ner. Exactly as the Tchaikovsky theme music announced the Maxwell House music program on station WQXR, he would walk in the door. Only all at once he didn't. It was after he took me to the office one day and Truda, a woman there, took me to the "little girl's room" and told me that really she only wanted "a *little* piece of Daddy." Or that's what I later passed on to Mummy. "I met such a nice lady at Daddy's office," I said, "and she told me that really she only wanted a *little* piece of Daddy." Mummy cried, cried, cried. I couldn't understand why, only that it was my fault. Every night after that, when dinner was on the table at 7:00 and the Tchaikovsky piano concerto began and Daddy didn't come, she would cry and cry and cry.

I *never* cry in front of her. I only do it by myself, and then I save things up and cry about them all at the same time. That way you can cry for hours and get it over with. The best time is in the dark before you go to sleep so your eyes have time to get better before anybody sees you. Once in Croton Mummy caught me, and soon afterwards she gave me a Rorschach test, planning to find, in my ink-blot interpretations, the key to my dissatisfactions. I made up silly things, so she took me to a doctor who asked me questions, spying for her. I wouldn't talk.

A long time later, when the FBI gave out pieces of its files, it turned out they'd also been interested in Truda from the spy office. According to their researches, she was a Czech who had married a Russian and been a medical student in Moscow. They also said that "her husband had been placed in a Soviet prison camp" and hadn't been heard from since; "that she associated with a British Consul General at Moscow, Russia, in the summer of 1941 and that at that time she obtained a British passport which is believed to have been stolen, and that this passport was signed by the British Consul General while he was in an intoxicated condition." The next job she got in Moscow was in the office of the U.S. military attaché, but she was "discharged from this position for being 'too hot to handle.'" They said, "SHE IS SUSPECTED OF BEING A MEMBER OF OGPU" (the name of the Soviet secret police in those days).

Providing her vital statistics seems to have brought some G-man out in a sweat. Where other people are described clinically, Truda tapped another dimension:

Height:	5'4"
Hair:	Blond
Eyes:	Very attractive
Complexion:	Very beautiful
Languages:	Speaks very good English; also speaks German, French, Czechoslovakian and Russian

At home my mother works on stories and novels and is always trying to get back to her typewriter from whatever childish or domestic distraction has summoned her away. There is a pencil in her teeth to remind you of where she would rather be. The pencils are all chewed. Her hair is messy, and she has a scattered air. You can't pin her down, but she definitely isn't all here.

If it's not another place she'd rather be, it's another time. Her specialty is nostalgia. I have a grudge about this: she so obviously prefers her life before we existed. The expression of her deepest sorrows is her music. She seems to see herself wrapped in protective arms, sailing around a ballroom in a mile of satin and lace. "There were angels dining at the Ritz, and a nightingale sang in Berkeley Squa-a-are . . . " (often hummed, not sung, because of the pencil). Her eyes moist, sniffling, self-pity closing in a tide above her head. "If I loved you . . . words wouldn't come in an easy way . . . " She can turn any old song into a weepy.

If she weren't crying all the time, she'd be still more beautiful, though her eyes don't work too well even when they're dry. Nicky and I have spent our childhood searching for her damn glasses in the mess, which of course she can't see any more than she can see the glasses. Another thing she can't see is how she looks to us when she's at home, or else she doesn't care. When she passes a mirror she has a special trick she pulls, holding her stomach in and standing up really straight, and on her face she gets this *face*—not at all like her true face, but a sort of fluttery pout. The second she's past the mirror the whole thing sags back to normal again. Like other people with a mirror face, my mother is unconscious of it. Anyway, who cares? The mirror that counts is in the eyes of the nearest man.

Beauty is weird stuff. What is it, anyway? Maybe some aspects and kinds of beauty are obvious to all; others just have to be taught, it seems to me. Grown-ups drone on about it all the time—what it was (for them), what it will be (for us). To a child, looks have no time dimension: a wrinkled skin was never smooth, a fatness wasn't once a flatness; and any fiddling with what you look like, disguises with bits of cloth or paint, fools nobody. As my father says, "Never trust a man who parts his hair under his left armpit." Vanity's illusions, as transparent to the beholder as the pimples boldly bursting through the pancake: who're you trying to kid?

Take my mother's hands. She tears up photos that show her hands, as if with that act she can change them, just as she tears up any pictures she thinks unflattering, although the rest of the world can perfectly well see her "bad side" as often as her "good"; and she makes cautionary remarks to me about the undesirability of calling attention to one's more unattractive features. "In my case, of course, it's my hands." But what is wrong with them? It's true the fingers are knuckly and worn, nothing like the smooth white worms in the Jergen's Lotion ads; despite all the rings they are peasant hands, used hands. She had to use them plenty in Croton, shoveling the furnace full of coal in the winter, digging the car out of blizzardy snowdrifts. The point is that their relative competence and deftness cancel out cosmetic considerations to a child, who doesn't judge value from appearances, any more than from the color of someone's skin, until taught to.

A *child*, that is. To an adolescent—to this adolescent—appearances are everything. All my life till now I have been used to thinking: She is my Mummy and she looks the way my Mummy looks. Without instruction I thought only: Her hands are her hands. Whether typing or teaching me to knit, to me they're her most motherly, comfortable, womanly part. And what others call her beauty, what is that? All that concerns me about her hands or her face or her clothes, any of her, is the attention she pays to her looks, because it reflects her state of mind.

And this matters to me now more than ever. Dressing up for work or a date, she goes all out to look great. With her cheekbones and hair she could play third sister to Joan Fontaine and Olivia de Havilland. She has a particular style that goes perfectly with her feminine yet tailored look: soft, Chanel-type suits worn with one of a huge collection of shirts, the buttons always changed to special ones of silver, brass, pearl, ceramic. My favorite dress is heavy cotton with cuffs and waistband of deep green corduroy, full skirt of green flecked with red in the pattern, and antique-coin buttons she added herself. Her face, with its perfect lines and clear skin, needs no artifice, but she works hard on it anyway with the free-sample cosmetics and scents saved from magazine jobs, pouting coquettishly at her image.

But appearances, to my mother, don't count at home. It's a case of raddled old denims and a sour smell. She saves her glamour, like her charm, for the others. She doesn't wash her hair for us or even for herself; she rarely bothered even before it was cut in Croton, when masses of waves of copper-gold reached to her bottom, famous to those who saw it cleaned and brushed and fixed in all kinds of hairdos. I really resent it. I resent it most of all when my friends are around, heaven forbid, and she makes no effort for *them,* only for *her* friends. I'd like to be proud of her. She'd probably like to be proud of me too, but it's been obvious right from the start that my looks disappoint her. I resent that too.

It's impossible to forget the time she and her best friend, Alison, decided to discuss me and my looks as if I weren't there. We were in the garden in Croton by the big old vine-covered barn—the two women in their lawn chairs so wonderful-looking (Mummy dressed for a party, Alison too, slim, smooth, blond, icy, English), me at eight or nine hanging around dumpy and lumpy in my shorts and halter and scruffy sandals—and Alison was observing, "She has some good *angles*. Hair's a pretty color. Could be more of it. Not a bad bone structure. Marvelous thighs."

"She got Ced's good legs," my mother contributed.

I stood transfixed, a stone. Alison scrutinized the object further and then reached out and patted first its stomach, then its chest, like horseflesh at a fair or cuts of meat at the butcher's. "Now, if *that* . . . can just be got to move up *there*," she said with a crafty smile up at me.

There had been a time when I would think, studying my mother: That's how I'll look when I grow up. But gradually, and in some indirect way, she has made me understand that while I'll be acceptable, perhaps, not exactly an eyesore, being beautiful is something I'll never know about. She has made it clear (though what am I supposed to do about it?) that beauty puts a woman in a special category and you can get anything you want with it. Look what it got her—deb of the year (some prehistoric year); mobs of boyfriends (called "beaux") who took her gallivanting around Europe in yachts and Lagondas and private planes; even a rajah she later cajoled into supplying Robert Flaherty with the elephants for *Elephant Boy*. Really, history has moved too quickly for her. She was suited to the sort of life in which you dressed for dinner, came up to London for the Season, relied entirely on servants. You can hardly pick her out from the others in the photos of her youth—the Beautiful People lined up with their arms about each other's waists, one leg flapping in tandem with all the other legs, before some elegant European vista during the Great Depression, about which they had no clue. Other evidence of these times survives most vividly in a profusion of traveling cases: fitted pigskin cosmetic cases, medicine, brush, and jewel cases, all embossed and stamped with her initials, the big ones overlaid with stickers from the best hotels in Paris, Rome, Cannes, Biarritz, Salzburg.

In the end, perhaps bored with it all, she'd made a proper marriage to Clive Castle, a dapper young man who misinterpreted her motives and threw himself into gallivanting along with her. Work—beginning as a lark with what she knew best, society gossip—seemed to come to her as an enormous relief, and evolved into her own page where she could write what she liked. The proper marriage ended as casually as it had begun, leaving her only a surname.

"It had never occurred to [her] that she might work for a living," she wrote in one roman à clef. "None of the girls she had been to school with had expected to work. Her father had never even thought of it; certainly he had given her no sort of training that would have made it easier. In any case . . . it would be her husband's duty, and presumably pleasure, to support her." However, in the next novel she had already assimilated the idea of herself as "the career woman whose stock in trade is charm and wit, rather than intellect or aptitude." Lord Beaverbrook thought enough of her to appoint her hostess at his business lunches, to promote her romance with his film critic, and to give her a page of her own too. In that novel he is "Lord Watermill": "'Good girl, this,' he would introduce her to Prime Ministers or labor leaders or effete members of the aristocracy hanging around hoping for jobs. 'Clever girl.' And his eyes dwelling affectionately on her added: 'Pretty girl.'" Repeated himself a little, it seemed. My father wrote of going to see the Beaver to announce his departure on a world tour, to this reaction: "He evidently thought me a trifle mad to throw up my fat weekly paycheck for this wild goose chase—and above all to leave Mary, of whom he said he was very fond. 'Good girl, that,' he said, directing his piercing gaze at me from beneath the tangled bushy eyebrows. 'Clever girl.'"

Molly Castle, billed by her paper as "Britain's Number 1 woman journalist," "The Girl Every Woman Reads," and "the most highly paid woman on Fleet Street," was a star, and enjoyed filling her weekly page. She wrote about fashion, food, society, and other stars. The *Daily Express* then had the world's largest circulation after *Pravda*. Even after my birth the column continued from California, my debut headlined, ". . . And Here Is SALLY CASTLE," with a photo, age two days, taken by Twentieth Century-Fox. There followed months of tips to new mothers: "Put Baby to Sleep on Its Tummy," or a story called "WHEN SALLY YELLS," advising, "a lot of handling is bad for baby's nerves, and rocking him to sleep will make all but a little prospective sailor feel seasick."

Another novel followed. But now, looking back on it, no accomplishment seems to count as much to her as having been a household face, thanks to the newspaper plastering her image everywhere, even on the sides of buses. "Let's go down to the corner and look at Molly!" her father used to say. She actually seems as pleased with that as with anything she has done.

Even though she makes a living out of them (and even though one of her favorite research topics is Mary Wollstonecraft and early English feminism), she has little use for other women, especially those who aren't beautiful or clever. And education—apart, of course, from music, painting, dancing, horseback riding—is neither here nor there for females, unless they're bluestockings and "frightfully plain." (And you're a long way from *that*, she implies to me patronizingly. Matronizingly?) You find a man. The search for one will educate you. If you're too intellectual they won't want you anyway. But never forget that it's just as easy to fall in love with a rich man as a poor one.

"Oh, can it, will you?" I blast back at her. "What a load of hooey." There come moments when, with J. Edgar Hoover's nightmare plot thickening, the trivial concerns of the woman drive me crazy. "Do you realize that Daddy has to testify in Washington tomorrow? What if they deport him?" Not least because I share them so much of the time, both genuinely and to blot out the other reality. "What's going to happen to us? And who cares how we look when it does?"

But of course by now she is crying. She is so *needy,* and I never get a chance to need anything. If you asked her what was the matter, she'd ignore the real reasons and say that I was beastly to her. I am beastly, and I'm rude, nasty, selfish, uncooperative, truculent, impossible. My being a loathsome brat at least confirms that she has good reason not to love me; my being awful makes sense of her misery, which otherwise threatens to engulf us in craziness.

There is more to it, anyway. "You are in my light," she says as I cast a shadow over the page she is trying to read; it is just another indication of my inconvenience. But is there another meaning? Maybe, while my looks will never equal hers, she would be willing to trade places anyway, for the sake of my youth. I get that feeling. Other mothers seem to recognize, if only implicitly, that they should move over now, it's *our* turn. Not my mother. It's always her turn.

Nicky is the focus of her life. Sometimes she tells one of her vast collection of stories about our early childhood, when one of us supposedly said something too too amusing, but in entertaining her friends she usually misattributes tales about me to Nicky. Then there is: "Nicky's the musical one," announced to all and sundry, "and Sally's the artistic one." Nicky has been so often diagnosed as unartistic that he goes spastic at the sight of a pen, and even though I tie with him for top place in the aptitude test at the Bronx music school she takes us to on Saturdays, she makes me feel there is no point in my continuing with piano lessons. In one of her novels the Nicky character is fanciful and creative and the Sally one is "the down-to-earth realist." "Sally is so self-reliant," is another myth. Is there a choice?

In my opinion she loves my brother and not me, and I'm very touchy about the unfairness. He maintains a scrupulous neutrality, young smellysocks, and Mummy lies about it just as she lies about her age and money. When challenged, she acts like she completely believes herself. She cried for a whole day when I opened her bank statement and then forgot to reseal it with the address showing through the window in the envelope. I only wanted to know if it was true that she's too broke for me to go to college. There was more of a nest egg than she'd ever admitted, but that was for Nicky's education probably. She cried for *two* days when I found out she'd once forged her papers, eons ago, changing her birthdate from 1903 to 1908, and I told Nicky, who squealed on me. What's the point of fooling the world over a lousy five years when you're that old anyhow? I know the way I act won't make her love me but I want to get back at her. She wants me to be nice first and *then* she'll love me. I want her to love me and *then* I'll be nice. That's the way she loves Nicky and the way Daddy loves me. It seems to me you ought to be able to expect that from your own mother.

Also, decent meals. Let others sneer at school lunches: we think they're great and we survive on them. Macaroni and cheese, pork and beans, chow mein, junket and Jell-O and butterscotch pudding hit the spot.

In Croton we had Dilsey Lee to feed us. She did much more: she gave up her life for us, with nothing left for her own comfort but Jesus. So old her parents were born into slavery, she had real gold teeth and "arthuritis" that served as everyone's barometer. Her laced corsets were too stiff for her to bend in the middle, and there was one enormous bosom across her front. The sayings and stories of the Bible were like personal memories to her. She praised the Lord and hummed her hymns: "Rock of Ages" while she braided rags and old stockings into rugs; "What a Friend We Have in Jesus" as she washed and ironed, swept and mopped; "Jesus Loves Me" as she stewed tomatoes with white bread and sugar. Humming and praying, Dilsey tapped lightly round the kitchen, chopping, rolling chicken wings in spicy flour, frying. "Oh, life," she'd sigh, or "Makes it nice." We adored her and her food: dumplings and fried chicken and string beans boiled in bacon grease for a day or two till all the vitamins were safely eliminated. Who cared about vitamins? The food was full of love.

The stuff my mother gives us no one would believe, never mind eat. "No Englishman understood about hamburgers," she'd written snootily in one novel, as if she understood about them perfectly. "They called them rissoles and had them on Tuesday made from Sunday's joint." Her own cooking prowess might be gauged from her first book, *Around the World with an Appetite,* a sort of witty travel cookbook, with favorite dishes encountered in an anecdotal series of journeys. It's just as well about the anecdotes, as the recipes are a little chancy. Maybe she ate the food in a restaurant and then tried to figure out backwards how they'd cooked it.

MADRONELLA SPAGHETTI

1 pound spaghetti
1/4 pound grated Parmesan cheese
juice from tin of tomatoes
3 cloves garlic
1/4 pound butter

Strain the juice of the tomatoes, add pint water, bring to the boil. Throw in the spaghetti, add pepper and salt, butter, garlic, stick of rosemary. Boil quickly for 15 to 20 minutes until juice is almost used up (watch out the spaghetti does not stick to the pan).

I suppose we should be grateful she doesn't attempt this dish for us, or hamburgers either. What we do get is burnt or raw, usually both, the chicken charred but bloody and the frozen beans still icy in the middle. Everything has a skin or singed edges, if not rubber bands and giblets in paper bags. I've grown up thinking spinach melts, since it never comes without a puddle. But lumps are the real specialty of the house. There are the lumps in the instant mashed potatoes that burst into powder on your tongue, solid lumps in gravy that could be almost anything, and the lumps composed of some experimental substance that she is still working on incorporating undetected into the meal.

We are like two lab rats for her fads and theories. Long before anybody in the world has heard of wheat germ and blackstrap molasses and seaweed and brewer's yeast, she sneaks them into anything gooey enough to bury them in (e.g., Franco-American spaghetti, Dinty Moore Irish stew). If it tastes like puke you can bet she's humming around in waltz tempo, halo freshly polished. But it's the principle of the thing that defeats her—the failure to consider that for us to eat the stuff it has to be edible. Our refrigerator is the usual repository for these substances in various stages of fur growth and rot development. I'm the one person in my bacteriology class who doesn't have to think twice about where to find an interesting sample for the petri dish.

Meanwhile we fill up on Cheerios (Lone Ranger), Wheaties (Jack Armstrong), Shredded Ralston (Tom Mix), and Kellogg's Pep (Superman). My all-time taste treats are:

1. Good Humor raspberry popsicle
2. Nedick's frankfurter
3. Orange Julius
4. Devil dog

The trouble is that Mummy's dietetic theories have got me feeling guilty about eating things like that. It's almost okay to stuff yourself, even to get fat, as long as what you do it with is made of whole grain. Nicky, who isn't plagued by guilt for some reason, sucks Necco wafers nonstop, and his teeth are always bothering him.

And of course our mother the cook can't eat her product either. That wouldn't matter, since she's always on a diet. But she is as hungry as we are, and so at off hours you tend to find her wafting around in the kitchen, her left hand unaware of what her right is doing, which is: thickly buttering and honeying a slab of brown bread, hypnotically conveying it to lips and teeth. Some might view this as verging on the hypocritical, except that the trance she is in obviously precludes responsibility for her actions.

What *is* she responsible for? Needless to say, she is completely uncooperative in my all-American invisibility project. With Daddy's dread of spectacles, I fail to see how he stood a minute of her public mode. She always says exactly what she has in her mind. "I say!" she hails a gas station attendant while Nicky and I hunt for somewhere to hide. "My man!" (Overcoming his astonishment at being addressed as some sort of flunky, my man warms up and is soon ready to be trodden on.) Because of her obsession with weight, she is prone to roar, on espying an excessively large person in the aisles of the Grand Union, "How *fat!*"

The shame of it. "Mummy, please don't say that."

"But it's *true*." She seems to think that by humiliating people who are disfigured in some self-induced way (in her opinion), she is helping them out. I think I'll go wait in the car.

She may be a social snob, but a cultural one never. Far from it. As well as her thirties tunes, she unashamedly loves Chopin, Rachmaninoff, and all the music that highbrows ridicule as "semi-class." She devours romantic novels and women's magazine love stories, not even pretending they are models for her own efforts. She has no time for fine art, weeps through soppy TV dramas, and if she didn't have to work all day she'd be hooked on soaps. Ideas, philosophies, systems don't interest her in the least unless they have some immediate practical application.

I wish I could talk to her about the politics around here (or to anybody besides my father, whose views are so predictable you don't even need to talk to him to know what they are). Other children can't get their mothers to discuss sex; with me, it's politics. "What do they mean, what are they talking about, *un-American?*" I'd like to say. There isn't anyone to say any of it to, that's half the problem. "The way they say *un-American* makes it sound like *inhuman*."

Doesn't she have an opinion?

"An opinion?" I can just hear her snort. "Not bloody likely. The last time I had an opinion look where it landed me." Perhaps she thinks the political beliefs she once shared with my father were her own idea.

According to another novel of hers, *This Is Where We Came In*, the character based on my father writes her a letter specifically instructing her to talk to me—still in the womb—about politics (name and sex changed to protect the innocent):

One thing, Jane, you must tell your son [in this one he doesn't yet know it's his son too] when the time comes for him to know the realities in which he must live and die. . . . There is nothing so important that I can hope for him except that he will be on the right side, the side of democracy and peace and world brotherhood. That for those things he will fight a good fight. That he will regard all those who are on this side, whether they are black, white or yellow, as *his* people; and all others, whatever language they speak, as his enemies.

The fact is, she doesn't see the point about these *sides* of his because she doesn't see the sides. She is oblivious to races, colors, countries; not so much unwilling as unable to divide people up as he does in order to identify the unfortunates or whole classes of enemy. She has his fictional persona say— in answer to the question "What do you believe now?"— "All I know is that I've never felt comfortable sitting in the rarefied, perfumed atmosphere on our side of the fence." She's always felt fine on any old side of the fence, as long as she liked the company. Apart from missing a familiar ambience, or the nightingale in Berkeley Square, nations are meaningless to her, so the idea of nationalism wouldn't detain her long enough to oppose it. Throughout her English education, for instance, she swears that America's War of Independence was simply never mentioned, so that when she visited some cousins in South Carolina at eighteen, and got off the boat to see two signs, U.S. CITIZENS and ALIENS, she burst into tears and helplessly awaited a rescuer, wailing, "But where do *I* go?"

So me and my monologue, we end up on the roof. "I mean, *anti*-American I could understand, but *un*? Americans are all kinds, Americans come from everywhere and believe in everything and look every which way. What is an American? If they can't answer that, how can they tell an *un*?"

3

THE BOGEYMAN

Better dead than Red? Better dead than a scoundrel.
—BERTRAND RUSSELL

Name:	CEDRIC HENNING BELFRAGE
Place of birth:	London England on November 8, 1904
Height:	6 feet
Weight:	175 pounds
Eyes:	Brown
Complexion:	Fair
Hair:	Brown, gray, bald
Appearance:	Walks fast, erect, military bearing, dresses neatly, usually wears no hat

Our father is tall, bald, and bony, with big bushy eyebrows and amazing sapphire-blue eyes. By far his most startling feature is the blueness of his eyes; if the FBI can't get that right, what can they? Women go wild for him, even though he's looked very *old* all my life. Now he lives with Jo Martin, his fourth wife (if you count Anne Marie third, since having a child counts to me), only they're not married yet because she is in medical school and his politics might get her thrown out if they went public. There was no single

moment when it was announced that he was living with Jo
(Not Done); I guess that's where he's stayed since he
stopped coming home to Croton. They have a floor-through
in an old brownstone half a block from the Third Avenue el
on 65th Street, a narrow railroad apartment with thick
chalky walls and tin ceilings. There's no sink in the bathroom, so you have to brush your teeth over the tub; the ice-
box, with its electric coil on top, is only one evolutionary
advance on a box-with-ice; the garbage dumbwaiter broke
eons ago, and rubbish seems to have flaked haphazardly
out of people's back windows and accumulated in the airshaft.

The apartment is small and rudimentary, without room
to swing a mouse in, but shipshape, snug. You can see the
details have been given thought. Lots of books, maps, hand-
woven mats, Mexican rugs, African sculptures, an Egyptian
patchwork here, a Picasso poster there, the Weavers on the
phonograph. Basic ethnic. One glance and you know their
politics.

I don't go there much, since Daddy usually visits us, but
when I do I feel peaceful. Jo is peaceful too. She smells nice
and goes perfectly with the apartment. Sleek black hair
pulled back in a bun, Spanish face, voluptuous shape, red
and black peasanty dirndls, a silver hand-crafted thing on a
thong around her neck. Her cooking is in character, exotic
and ingenious, and infinitely expandable in case of last-
minute drop-ins. It's fun being there in the evening because
the three of us go to the kitchen to make dinner together
and they drink Manhattans while we chop and mix; there is
music, and we're singing and happy, and the meal is delicious.

My father is the only father anybody has ever seen who
cooks and washes dishes. How proud I am! How ashamed!
It's typical of everything he does and the way I feel about it.

Jo has had a hard life: she grew up in a community of
Spanish immigrants in Tampa where everybody had tuberculosis (her own was what first gave her an interest in
medicine) and some of them didn't survive it or the poverty.

But she is grudge-free. Sometimes she sings in her wild, tone-deaf way:

> *I don't care if it rains or freezes*
> *For I'm safe in the arms of Jesus*
> *I am Jesus' little lamb*
> *Yes by Jesus Christ I am.*

Whenever she feels wrought up she moles into some closet and flails around in there for hours, flinging contents out all over, then neatly reassembling them. But she doesn't take anything out on people. She never plays games with you—no blackmail, no power ploys, no conniving. Neither does my father, although he is charming to a degree that is hardly believable until you get the hang of it. He is so *nice.* He overwhelms you with kindness, and it never flags, after years in this What's-in-it-for-me? city. Ordinarily, charm is something people don't waste on their families, the usual bunch around the place. He's different. He makes an effort with everyone, only it never seems like an effort. He's even nice in the morning—he gets up first and squeezes juice, brews coffee, pets people awake, sweet-talks them when they're grouchy or hungover, makes it worthwhile to get up. All day he has you feeling good, doing automatically what he sees is needed, not expecting credit, and throwing in the odd Sophie Tucker number for the hell of it. At night he's the last person to go to bed after he has emptied the ashtrays and straightened the rugs and cushions so it will be pleasant to wake up to again.

This is maybe how he atones for a childhood in a twenty-room house with six resident servants, excluding governess (not considered a servant) and coachman (who lived above the brougham in the mews). His father, who died before I got to know him, was a fashionable London physician, and such perks were only to be expected in the Edwardian middle class, but Daddy grew up feeling guilty about them. He was the youngest of three sons, all sent to public school and Cambridge but only one coming out according to plan. The eldest, Bruce, had not altogether respectably "gone on the stage," and ended up reading the news on the BBC at a time when such voices came from men wearing dinner jackets. He became famous in 1940 for having cleared his throat and carried on with the news after the studio took a direct, audible hit from a German bomb. Only when I got to know the middle brother, Douglas, in England and saw the form and content of the person merged in a consistent, comprehensible *type* did I understand the world's confusion over Daddy. Douglas was a doctor like their father, and he was what he had been designed to be: a caring conservative gentleman.

Cedric was named for Little Lord Fauntleroy but would have no part of the role. In his autobiographical book *They All Hold Swords* he writes of the rebellion's early beginnings in constant childish arguments such as the one provoked by the "tweenie," or "between maid," the more usual name for the kitchenmaid, who came last after the cook, the upper parlormaid and housemaid, and the under parlormaid and housemaid, and who caused him "to madden my mother with the question: 'How can a maid be between? Between *what?*' I came to see that she was between plenty—all of it on top except the ground."

Sydney Henning Belfrage, M.D., MRCS, LRCP, had obviously played a large role in goading his youngest son toward mutinous politics. The doctor descended from a long line of Scottish clerics who may have contributed some aberrant genes. According to a nineteenth-century family tree, "a certain Friar Beverage or Beveridge, who may possibly have been a monk of Culross Abbey, was burned to death on the Castle Hill of Edinburgh in 1538 as a martyr to the new faith." Later came the Reverend George Belfrage, who, having attained an arts degree from St. Andrews, Edinburgh, was ordained in 1647. "He lived in troublous times, and suffered for his attachment to the principles of the second Reformation. Being among the Nonconformists in the time of Archbishop Sharpe, he was first suspended, and then deposed from the ministry by appointment of that Prelate."

Further men of the cloth turned out to be extra-pious "Secessionist" Presbyterians in Scotland who required strict adherence to the letter of biblical law. One ancestral divine, the Reverend Dr. Henry Belfrage, D.D., born 1774, defined this law in a series of catechizing volumes, and even devised newer, more exacting rules and prohibitions. "Let the books which you read be of a grave and moral cast," he directed in *Practical Discourses, Intended to Promote the Improvement and Happiness of the Young,* published in 1817. "The loose dialogues of plays are unfit to be perused, as well as heard, by those who wish to keep themselves unspotted from the world." He believed that "childish levity, excessive hilarity, or a satirical humour" were "allied with malignity."

Most vital was the proper observation of the sabbath. In *A Monitor to Families; or, Discourses on Some of the Duties and Scenes of Domestic Life,* Henry outlined one's Sunday obligations, which included church three times and otherwise sitting in sober silence, curtains drawn, with the father of the household enjoined to educate the children and servants in the evening and "examine them as to the discourse which they have heard." ("It is said to be a practice in some places to make this a day of freedom to servants, and to allow them to spend it where they please. Such conduct must be severely condemned. . . . Such indulgence deprives them of a season very favourable to their moral improvement . . . and engages them in scenes perilous to their virtue.") Entirely forbidden on the sabbath were "journeying, walking, and visiting, indulging in amusements and recreations, reading [anything but the Bible], needless indulgence in sleep, lolling at the fire-side, sauntering about gardens or fields, engaging in vain conversation or games. . . ."

All conversation unsuitable to this day must be avoided. . . .
A day so solemn calls for gravity strict, yet mild, and the

heart must be strongly addicted to folly which can suggest
or relish aught that borders on levity.

Oh! when will men live to God, if they will not on his
own day! and when will they prepare for eternity, if they do
it not on the Sabbath!

The next ancestor to make a mark was the one who got
away, my great-grandfather James. His story is so absurd
that all one can do is consider it and sigh, or shrug. Tired of
this austere and wrathful religiosity, James took off at the
age of fourteen, sometime in the 1860s, and walked to
Glasgow. Presumably even more tired by the time he got
there, he sat down on a doorstep and fell asleep, to be
kicked awake at dawn by a brute shoving a broom into his
hands and ordering him to sweep up. "And do you know
where that was?" the story climaxes. "Younger's Brewery!
And do you know where he finished up? Chairman of the
Board!"

Be that as it may, James certainly moved finally to London, rich enough to provide his own sons—among them my
grandfather—with a substantial inheritance, which in Sydney's case was frittered away in its entirety on the stock
exchange during my father's childhood. Apparently this
leakage occurred invariably during lunch, when the broker
for some reason chose to telephone. Otherwise, we might
have been rich. What would that have done to Cedric's politics?

Daddy's mother, my granny Grace, brought a different
stamp to the Belfrage clericism. The daughter of the Canon
of Gibraltar, she was a sweet, giving, tolerant lady. Sydney,
as though Calvinism were a dominant gene, was of a sterner
substance. Photos of him always stopped my breath: his
enormous height, electrical presence, huge white brows
above implacable eyes. A bit like Daddy if Daddy were
twice as tall and three times as fierce. But while he may
have loomed like a lighthouse, with a beamlike look to
match, it's hard to imagine the doctor as really ferocious;
after retirement he spent his time doing petit point with

Grace's help. Maybe he was also a little afraid of his youngest son, whose notions were quite beyond his comprehension. "Why don't those people give their money away?" he asked Cedric about a wealthy socialist they knew. "That's what socialism means, isn't it? Can't understand these fellers! So dashed inconsistent!"

Sydney's specialty was nutrition. In a half-dozen books on the subject, his true concern was to be found among the chapters on vitamins and roughage: *constipation*. According to his theory, a failure to produce "two or three evacuations daily, [preferably] in the squatting position," caused "intestinal toxaemia, i.e., a poisoning of the body caused by the absorption of 'toxic' or poisonous substances from the bowel. . . . Every tissue and organ exposed to the poison undergoes a degenerative change," and since the poisons seek the weakest link, "rheumatism, cancer, tuberculosis, and most nervous disorders such as epilepsy, insanity and neurasthenia" can result. Further conditions arising from constipation include "premature ageing, chilblains, flat feet, spinal curvature, arterio-sclerosis, goitre, epilepsy, diabetes," and more or less everything else. Better far, my grandfather held, to emulate "the brute and the savage," and "allow free and fair play to the colon."

"It is no exaggeration to say that constipation may well bring the downfall of civilisation in its train," he warned in 1926. His sons were out of earshot by then, though it can't have been simple growing up in a house where a seven-foot-long mantelshelf in the bathroom contained every known form of laxative.

When at home with his parents, Cedric would join his father's weekly expeditions to the public library. The doctor was in the habit of asking the librarian for recent works of his favorite authors, and one week, having requested "the latest Strachey," he took home the offered volume and settled into his armchair to begin reading. The son was near enough at hand to hear the father's exasperated snorts as he turned the pages, and then to observe him flinging the whole thing disgustedly to the

floor. This was enough to interest Cedric. He retrieved
the book and discovered that it was not after all the latest
Lytton Strachey, as his father had intended, but *The Coming Struggle for Power* by Lytton's nephew John. The
wrong Strachey. Anything that revolted his father that
much was good enough for him.

For years my father remained "a victim of the delusion
that because I had rebelled with my brain and my feet
against my gentleman background, I could run away from
the gentleman in my spirit." In the twenties the first running
away had been from Cambridge to the Devil's Playground,
"that nest of rogues and low fellows," in his father's
words—Hollywood. America was the place for him—"raw,
spacious, restless, uncoagulated America." After a period of
starvation he began to sell articles to film magazines at
home, becoming "a reporter of and commentator upon the
wise sayings, gay doings and amorous adventurings of that
group of human beings who (mainly because they were con-
structed in a certain shape) had been selected to channelize
in shadow the unfulfilled longings of the unrewarded
mass." He was obsessed with films in the same way as with
politics later, seeing in the cinema the first universal language, the means to create one world. Everyone everywhere
experienced Chaplin and Keaton *together,* laughed *together;*
maybe at last here was the way to build a world *together*
too. The talkies wrecked that one.

He became Sam Goldwyn's press agent and the fourth
husband of a silent film star, Virginia Bradford. She had a
hick southern accent, and the talkies wrecked her too. But
at that point Goldwyn came to the rescue, assigning Cedric
to London. There Virginia went too far by seducing all of
his friends, both brothers, and even his father. Whenever I
asked my father what had gone wrong with his first marriage, he would only say, "She threw telephones at me."
Transfixed with awe at this use of the plural, I would be
diverted from any further inquiries, for there was something
truly impressive in this wanton waste of telephones, of
which everyone normally had but one, found in one place,

extremely heavy and black. But in the end Virginia would collect eleven husbands, so it was not just telephones she was wanton with.

My mother was Daddy's second wife, and he was her second husband. His version of their meeting on the *Daily Express* is in *They All Hold Swords,* where he refers to "the almost unnaturally calm and pleasant atmosphere that surrounded Mary."

> I told myself I wanted nothing of Mary but the balm of her womanly companionship. She sensed my state of mind, showed her friendship for me in a hundred simple ways, gave me tenderness and love, and asked for nothing I was not ready to give.

They lived and worked on the paper together, with weekends in the country. But the journalism that she loved was making him more and more restless; despite Beaverbrook's wooing with progressively bigger carrots, he resolved to travel around the world, but soon realized he shouldn't have left "clever girl, that" behind. From the South Seas he wrote to her:

> Sometimes I get so desperately lonely for you, darling Moulie, but I always think how unendurable the pleasure will be when we first are in each other's arms again after this long separation which I have been so eccentric as to inflict on us. Next summer, if things are still peaceful in England, we will have the grandest country estate obtainable with seventeen butlers (that is if you want them).
>
> I shall spend the rest of the afternoon thinking exclusively about you and how much I love you, everything there is about you, and always shall love you. I love you because you are gentle and because your skin is warm and tender and because your voice is sweet and soft and pours outrageous flatteries into my vain and skeptical ears.
>
> I knew before I started that this trip would have some major effect on me in changing my outlook, or at least in

settling it. The effect has been produced and this is it. Every new bit of the world I see and every new person I meet makes me feel more overpoweringly that you are my world and that I love you always more, always more, until I am ready to burst with it.

Otherwise I am as before—a child of nature, wistful, capricious, dazzling as May morn, drinksodden and owlish, hero of a thousand loves, pawn of fifty Beaverbrooks.

My darling, if I don't keep right on loving you best in the world it will only be because I am dead. . . . Your Cedric.

They arranged to meet in Hollywood, when his round-the-world trip took him back there. In *Away from It All, an Escapologist's Notebook,* he describes his reaction to seeing her again:

Nothing I had been able to dream about her during our long separation could compare with the reality. I was immediately strengthened by her presence, and scales seemed to fall away from my eyes, and the ground I trod with her was firm. Our deep intimacy was resumed instantly as if it had never been interrupted.

After their reunion they tried the London newspaper scene together for a year, but he again grew restless and took off, this time with her. They traveled through the Soviet Asian republics, Siberia and China and across the Pacific, back to Hollywood. Throughout the trip she was pregnant with me. There is a photo of her with a big belly in Baku against a backdrop of a flowerbed planted to resemble Stalin's face. They didn't see evidence of famine in the Ukraine or the start of the great purges, they saw breakneck progress in Soviet Central Asia, which had started out on a par with India or Egypt; they saw a country that had abolished unemployment in a world otherwise crumbling in the Great Depression. As usual she looked at things in her slightly wonky way, describing the Kremlin as "shimmering in the heat, its red-brick fortressed walls picturesquely enclosing the flourish of large gold pawnbroker signs which sit on top of most of its inner buildings." But my father was getting politics the way some people get religion, so that by the time they were house building in Laurel Canyon he was already guilty of being what the witch hunters later called a "premature antifascist."

While rejecting the substance of every identifiable idea ever taught to him at home and school, my father kept a grip on his British style. Humor, dry. Reserve. Very far removed from anyone's emotional upheavals. Excessive behavior is foreign to him and seldom occurs when he is around. My mother's scenes make him hide in the bathroom. Language: urbane, amusing, articulate. Neatness, symmetry of movement: nothing fussy or fidgety, but a kind of very careful grace about the way he slices bread or wraps parcels or tamps the tobacco down into his pipe and pats the tin top tight again, the way he unobtrusively orders things in line and scale when he sets the table. He arranges flowers and prepares meals and doesn't bother about what men are supposed to do and women are supposed to do. Unfailingly considerate and sweet-tempered: this is the Daddy I grew up with, and it makes no sense that they should want to put him in jail or get rid of him. He is so nice to have *around*. He does have a tendency to make speeches sometimes; most of his friends do. The point is, he explains things, he is witty and completely patient, he knows all the old English music hall songs, he organizes life to take the sting and craziness out, and he is never mean. Everybody loves him, as far as I know. He has no personal enemies, only ideological ones; and those enemies have certainly never met him or they'd see he only wants the best for everyone, even them. His ideas are divisible into the simplest possible terms so that I, a child, can understand. Yet he never treats me as a child.

Once when I was six or seven we were walking along near the spy office at Rockefeller Center holding hands. I almost had to run to keep up with his long strides. He was

telling me about the war, and how he had to go to Europe
to help fight Hitler. As we walked we saw coming toward
us another little girl, a pretty, dark-haired little girl, with a
woman. He greeted the woman, who replied in a voice with
an accent. They passed on. He explained that the woman
and the girl were refugees who had had to run away from
the Nazis, because otherwise Hitler would have killed them.
Hitler didn't like little girls who looked like that. He only
liked little girls who looked like me.

Daddy talked about how the most important thing is
human life, and how some think that property is more valu-
able than people, or that animals count more, but it's
important not to be fooled. The English, for instance, get
soppy about their dogs, but they don't mind a bit about
massacring "natives" with dark skin. And everywhere the
laws are stronger against thieves and burglars than against
people who hurt other people—except the really big thieves
and burglars, who get away with it.

He explained about God being good with an *o* taken
out, about Jesus being maybe the greatest man who ever
lived, but *real,* not some holy haloed church creation, so
that we can be like him too if we try. Early Christians held
all things in common and shared just the way Jesus said to;
in fact, Christianity and communism are really the same
thing. It's all about not being selfish, since there is enough
of everything for everyone. But it wasn't going to be easy,
because "all the people who have ten times or a hundred
times more than they need are going to hang on to it like
mad in case some of the other guys get a little of it." Didn't
that all make perfect sense? Any kindergarten kid could
grasp what he meant. The snag was that since kindergarten
is all about learning to share, a lesson you have to unlearn
pretty soon afterwards in order to get along in the world,
maybe *only* kindergarten kids could grasp what he meant.

As time went on, his explanations got more complicated, but not much. It was all summed up by the Sermon
on the Mount: the brotherhood of man, compassion, truth,
mercy, justice, love. Blessed are the meek, for they shall

inherit the earth. The point about Daddy is that he lives it, he makes it all seem possible, plausible. How can the world deny him? He's always helping out people in trouble. He has what he needs: one suit, two pipes, and a typewriter; he doesn't covet anybody's goodies. His life is pure simplicity. Maybe it has to do with having been brought up by the English cold-shower crowd, but Daddy revels in quite ordinary comfort—you can tell he really enjoys being warm and well fed, as if these are unexpected blessings not his due. It is a pleasure to witness his pleasure.

But it's not always easy to see things his way. He has made me aware and ashamed of how rich we are, even though we have nothing. I have to imagine people poorer than us, since I never see any. There are no beggars or bums except in Depression photographs or on the Bowery, and none of that is real life, any more than pictures of the battles in France or exotic stuff in the *National Geographic*.

Everywhere he goes there is motion and music and a sense of involvement; only Mummy, so estranged from her own life and so anguished by his absent love for her, refuses to enjoy herself when he's there. People generally treat each other with respect in his presence: they get funnier, nicer, as if to live up to him in some way. Even when they're only speaking about him, they light up. All kinds of people, especially when they've had too much to drink, are forever cornering me to say, "Your father is a great man." But that is self-evident. The fact that the world persecutes him gradually makes sense too—it seems he is an affront to them.

Daddy has an interesting way of making me behave. When I am bad, he clicks off. The lights go out, the sound, the power. He leaves the room, and it is only protoplasm still breathing in that chair there, glassy-eyed, absent. When he goes blank like that and I am being especially obtuse, I pile into him and try again; but when the most emphatic behavior still achieves no response, I have to stop and think: *Why isn't this working?* It isn't hard to pull myself together after that, although at times quite a lot of experimentation is required before I get it right, or stop getting it wrong. But the great advantage of it all is that afterwards he has no apparent recollection of my mistake; he never has to forgive me, as he hasn't heard, so the record stays stainless and I am still, in his eyes, perfect.

He is the strongest force around me even when he is oceans away. He's the one who loves me. Anyhow, I'd rather be ignored by him than "loved" by anyone else, since he's the one person who knows how to treat you decently.

I think of being small, bathed, wrapped in a big soft towel, sitting with my feet in his lap while he gently cut my toenails. Mummy couldn't cut them without hurting. There was no point either in getting sick unless Daddy was around. He brought you a new book to read every day and trays with delicious things to eat beautifully arranged on a cloth with a flower in a little vase. *She* cured me of being sick when she heaved me a tray with the usual on it plus ants. *Ants.* I fell into a feverish dream with ants crawling all over me, and I woke up well. I never bothered to get sick again when he wasn't there.

The most important thing he does is make you laugh. "Fun" is something we never, never, never have when he's not home, with the atmosphere negatively charged in deference to my mother's suffering. If you want to laugh, go someplace else. When he comes it's different. After I grew too big to walk up his long legs, he taught me double solitaire, and we still hoot and scream and nearly come to blows dumping our twos and threes on each other's aces. But we have fun doing anything. Even washing dishes is fun. He gets me and Nicky singing "Sweet Fanny Adams," or "Fuck 'em All," or "Roll Me Over in the Clover" with about a hundred verses. None of them seems rude until a decade later.

But my favorite thing in the world is Christmas with Daddy. For a godless Red materialist, he is amazing at ceremony. He gives special creative attention to decorating the tree with handmade ornaments he brought back from Germany—a set of cut-out wooden figures wonderfully painted with the holy family and masses of angels and wise men bearing frankincense and myrrh. Every strand of tinsel is separated reverently with talk about how they're meant to represent icicles after all; then he stands back like a painter at an easel to gauge the effect and check that each has been hung in a true vertical. The air is full of music. He knows all the verses of the carols and has taught us to sing the harmonies. One Christmas Eve in Croton we walked and sang for miles through snowy woods and fields to people's houses, collecting friends, roaring out our carols, demanding figgy pudding, getting hot drinks and warmth around their fireplaces, before moving on. It was enough to make you believe not in some mere Santa Claus or even Baby Jesus but in magic, in *childhood*.

The strange thing is how near the surface, no matter what, are the ideas that consume him. In an article for the London *News-Chronicle* to celebrate my birth, he wrote:

> We do not know whether in ten years, even in one year, the structure of our present civilization will still be standing, or whether it will be a stinking ruin. We do not know which of us will live, or, living, will be on a daily rack of torture devised by our fellow-men who think differently from ourselves. We do not know whether our family will be allowed to remain together even if we live. We are not sure what will happen tomorrow. We know only today.
>
> The sunshine must look beautiful to my daughter. Only she cannot read the paper that is thrown in the morning on our drive, so she does not know she has been born into a world of blood and iron and hatred, a world in which unreason, like a homicidal maniac, is loose.

The first thing he did when he came back from occupied Germany was to resurrect this piece to use as the foreword to a seventy-five-page book he wrote for me, really a kind of letter to his daughter, "on the occasion of her tenth anniversary." He called it *The King Is Naked: A Primer of Heresy for My Firstborn.*

> You are beginning your eleventh year in the world and your mind is spreading out wings. The things that are stirring around now in my typewriter will catch your interest as and when you realize that they affect your own life. As an American wisely said, everything starts with self—it's only when everything ends with self that we go off the rails. Your happiness in the future, whether you like it or not, and you probably don't, is bound up with the subjects raised in this letter and the decisions you make about them. If, when you do get to thinking seriously about them, you find that my ideas don't match up with your own experience and observation, don't hesitate to call me a liar or an idiot. I have been called worse things, if not by worse people. It isn't important that you should agree with me but that you should make up your mind, know what you think and why you think it.

Subheadings include "Governments and Wars," "Words," "Change," "America," "England," "Russia," "Liberty," "Bogey Men," "Love and Hate," "Reading the Papers," and "The Future." Under "Words," he refers to a dictionary he'd given me for my birthday:

> . . . you're getting now to some of the longer words which are in constant use in the papers, in speeches and in general conversation—words like "democracy." And I have to try and explain to you that whereas "democracy" really means what Abe Lincoln said—government of, for and by the people and not by one man or a small group, many users of this word nowadays do not mean that at all. There are men and women in America, just as there are in other countries, who don't at all like the idea of "the people" running the government. They enjoy a very good, fat life and they are afraid of "the people"—which includes dirty working men and even literary bums like your father—taking it away from them.

Under "Change":

> Whenever you hear screams of "revolution" and "un-American," just remember these simple facts. There is nothing un-American about change, any more than it is un-Chinese or un-Eskimo. Nor does wanting and helping to make necessary changes mean being against the ideas of Washington or Lincoln; indeed, just the contrary, for the greatness of these men is that they led people through the greatest changes ever made here.

And "Socialism":

> I doubt if one American in a thousand could tell you exactly what socialism is, although it is the one overwhelmingly important idea in the world today. . . . The word you do see and hear all the time in these discussions by people standing on their heads is "communism," but probably even fewer Americans could define that word than could define socialism, and it is almost impossible to find the word correctly used in any newspaper. Communism originally means sharing everything in common. It has been tried at various times through history by small groups, including the group of fishermen and working people who went about with Jesus in Palestine. But it has never yet been practised by a nation.

No country at present was economically ready for communism, he wrote, including Russia. Russia wasn't communist, it was socialist,

> because everything connected with the producing and distributing of goods is centrally owned and organized and the government tries to divide up what there is as fairly as possible [and] looks ahead to a day when communism will be possible—when money will be done away with altogether and people will just help themselves to whatever they need; and when there will not even be any government in the

sense of a maker and enforcer of laws, because if you have
everything you need there is no need to commit crimes.
Because that is the final aim of the party that controls Russia, it calls itself the Communist Party. . . .

His complaints about the world as it was presently constituted particularly spoke to me, whose life's great moan
ever since Nicky was born had been "*It's not fair.*" But I
remember feeling not only bored to death but vaguely
insulted by the tone of all this—talked down to. He had lost
touch with me in his two years away and now misjudged
my level, as he never had before. Around the same time,
when I was ill with some pox or other and he was going to
visit Pearl Buck, I asked him to bring me her autograph. He
did better, returning with a signed book of hers—but it was
a children's book, with a note beside the price on the flyleaf
about being "suitable for ages 10–12." My disappointment
was terrible. I was ten but had already read *The Good
Earth.* I blamed her more than him—after all, she wrote it
for some category I was supposedly part of. But then, I
never blamed him if I could help it, from a simple failure to
differentiate the woods and trees. His grace and affection in
small matters overwhelmed and obscured the view of the
larger matter: *he left me.*

If I had been less sniffy about *The King Is Naked,* I
might have paid more attention to what was undoubtedly
the most important section, the one called "Bogey Men,"
because it was a warning, intentional or not, to prepare me
for the day when he himself would be called names.

We don't yet know how to get along without a Devil. We
ought to see our world as made up of groups acting in certain
ways because that is to their interest, and judge them by
whether their interest is for or against the general interest. . . .

There has always been some group that filled this
Devil's role and so kept people from thinking out the real
causes of their troubles. Hitler used the Jews for this purpose, and they are also being used, increasingly so, by vari-

ous groups in America. In the south they use the Negroes, and all over the world, but especially here, communists are a favorite choice for Devil. People go completely mad on the subject of communists. It is of course important that they should never find out what communism really is, for if they did they would be compelled to use their brains. As it is, using only their emotions, they can blame everything that goes wrong on communists, whether it's a war or a strike or a food shortage or merely that their hair is falling out.

In closing, he wrote:

There isn't really anything to be scared of. Not even the atom-bomb is worth a single sleepless night. At the worst the atom-bomb can only delay the arrival of the new world of plenty. It can blow cities and their populations, but not ideas, off the earth.

Nothing was ever so worth working for as the new world that is now almost within our grasp. And the world we know now, while it is filled with hatred most of which is caused by ignorance, abounds also with love and the desire and capacity for love.

You are lucky, not unlucky, to have been born just now. Don't be afraid.

And yet of course I was afraid, though less of the atom bomb than of losing him again; and soon after he finished *The King Is Naked,* in 1948, I did. It wasn't a war this time, it was the founding of his newspaper. Everything changed completely. Life was full of fund-raising benefits starring W. E. B. Du Bois and Vito Marcantonio, folk singing, frenzied deadlines, the opposition hotting up. He came to Croton to see Nicky and me on Tuesdays after the paper was put to bed; the other nights he must have been with Jo. After dinner, cooked by Dilsey, we'd play poker, parcheesi, gin rummy, cribbage, concentration, Monopoly, Chinese checkers, canasta. Anything with good solid rules. It was all we could do, the four of us together, without fighting and

Mummy ending up in tears. She usually ended up in tears anyway.

The *National Guardian* was started in support of the Progressive Party's presidential candidate, Henry Wallace, who stood for peace and a revival of New Deal policies. They lost the election, of course—though for a while there had seemed no "of course" about it. After all, Wallace had been Roosevelt's vice-president until Harry Truman replaced him in 1944, just in time to inherit the presidency when FDR died the following year, and Wallace alone offered the people what my father and his friends thought the people wanted—so why not President Wallace?

Well, it was a disaster. Wallace got no votes to speak of. Truman beat Dewey by stealing Wallace's issues, which he proceeded to ignore once in office. And one of President Truman's first moves was an executive order requiring all federal employees to sign a loyalty oath and swear that they were not now and had never been members of the Communist Party. The idea took hold, and in no time, state and city administrations, even schools, hospitals, universities, had their oaths in place. Thousands of *Guardian* readers were caught up in the witch hunt, lost their jobs, were blacklisted. Now they really had something to fight for.

The benefits and deadlines continued, and the people's music played on: Pete Seeger was singing, Paul Robeson was singing—spirituals with the resignation changed to resistance. In "Ole Man River," you don't "git a little drunk," you "show a little grit (and you lands in jail)," and none of that defeatist crap about "I gits weary and sick of tryin', I'm tired of livin' and scared of dyin'," because now "I keeps laughin' instead of cryin', we must keep fightin' until we're dyin'." All the old hopeful workers' tunes could fool you into thinking that we'd prevail, that the world was a generous place, even while the opposition was pouncing.

One day in early 1953 they meant business. They sent Daddy a subpoena from the House Un-American Activities Committee (HUAC). What did they have to go on? His FBI file begins with a 1942 entry:

> On checking a reference to Mr. Belfrage, Supervisor xxxxx
> ascertained that this individual is apparently a rabid Com-
> munist. He is at least definitely radical and a fellow traveler
> of the Communist Party. Our files contain numerous refer-
> ences to a Cedric Belfrage xxxxxxxxxxxxxxxxxxxxxxxxx

According to these references, he had been: a delegate to a
California State Conference on Civil Rights; a contributor
to the North American Committee to Aid Spanish Democracy; a guest in 1937 at "a stag dinner on the ranch of
Lewis Browne, a prominent Trotskite [*sic*] and an author";
"a delegate on the Film Committee to the Fourth American
Writers Congress at New York City"; an editor of *The Clip-
per*, official organ of the Hollywood Chapter of the League
of American Writers, which had "well-known Communists" among its members; "an instructor in the School for
Writers, sponsored by the League (of American Writers),
teaching the subjects [*sic*] entitled 'Non Fiction'"; one of the
"Committee members of the National Committee for
Human Rights"; and "a sponsor of the 'Rescue Ship Mission' an organization . . . to rescue Spanish Loyalists from
Spain and France."

In a 1944 update—presumably to check out the man
who was about to work for Eisenhower in Germany—a
confidential memo to the Department of State, signed "J. E.
Hoover," repeated the above and added more; by then my
father was further incriminated by the revelation of past
membership in "the Hollywood Anti-Nazi League."

By the fifties the FBI was getting help from the public.
One document in my father's file that is less censored than
most seems to be a form letter thanking one of these patriots:

> Dear xxxxxxxxx
> Your letter postmarked April 9, 1951, has been received and
> I sincerely appreciate the interest which prompted you to
> bring your observations to my attention.
>   In these vital times it is particularly important that the
> FBI receive the aid of all loyal citizens and that information

of value be brought to our attention. Enclosed is some material I thought you might like to read.

Sincerely yours,
John Edgar Hoover
Director

Enclosure
Commmunist Threat in US
How Communists Operate
Hoover Answers 10 Questions on the FBI
President's directive & Mr. Hoover's statement 7-50

The people on the *Guardian,* independent radicals supporting national liberation movements, civil rights, and civil liberties, see themselves as guardians of the "decent popular tradition of America," of "Tom Paine, Tom Jefferson, Abe Lincoln, and Franklin D. Roosevelt." They are perceived by others as dangerous traitors, as *evil.* This is what slays me. How can I associate my gentle father with what they teach in school? With the mob's hatred and my schoolteachers' whimsical grades and the newspapers' vilification and the government's threats? Representative Harold Velde (chairman of HUAC), Senator Joseph McCarthy, and his investigating committee's chief counsel, Mr. Roy Cohn, say they are defending freedom against these rats and scum who are part of a global plot to enslave the world; Daddy says *he* is defending freedom while they are trying to enslave him. They say he is subverting democracy and undermining the Constitution; he says they are subverting democracy and undermining the Constitution. They say that he and his kind use "treachery, deceit, infiltration, sabotage, terrorism and any other means deemed necessary" and therefore don't deserve to be free; he says he loves America and they are hypocrites, betrayers of Jefferson and the Bill of Rights, not to mention Roosevelt's New Deal. They say New Deal, big deal, Daddy is a revolutionary who would liquidate those who disagree with his beliefs; he says they are the descendants of revolutionaries who fought for his right to disagree with their beliefs, and who is trying to liquidate who around here anyway? You could almost make a snappy variety routine out of it if only the congressmen didn't have all the power and the witnesses all the fear. With that kind of imbalance, witnesses didn't get to be funny.

There was nobody who could remotely share any of these concerns with me. There was nobody around who even thought about anything like that. Better than thinking about it anyway was just to keep the head down and work on being invisible.

Who says you have to be only one person, anyway? After all, I'm not just the daughter of a Red and a weird Englishwoman, I'm also a real American teenager. That is, if I can just bring it off. It's hard work keeping everything separate, but I'm learning. All I have to do is go downstairs to the Giglios.

4

RUNNER-UP

In dealing with a male, the art of saving face is essential. Traditionally he is the head of the family, the dominant partner, the man in the situation. Even on those occasions when you both know his decision is wrong, more often than not you will be wise to go along with his decision—temporarily—until you find a face-saving solution.
—SEVENTEEN MAGAZINE'S BOOK OF YOUNG LIVING

The Giglios moved to Spuyten Duyvil from a suburb like the one we came from, but the way Debbi talks about her hometown makes Croton really sound like the sticks. Everything about her is like that. She's only a year older than I am, but she's already gone steady with a boy for ages. The nearest I got to boys in Croton was looking up their last names in the phone book. Her boyfriend's name is Wolfe,* "but he isn't Jewish." He's captain of the football team, and she a drum majorette. She would be. Debbi has success written all over her: she has personality. If you have personality, popularity just comes naturally. Maybe I can learn from her how to get a boyfriend. For ages now I have been consuming the magazines to find out how to go about it ("Dating Secrets of the Stars," "10 Guidelines to a More Beautiful Bust," "Understanding the Psychology of the

Male Sex"), but something goes wrong, if not because my foot is in my mouth more or less permanently then because I'm marked as different, unacceptable to parents. Number One, unlike Captain Wolfe, they *are* Jewish—people just are, and definitely everybody I love. No need to go into that with Debbi. Two, just wait till other people's parents find out about *my* parents. All they've got to do is hear my father's name frothing out of Senator McCarthy, in the same breath as "a conspiracy so immense, an infamy so black, as to dwarf any previous such venture in the history of mankind." No need to go into any of that either.

The perimeters of Debbi's world are manageable and cozy; a person can cope with what's inside them. Not too good at school (Walton, not Science), she's got all it takes to fulfill her ambition of becoming an airline stewardess, and she invariably has the right retort, smart but not smart-alecky. She's never at a loss for what to say, how to butter up the teacher or put a boy at his ease. The fact that her eyes are kind of close together and her nose a little big is no big deal next to her pep; also, she is really stacked, as they say, with this big bust and weensy waist a boy's hands can fit around. And does she know how to dress! Always the faddiest thing, but *quality*, and fitting right and starched and ironed. Her mother takes care of that. Debbi is some dancer, too. No step too tricky, and she can even do a few soft-shoe routines. She got hold of these fantastic dancer's mesh hose, a tuxedo jacket, top hat, and cane, and with her hair tucked up but the rest really bouncing, she can knock 'em dead dancing and miming the words along with the record of "I'll Build a Stairway to Paradise."

Debbi's real name is Desilda, after her father, Desider-ato, and her mother, Matilda. I call them Mr. and Mrs. Giglio. They call each other Mr. G and Mrs. G. He is an encyclopedia salesman recently promoted to head "*the whole Eastern Sales Division*" (always spoken in italics), the reason the family moved to the city. The Giglios have this reputation for being in love. Once, a neighbor caught them necking in their car at night, and everybody thought it

was real cute to have three kids and a twenty-year marriage
and still get a charge out of necking in cars. They're always
cheerful, these two. They have beautiful mouthfuls of teeth,
and they smile, smile, smile. Mr. G because he's such a success, I guess, and Mrs. G because Mr. G is such a success
and she is helping him. They have no room for sadness.
They thank God. Just as they named their oldest daughter
after each of themselves, they went half and half on her religion: since Mr. G is an Italian Catholic and Mrs. G a German Lutheran, they got Debbi in with the high-church Epis-
copalians. God gets the credit anyway, no matter how you
worship Him, and the Gs live by the rules.

Being at the Giglios' place is in many ways like still living in Croton; and knowing Debbi is almost like having a
second chance. A lot of kids in my class there also had Italian names—Luposello, Fittabile, Ottaviano, Zulla, Manzi.
Like the Giglios, they were terrifically proud and happy
about being American, with everything to be proud and
happy about. Why make waves? Why read a book if you
know the RBIs of the whole Yankee line-up by heart, or the
kind of kick pleat a pencil skirt ought to have? This stuff
they don't tell you in books.

Just as Debbi has her kick pleats down pat, her mom
knows the whole A to Z about keeping a nice home. Their
place smells of soap, cleanser, floor wax, metal polish, disin-
fectant, window spray, bleach. They have the right new car
every year, the wall-to-walls with the oak-leaf pattern and
the old-American colonial-style maple furniture, the latest
never-before-seen labor-saving appliance (steam iron/waffle
iron/electric blanket/garbage disposal/Waring blender), and
they're hooked into installment plans. Mrs. G is a red-hot
shopper with a nose for the new. Chlorophyll comes in?
She's got it—in the soap, the deodorant, the gum; and the
new chlorophyll dog food almost makes her relent in the
kids' campaign for a pet if they could just find one that
didn't shed or shit. The Giglios are the first on the block to
be painting by numbers. The minute someone comes out
with the felt circle skirts with the appliquéd poodles on

them, the girls have one each. Mrs. G raids Manhattan for
the latest gadget for the house; the United Parcel truck is
forever pulling up at the door. She won't take any bull from
the furniture companies. The merchandise comes with a
scratch, she calls up right away. "Hello, Better Business
Bureau?" etc. But once it all passes muster, it's really taken
care of. Mrs. G scrubs it spotless, then she polishes it, then
she rubs and rubs it. She coats Johnson's Wax on her plants
so the leaves are easier to dust. She'd coat it on her daughters if she could.

Besides Debbi, there are two once-identical twins of ten,
named Cherilee and Happilee, both called "Twin." Happilee, whose name sounds especially cute next to a surname
pronounced "Giggly-o," unfortunately sucks her thumb,
which has made her upper lip protrude, and there is a lot of
conversation about the orthodontia problem. They paint
bitter stuff on her thumb and make her wear gloves to bed,
but she can always get that thumb in there. It really is the
only cloud on Mrs. G's horizon, unless you count Debbi's
acne. Of course, it isn't strictly speaking *acne,* I mean she
isn't *diseased* or anything, but she's always picking pimples
and leaving blotches worse than the pimples. "But at least
they aren't pus-y," Debbi says. She spends a lot of time in
the bathroom ransacking her pores for blackheads, white-
heads, pinkheads, and old scabs, gouging them out with
crescent fingernails and pins. The result is scarred but clean,
symbolic proof of purification.

Purification is what it's about. "My mother will *kill* me
if I'm not home by 10/I don't clean the icebox/I forget to
buy the milk," moans Debbi, and I am imagining, *kill?*
What does it mean? Physical contact at least: thwack!
thwack! Stinging abuse, raised voices whose volume con-
ceals the knowledge that somebody cares about you and
wants you to be a certain way enough to go out on a limb.
All the kids I know are forever bellyaching about parents
who harangue and browbeat them to clean their plates,
wash their hands, do their homework, get their elbows off
the table, act their age, be nice. With nobody to tell me to

do or not do anything, I have to invent who I am and get there by myself. But who? And how? It's easier to pretend I'm a Giglio.

However. Running and running, never catch up. Swinging and swinging, never hit the ball. Everything I do, this girl makes me feel dumb, ugly, poor, pathetic, dirty, wrong. That I have to baby-sit to make my own spending money, as I have done since age thirteen, instead of getting the folks to cough up an allowance, is too pitiful to discuss. That my parents are separated strikes Debbi as simply unacceptable, and I wouldn't dare reveal the disgusting fact that my father is living with another woman *out of wedlock*. She already knows my mother goes downtown *to work* instead of to shop. On top of that, my mother uses curse words, although most of the time only "bloody" or "bugger," and luckily nobody knows what those mean. Even the foreign way she's called "Mummy" instead of "Mommy" is impossible. And we have the wrong kind of car (a five-year-old Willys *jeep*, hardly used anyway since we left Croton and never go anywhere), and junk all over the apartment, and listen to longhair music and eat wacky food and don't go on vacations out west, and MY FATHER IS A RED. The whole of our life is unspeakable, in the sense that you do not speak of it.

And me, I can't do anything right, and I never think of cute, funny things to say. Obviously and first of all, I don't know how to dress, and I haven't got anything to dress in anyway. The fact that I go to Bronx Science means I am a brain, an obvious handicap to the repartee, the only appropriate use of the equipment. I don't own a slip, and when I get one it shows; I can't make spit curls, and when I learn they fall out; my dickey is crooked, my cuticles are chewed. Despite all this, some boys seem to like me, but Debbi makes me feel that's because there must be something wrong with me—probably they think I'm easy or something. If not, there must be something wrong with them.

Practically everything is wrong with me. You only have to look at Debbi to see what it is. I do all the regulation things, wear spike rollers to bed, stuff tissues down my bra, starve. I don't know which is the tightest, my panty girdle, my cinch belt, my pointy heels, or the smile fixed to my face to disguise all the pain. It's just that with me, none of it comes out right. When we went and bought the same clothes for our combined fifteenth–sixteenth birthday parties, Debbi's black velvet skirt fit snugly around her gorgeous curves and mine looked like a laundry bag; her orange cotton puff-sleeved blouse was starched and full of tits, and my powder-blue one sagged down my flatness and wouldn't puff. I feel constantly embarrassed, a loser, and even after Benny from the neighborhood tries to convince me, "You're better *looking* than she is, so what's the big pro*duc*tion?" I just think he's lying or counting things that don't count. I mean, he might think blond is better than brown, but what does he know? The point is, curly has it all over straight. Brigitte Bardot has an eighteen-inch waist: that's only about a foot smaller than mine. The world wants you thick here and thin there, this long and that short, these big and those small, and with me it's come out the exact opposite. What am I supposed to do about all these freckles? If only I hadn't kept twanging my braces with my tongue I might have straight teeth. Why do other people look born neat and five minutes past the mirror I'm like an unmade bed?

But if we're talking items and priorities, it's cleavage that counts. The whole world is an advertisement for knockers. Here is *Time*'s review of a new movie: "Sophia Loren, the bosomy beauty starred in this Italian picture, is running chest and chest at the European box office with Gina Lollobrigida." The film "gives visible evidence that her reputation is not inflated." Then they provide Sophia's age, height, weight, and the vital 38-24-38, one inch more in all major circumferences than Marilyn Monroe. Her performance is not discussed, nor are the script, direction, or other actors. Even if you're cute and popular, with a swell personality, they still look first at your boobs. I find out firsthand when I get cast in a play at a local boy's school

and they make me wear falsies. "It's *okay*," the director
reassures me, "it's only a *play*, they're just like *makeup*,"
but when I submit and walk onstage there is a pandemo-
nium of wolf-whistling. Funny how nobody ever reacted to
me like that before. My mother purports to address my
plight with, "I daresay one day you'll be pleased, because
when you're older they won't sag." Who cares about *older*?

These are just details, anyhow: Debbi has a family, a
real honest-to-God all-American family that sits around the
table doing a Thanksgiving imitation every night. Can't do
anything about that, any more than wishing will make the
Dodgers beat the Yanks this year. But I copy everything that
seems transferable. For my birthday Debbi gave me smoking. Now I end up going dizzy daily on her Viceroys. I start
inventing blemishes to squeeze, leaving scabs and craters
like hers in my skin, and toy briefly with ending my name
with an "i." Her ambition to be a stewardess becomes
mine—on international flights, though, in order to meet a
more broadminded Mr. Right; she's happy with domestic,
"'cause that way you don't have to learn a foreign language." I sunbathe with her on her terrace—that is, she
"works on her tan" and I try to join up freckles. I shave,
pluck, tweeze, and wax *unwanted hair*, which is harder for
me because mine is too light to show. I buy eyelash curlers
and try to coax my invisible blond lashes into Debbi's Ava
Gardner–style fringe. I get saddle shoes like hers and try to
keep them not just white but *shiny white*. I imitate the exact
height she rolls her dungarees up and her white socks
down.

Underneath I know what a coverup it all is. I know all
that counts, really, is that my father never comes home anymore. Why should he want to? The atmosphere is humid
with tears. Sometimes the way he looks at my mother it's as
if he's never seen her before and wishes he hadn't now,
either. That's worse than anything.

It's better to concentrate on the Giglios. I can't keep
away. I am definitely in some kind of trance in this whole
matter: why do I hang around there all the time? The

minute school is out or it's Saturday morning, I'm in the elevator going down to Debbi's. My mother thinks I'm nuts. She took one look at Mrs. G and never wanted another. Boring, she says. What does she know? Her notion that we *outclass* my Norman Rockwellian models is greeted with one great Bronx sneer. I'm interested in performance, not that European eyewash about class. I learn things from the Giglios, things about how to dress and act and be. Like, my mother says it's better to have one "good" outfit than six cheap ones, but how's that supposed to work if you have to wear something different every day?

Debbi is on the ball: she knows what I want to know. I feel incredible gratitude for any advice she throws my way—tips about accessorizing, the right direction to twirl the pincurl, etc., not to mention serious guidance like the importance (almost as critical as changing from suede to patent leather in the summer) of making an entrance, how when you go into a room "what you got to do is you pick out a chair that is color-coordinated with your outfit." I spend months practicing this. Unfortunately, if there is anybody else I care about already in the room, sizing up the upholstery gives way to seizing up entirely until I find a way to sit anywhere at all. And then it's on somebody's orange flowers, and me in my pink stripes. I am just *hopeless*.

The best lessons from Debbi emerge when she recounts her various challenging encounters with elders and betters and boys. "How I talked myself outta this, outta that . . . " is the running theme:

"So this fella goes ta me . . . so I go ta him . . . then he goes . . . "

"He didn't! Jeez, is he obnoxious!"

"Yeah, and does he think he's God's gift, I'm tellin ya, it's pathetic. So no kidding around, then I go . . . "

"Wow! You said that? That musta really gotten him! Boy, did you ever tell him where to get off!"

"Yeah, well, like, what a shmoe! Whatta nerve on him! Talk about an overstuffed outhouse! Is he a nothin'!"

In Debbi's stories she is always the innocent victim who

wins out. "So he's takin' me out in his Pop's new De Soto, and we're moochin' around, and he goes, So howsaboutit, kiddo, ya wanna brew? and I go, Not me, Daddy-o, I'm drivin', so he goes, Izzatso, get you, since when, you can't drive, and I go, Ya wanna bet? So he gets me on his *lap*, right? and I'm havin' conniptions, li'l ole me at the wheel and what can I do? I'm drivin', what a panic, and all of a sudden I get this *feelin'*, you know? Like I'm sittin' on somethin'? and I go, Crikey, either this car is bumpy as all get out or you got a extra beer bottle in your pocket. And then I realize! I coulda *died*, swear to *God!* Story of my life. Wasn't that just George?"

Nothing like that ever happens to me. I'm not too sure what she's talking about anyway, I just laugh when she does. But it's obvious that an afternoon with Debbi is worth a week at school. One of these days I'm going to figure out about boys.

Gradually I glean a few rules.

1. Never show your true feelings. The more you like a boy the more you ignore him, or if necessary treat him with sarcasm.

    (a) Never mean what you say.

    (b) Never say what you mean.

    (c) Be sincere.

2. What you have to do is convince them they're superior; that's their problem. Girls have to pretend it's true; that's theirs. Perish the thought you should be accused of "playing games." This one is like the eleventh commandment, the one about getting caught, because it's what boys say you're doing when you're pretending they're great and it shows.

3. If you're stuck with some creep, you can string him along till you meet someone better, since what counts is having a date Saturday night, never mind who with.

    (a) Make sure you meet his buddies. Who knows, one of them might turn out to be the love of your life.

4. You also need to make friends with girls—they might throw some brother or halfway decent reject your way; but

never trust them since they're the competition and they'll use it against you. See 1(a) and 1(b) above.

5. Boys are only out for one thing. You have to prevent them from getting it. Otherwise they won't respect you anymore. It's a moral duty. There aren't too many moral duties in this game, so it's easier to keep your mind fixed on the one.

Sort-of-Rules: Here comes the tricky part. There's a whole rigmarole of stuff you *do* have to do with boys, and Debbi has these sort-of-rules for when you do it. Kissing on the second date, a little necking maybe on the third or fourth if he's really cute and he respects you. Then starts the problem with the hands. Above the waist, below the waist, outside and in. But that's for much later, when you've gone steady for ages or get engaged or at least pinned.

Debbi pays a lot of attention to her virginity; it's her main selling point, after sex appeal. A sexy virgin is what you have to be. Sex must be pretty horrible anyway, we figure. Debbi found a copy of the Kinsey Report, and we read that 42.7 percent of American women have sucked their husband's cocks. Ick!

I have more ammo against males than Debbi any day of the week. Upstairs in our apartment is a book that makes the Kinsey Report look like Mother Goose. In her spare time my mother free-lances medical articles and ghost-writes books for psychiatrists, and she's accumulated a large library of source material. One book is about sexual psychopaths who did things to women like rip open their stomachs and coil their intestines neatly beside the body or bite off nipples and swallow them. There are photographs of the corpses. Some of them don't even look like people anymore, so a pencil or some familiar object is in the foreground to give it scale. One picture always gets me, a mug shot of a necrophiliac who worked in funeral homes so he could do things with the bodies after hours. In the photo he looks gentle and ashamed; it doesn't seem to me that he belongs there, since he never hurt anybody. But of course even he is a guy. A woman wouldn't get up to anything like that.

I'd never show that book to Debbi, not just because it would shock her but because it's another example of the unnaturalness of my life, that I could have a mother who would own it in the first place. Anyhow, it has nothing to do with *boys*. I can't imagine one of the guys from the neighborhood, even Bob the acolyte, biting anybody's nipples off. But just to make sure, I'm not letting him anywhere near mine.

I keep notes in my diary, in the mode of the magazines. "Oh what a fool I was!!! I believed him. I thought he really *did* like me. *Nothing* could have been farther from the truth!" He (or another he, or yet he-three) is "the swellest guy, but the *swell*est, that you'd want to meet," or "such a bubi, a real doll, quite a challenge"; or "Is he a nebbish: Ugh! An absolute *shmoe,* an infantile creep." Often the characters referred to under one heading are the same as those in the other; only the times are different. Never mentioned are actual mortifications like what happened six months ago when I was still a real baby of fourteen and my mother got a friend's son to take me for a horse-and-buggy ride around Central Park. I was too embarrassed to tell him I was allergic to horses and didn't have a handkerchief, so I spent the whole ride pretending I wasn't wiping snot up and down my coat sleeve.

In the inside front cover of my diary is a chart of boyfriends coded according to how much I like them, kind of personality (introvert/extrovert), whether they have kissed me, hair color, and religion. One of the magazines has recommended this "as a means to identify the emerging pattern in which you will find yourself." That's what this is all about, and *yourself* is just one thing: the kinds of boys you like. If most of mine turn out to be red-headed Jewish extroverts who kissed me, then I will end up wed to such a being and be defined at last. (The religious angle is my own: no magazine would include anything that might be construed as a suggestion to cross that line.)

I would die if Debbi knew about my chart. For that matter, I would plotz if she laid eyes on some of the specimens from Science I'm starting to go out with. (Well, we don't exactly "go out." We do things like take long walks down the river and over the George Washington Bridge to the Palisades, much more fun than chicken runs and booze. Or talking to Steve. Steve and I *talk* together. Also we kiss together. We have tongue language. Two kinds.) She'd think they're real jerks. Maybe they are. So what? I like them. *Wanna make somethin' of it?* I say to her, but only in my fantasies.

Every minute there's a new terrific crush on somebody. The first crush-of-the-day depends on who's waiting at the 10A bus stop, Bill or Eddie. If they're both there it's even better because I can love them both. Then Steve or Marcel or Arnie or Jonny from this class or that in the morning, Aaron or Mike or Gordon or Lew in the afternoon. Also there's Manny and Mickey, who stoop to look at me from their half-year ahead (*so* mature). Then there are the boys in the neighborhood and the church club. They're really complete poopheads—if you pooled all their brains they would still not amount to one moron—but they have cars and cute crewcuts, they know their way around the local bars and drive-ins and how to dress, all amounting to a certain veneer meaning that they'd pass Debbi's test. "They know how to treat a girl," she'd say. That means they bring you a corsage before a big date and light your cigarette and open the car door for you, closing it after you've got all your crinolines packed in, and they never curse without apologizing. It also means they manhandle you into dark corners at their make-out parties and you have to endure their breath and spit and paws all over the place. It's hard work having a crush on them compared to Steve at school. Steve is like me, a person. I don't know who these other guys are. They're not so sure themselves. *Boys.*

But in the end everything depends on whether I am in love today or not. It's not that I'm fickle exactly, just that if I am in love today then I love everyone, and I love them for what they are, which mortifyingly enough is usually just what the magazines would dub well under par, if not out-

side consideration. Bill-at-the-bus-stop is lovable specifically
for his shy shame about his acne, Eddie for how he hides
behind his Clark Kent glasses, Steve for his blushing stam-
mer. That is what makes them human and worth loving in
the first place, because they can't get away with acting all
tough and invulnerable.

The trouble is they're all Jewish, and they have parents.
There is this running mother tantrum on the theme: Get
that shiksa out of my life. In what way am I in her life? I
went to one movie and a few walks with her son. Drama.
There is something unreal about being oppressed on the
grounds of my belonging to the oppressive majority, when
any nitwit can see things are the other way around. However, it makes me more Jewish than anybody, if only they
would notice.

But then this son, braving it out on the shiksa front,
also decides to announce to his mom that my father has just
been denounced by Elizabeth Bentley, the "Red Spy
Queen." He might think it's pretty exotic, and naturally
nobody asks me what I think (I think nothing as a matter of
fact, but who knows that?), but for the parents, usually
panicked liberals scratching for some rock to creep under,
now it turns out I'm not just a blonde but a Red. Mostly
they're pretty ashamed of themselves and it shows in the
trouble they have deciding which excuse to use against me,
that I'm too American or too un-American. Of course you
can always take brave stands against these people, pity
them, defy them and whatnot, but when they're saying Kad-
dish for their son it doesn't help you down the aisle.

It's all so hideously depressing. Every day I get another
million miles from the true-life heroines of the success stories or the ads like "She's lovely! She's engaged! She uses
Ponds!" So it's back to the ironing board, down at the Gs'.
To straighten me out I need Debbi more than ever, living
proof of the way and the path. Even though I can't really
tell her a lot about my real problems I just live for my sessions with her, but they're pretty hard to come by, as Mrs.
G is forever sitting me down to tell me how she really got

Gimbel's to eat crow over the chipped saucer in the new dinner service, and incidentally to pass on her theories about life. "Bringing up children, it's like tending plants," she'll say, squeezing lemons in the new juicer. "You gotta watch over them and feed them and water them and cut them into shape, break off the bad pieces and get the little green shoots going. Every day it's an investment, so they'll grow big and strong and beautiful."

Part of the pruning process is to train the girls to be good housewives, so Mrs. G keeps them hopping by organizing giant clean-ups of rooms already sterile. "Desilda!" she cries if by some miracle Debbi and I are alone for a minute. "How many times I gotta tell ya. Your bathroom is all messy, straighten up your room, your sock drawer is a *sight!*" etc. Then she starts gabbing at me, and when I am finally released, full of lemonade and cookies, I find Debbi surrounded with and refiling the contents of her closet or scouring the bathroom ceiling, yelling, "Twin! Get the Ajax!" and I feel conned, not only because the Giglio place is never perfect enough to satisfy Mrs. G and there will never come a time when I can just be with Debbi and tear the secret out of her, but also now they are embarrassing me again, because here we have an actual *home,* with a *homemaker* in it, just like the ones in the magazines; and at the top of the building on the unscenic side is this apartment half the size of theirs, and theoretically I could be cleaning it up like they're cleaning theirs, only my mother is writing and I can't bother her with noise and it would take forever anyhow. We don't even have anything to clean with, and besides, the furniture isn't the kind you can really clean. Half of it is junk from some old hotel job lot, chipped and peeling, and the rest is very distinguished old English oak with crevices sealing in centuries of rancid crud you can't get out except by picking at it with a pin.

The best thing to do, as usual, is go up to the roof.

The roof of our building is bubbly black tar paper, with a four-foot wall around the edge and two elevator shafts, one

for each side of the building. I climb a ladder up one shaft
and perch on a special ledge where I can watch the world
moving. They say that this place is just above where the
Indians once sat as they waited for the tide to turn so they
could ford the stream—the island of Manhattan then was
an island only half the time, when the waters rose. Kappock
Street is a name from the Algonquin for "sitting-down
place."

As perfect as it is for sitting down, my place can't have
much resemblance to the Indians'. Everything is manmade
motion. Cars slow down to pay the dime toll on the Henry
Hudson Bridge in front of me, trains clack underneath my
feet to Grand Central through a slash in the cliff below,
boats bear freight and tourists past my legs around the
northern tip of Manhattan, planes make white feathers over
my head into the sunset (in my memory there is always a
sunset), and on Saturdays in the football season Baker Field
is full of fans screaming so loud you can hear what team
they're rooting for half a mile away.

And yet with all the tumult it is quiet where I am. I'm at
the highest point, the still center, the god's eye. Above it all,
that's me. Above my brother's lousy squeaking clarinet,
above my mother's contagious despair, above the fights,
above politics and what may happen to us because of them,
even above Debbi and her secret. She never joins me up
here. She tried it once, can't understand what I see in it.
Besides, her mother's always making her clean up. If my
mother ever said "Your sock drawer is a sight!" I think I'd
faint. Who ever heard of a special drawer for *socks?* Debbi
even has a special drawer for underwear, immaculate in
white and pastel subsections, interlined with scented paper
and sweet sachets. Even her days-of-the-week underpants
are in the right order. Me, I have a bunch of drawers with
every kind of junk hurled in: chemistry reports, curlers, old
sneakers. You never know what you'll find in our drawers.
"I bet you had interesting drawers," said a friend long afterwards, a friend with another neat mother, looking at me

wistfully with what seemed to be a pang of—surely not—
envy? Giving me a whole new slant on life.

When I'm on my elevator shaft, I don't lie. It would be
ruined for good if lies were allowed there. I even have to
admit the truth about the Giglios, what it is about them
that really draws me. With my parents' cynicism (on people
like these, at least, they agree) I can mock my model family
at the same time that I long to copy them. I have to shut
down part of myself with the Gs, though since it's the part
I'm least comfortable with, that's no problem. But when I
go to their place, if for some reason I intercept a look
between them, or if I have to go into Mr. and Mrs. G's bedroom, it seems like trespassing on some great mystery, stepping unworthy into a holy place. Only once before did I feel
this way: at the home of my cousins in England. *Here, people love each other*.

The Giglios have it all over the cousins, though,
because what they know how to do is fight with love. The
English don't fight. Scenes are so unpleasant. This must be
the secret of life, the ability to fight with love, and those
Italians in Croton knew it, and the Jews in the Bronx know
it, and I don't know it. How do you learn when the other
half of the fight just cries? How can love be real if you
can't be real in it?

I think about love on my elevator shaft. I think about
life. Life, I figure, is divided into six states of mind: ecstatic
happiness, happiness, contentment, boredom, depression,
and ecstatic misery. Let other people keep that stuff in the
middle: give me the *ecstasies*. The enemy is tranquillity:
boredom or contentment, whatever—Moods 2 through 5
are pretty much the same, equally to be despised. Reaching
a pitch of ecstatic misery, which seems more and more
available these days, is the best drowner-outer there is
except Mood 1. But how do you get more of that? Mood 1
comes out of nowhere in weird jolts—a blast of awareness,
all of a sudden this crazy choked expectant weightless

flight: *I have it all ahead, with nothing now to pay.* Such moments of pure, exultant clarity seem to have little relation to external causes, except occasionally in a moment of discovery. Once, my great ambition was to stand somewhere where no one had ever stood, see something that no one had ever seen. The disappointment when I learned that there was not an unexplored inch on the globe disappeared the day it occurred to me that just to crack open a rock was to witness a sight that had lain hidden, waiting for me, for millions of years. This kind of elation is substantial. There are the other, more ephemeral possibilities to be derived from a sudden pang of love for Bob the acolyte or somebody, but you don't get that sort of Mood 1 without Mood 6 for a chaser, because one minute you love somebody and the next minute you see perfectly how they don't love you back. Full to empty in a flash. But good or bad, you know it's ecstatic, because you can't eat and when your girlfriends ask you how you are you say, "I'm *dying.*"

Which brings me to death. Lately everything does. The roof is an obvious place for thoughts of death, combining lethal height and such singular solitude. My friend Rick, the one person from the neighborhood who feels as messed up as I do, introduced suicidal thoughts to me up there one night while we were watching the lights of the city meet the stars. He is a virgin, and he really ought to be trying to make out with me, but he gets so drunk that he smells nauseating and says absolutely anything that comes into his head, half the time some gobbledegook from Rimbaud or Blake and the other half his own garbled poetry about flying off the roof. I'm in a panic, partly because his loneliness is so terrifying I wish he would. But to get rid of it I mother him down off the ledge and back into the elevator to the street and into his car. His ideas stay behind on the roof, though, demanding to be thought about whenever I go back up.

"There are two of me," he'd said. So sad and gentle, the boy, the only other self-admitted split personality I know. "The one who thinks and the one who does things. The second usually obeys the first." He was leaning much too far over. "But when the second is hurt, the first *always* knows about it." What did he mean? You could tell he'd been watering his mother's gin again. It wasn't just the smell; although he's really good-looking, with deep bright eyes in a strong square face, he seems to sweat pure gin, constantly glistening with this strange stuff that's clammy when he brushes up against you, and his cheeks turn into patches of pink bright as shrimps. To top it all, they've cropped his pretty bronze curls and given him a military haircut that makes him look as if he's failing to impersonate somebody else. Nobody understands him.

One thing I like about Rick is that he never thinks about politics. He is absolutely oblivious to politics! There's no problem finding people who are apathetic, scared, or dumb. But Rick has another slant altogether: politics are *irrelevant*. He wants to be a beatnik—though can you be a beatnik all by yourself? You need to find your generation. But he's working on it, reading and fantasizing. He dwells in the land of life's higher truths. Where he got these big ideas in his sixteen, seventeen years, who knows. Not from his parents, who are divorced and only think of him, when they think of him, as impossible; they pack him off to the Admiral Farragut Naval Academy, which to hear him talk is modeled on a Nazi concentration camp. Not a lot of life's higher truths around Farragut. But he writes to me constantly, sending poems or quotations I don't understand, like markers on a route I cannot travel; and he takes me out when he's home on vacation. "Out" by Rick is the nearest bar that has good jazz, but then he gets stinko on straight shots with beer chasers, so it's back to the roof with me always connecting Bird to despair. Throughout, Rick is relating his latest observations on the horror story that is the human lot. I really, really don't want to hear. But when you think about it, his ideas are just more complex versions of my own. Ending it would solve everything.

Ever since the Great Depression, suicide from a tall building is definitely the American way. The New York way, for sure. Unlike Rick, though, I have this problem about jumping off the roof. My father would be really upset. If somebody loves you so much, even if they don't have the faintest idea who you actually are, you just can't do that to them. But one day an answer occurs to me. What if I assassinated one of the people Daddy's always mouthing off against? Why on earth, for instance, hadn't just one of the people who must have committed suicide in Germany in the thirties taken a potshot at Hitler? What did they have to lose?

I start compiling a list. It's easy. My old man has a whole pantheon of knaves, scabs, goons, and ghouls. (His favorite terms of opprobrium are, like him, part English and part American; there's also "familiars," for "finks," a word on loan from the Spanish Inquisition; plus the toadies, stooges, and sycophants who latch on to the above, but they are by their nature secondary.)

Witch-hunter-in-chief J. Edgar Hoover is the obvious front runner. In a way I'd prefer a nice foreign dictator— Chiang Kai-shek, Franco, Salazar, or one of those terrible Latinos, Trujillo or Batista or Stroessner, say—as that way you're more likely to get rubbed out quick in the crowd and not molder for years on death row. There's Pope Pius— Daddy *hates* Pope Pius. (Though he lately granted him absolution when Pius recommended clemency for Julius and Ethel Rosenberg after they were sentenced to death.) But Americans are really the ones who preoccupy him, and I can't afford to go abroad, so I may have to sacrifice myself. There's Cardinal Spellman. Either of the Dulleses, John Foster or Allen, would do fine. Or those guys he calls "the monstrous regiment of Macs," Senator McCarran, Attorney General McGrath, Senator McCarthy, General MacArthur? It turns out to be pretty complicated.

"Who's the worst man in the world?" I ask everyone I meet. Well, not Debbi. Her mind doesn't work that way. She thinks I'm out of my mind to mess around with Rick at all, especially when she hears he doesn't try to make out, which means "he must be a fairy." As for J. Edgar versus the caudillo of Spain, this is not a contest that interests her; anyway, she's busy rehearsing her new dance routine, "Love for Sale."

The list lengthens. Then out of nowhere some Science wisenheimer points out that you don't solve anything by assassination unless you have an alternative to go into the vacuum. Grudgingly I have to admit I hadn't thought of that; I guess it's true, even though solving anything except my own misery has been the last thing on my mind. So assassination just has to join the list of schemes that got nowhere, like the hole to China I started digging on Finney Farm with a boy called Dallas when we were seven or eight. As the ground got harder, we decided a secret underground playroom would be more fun than China anyway. Finally it was just a hole in the ground.

But interestingly, this new hole in the ground has metamorphosed. One night a black man in one of Rick's jazz clubs, tired of Rick's moaning, got me thinking when he muttered, "You know, you can only die once, but you can live forever feeling sorry for yourself." Then, too, I have grown so obsessed by my list that dying seems a bore by comparison. Especially since between the roof and the ground—it comes to me in a flash and with absolute certainty—I will suddenly understand everything. It's just too much of a swindle otherwise, life. The one thing it's got to do for you sometime is explain itself. What's the point? When did it start? Where does space end? (*How deep is the ocean? How high is the sky?*) What a marvel, finally to get it! So how could death be a punishment if it's such a thrill? As a matter of fact, in that case it might as well be postponed, since it has to happen anyway and something equally exciting might come along meanwhile. Unlikely, but possible.

An exciting thing finally happens. I come in second. In June 1952, Rick proposes me for queen of the hop at Farragut, and I come in second. You mean Me? It's flabbergasting. Well, they did only judge from a photograph. But there's a

nice ring to it: second. It means you're in the running, yet
you're only running *up,* so nobody's got to notice especially
and hate you for it. Debbi says something withering about
"How's he gonna hop without his hooch?" and I can tell
she's jealous. My mother, though, is delighted: she even
takes me shopping for a ballgown, a strapless to wear over
my crinolines, billows and froths of white tulle with more
tiers than a Christmas tree, and a stole, and a rhinestone
necklace (plain, could be diamonds?). Rick looks even more
handsome in his formal naval get-up and without the alco-
holic flush. He gives me an orchid corsage attached to a
transparent plastic bracelet, and I get a crown of flowers,
the one for the runner-up. We really look convincing.

The event palls quickly. Of course Debbi was right,
there is nothing to drink at the academy, even at the senior
prom, and Rick without gin is like Rice Krispies without
milk: inert. More than that, his sadness, when he is sober, is
so undiluted by poetry that he makes you want to burst out
weeping.

5

THE BLACK DRESS

The ex-Communist and ex-sympathizer of Russia should be tolerant of Communists and sympathizers. They too will awaken from their dreams.

—LOUIS FISCHER, *THE GOD THAT FAILED*

"And when I tell them . . . how wonderful you are," my mother is trilling, ". . . they wouldn't believe me. . . . They wouldn't believe me. . . ." Once, she alluded to something romantic involving this song that happened to her and my father at Claridge's, so I know when she sings it she is thinking of him.

But there are times when I suspect that she does things with other men despite being almost fifty, and the idea is revolting even if it isn't immoral. At Christmas it so happened that we gave each other almost the same thing, one of the new nylon half-slips. The one I gave her was plain. The one she gave me was lacy and pleated. She seemed disappointed, and since I didn't care, we swapped. On the other hand, I couldn't imagine what difference it could make to her, since who would see her slip? But there was a feeling I got from the coy way she acted that somebody

would. *At your age!* I'm thinking, and she knows I'm thinking it, and I know she thinks I'm a prig, and she knows how
much I despise her beautiful woman's vanity and most of all
her terror of getting older and losing her looks, leading to
this awful desperation about finding another husband first,
fast. But what she doesn't know, because she is too wrapped
up in pity for her situation, is how scared her daughter is of
being like that too.

"... You heard me saying a prayer for," she warbles,
"someone I really could care for. . . ." She'd prefer an
Englishman again, no doubt about it, because she'd like to
go back home to London, but Nicky and I won't let her.
Something along the lines of her first husband would suit—
an unexciting, unexcitable, dashing sort of swain (rich, goes
without saying) who'd look after her instead of landing her
in this sort of nightmare.

While waiting, she has a lot of beaux who take her out,
though none of them really fills the bill. There is Jules, who
is smart and handsome but badly crippled from polio and
much too young for her. There is Sam in Westport, Connecticut, a square-shaped old guy in a string tie, who is her
square-dancing partner: once a week she dresses up in circle
skirts and petticoats and do-si-dos out to the Willys jeep,
for once to remove that eyesore from among the shiny new
Buicks, Pontiacs, and Studebakers with their low-slung
chrome and their whitewall tires. A bald rich guy called
Eddie takes her to fancy restaurants in Manhattan; she
doesn't come home from work first before dates with Eddie,
and the next thing you know we own a new glass, fork,
bowl, or more curious knickknack, lifted on her usual pre-
sumption: "Nobody was using it." She and Eddie seem to
go to the Waldorf-Astoria a lot, judging by the inscription
on an increasing number of our knives and forks. The Wal-
dorf silverware is unusually unattractive and chomped with
other people's toothmarks, but within a year we have a
dozen everything, even the pieces there aren't slots in the
drawer for, like butter servers and small soup spoons (for
what? small soup?).

My mother has a different set of rules from most people. Maybe she got them from her mother, Piggy. Piggy used to take them on picnics around Cookham-on-Thames, where they had a cottage, and never bothered about private property notices—because, she said, "Whenever I see a sign saying No Trespassing, I think, '*That's* for the *oth*er people, as naturally *I* am welcome *ev*erywhere.'"

In the same way, my mother feels welcome, say, to that bough of dogwood blossoms from somebody's tree. When she's caught with the evidence—which is not infrequently, because she's quite open about it, there's no stealth involved—she always laughs and says (charmingly, disarmingly, like her own mother), "Nobody was using it!" Even if caught with the evidence by *the very person who in fact was using it,* my darling kleptomama only laughs some more and doesn't mind a bit.

Her friend Alison, who moved into the converted horse barn across from our cow barn in Croton, had six matching plates of a rare cobalt blue, with hand-painted flowers around the rim. Alison couldn't help noticing one day that there were only five matching plates, and soon afterwards that we had one exactly the same. What a coincidence! My mother was perfectly affronted to be accused of anything. It was all supposed to be hilarious: Mummy's little quirk.

This quirk also comes in handy for her failure to notice that she is cheating at solitaire, which she calls "patience." She doesn't smoke and hardly drinks: her vice is patience. And there are no two ways about it: this game has got to come out, because she has staked her life, in the form of a crucial wish, on the result. She wrote about her addiction in her fourth novel, *New Winds Are Blowing* (published five years after the events):

I took to playing endless games of patience with varying sets of rules. If it came out completely I would promise myself everything would work out all right in the end. There would be no divorce and he would get over the affair with [Truda] and settle down again happily. If it came out very quickly, he would even fall in love with me again. If I had to cheat to make it come out that meant I would have to work a little harder. Of course, more often than not it didn't come out at all, which was bad, but not fatal. It just showed that I was not on the right wave-length for the Fates and I would have to rephrase the questions and try again.

One birthday when I got a present of a cardboard wishing well with little numbers corresponding to I Ching–type fates in a booklet, she not only appropriated it because I wasn't using it, but lost all the little numbers that matched the discouraging fates in the booklet.

She's big on wishing, is my mother. Since it hasn't seemed forthcoming in the normal run of events, she has had to reinvent the pot of gold by hiding things from herself. Thus, for instance, various books contain dollar bills, or even the occasional five. She doesn't know which books or where in them; if she knew, it would ruin the surprise of encountering some loot. Just as well she doesn't, since any money I've encountered has moved on. *She* wasn't using it.

There is a peculiar attitude about things in my family. "Never own anything worth stealing," my father's practical view, has become willy-nilly the policy for the rest of us, for all that he has only an absentee ballot these days. It's not done to buy a new car, even though our old jalopy won't start half the time, because "cars," says he, "are just for getting from A to B." Americans may be buying three-quarters of the cars on earth this year, but they get no help from us. The national fantasy is the new car, but my father cannot imagine what all the fuss is for, and Mummy concurs not least because she is the one who gets to pay. (He provides her with a pittance for our upkeep, but only when the *Guardian* is giving out paychecks—far from every week, and the burden rests on her.) Other priorities are confusing. You'd think there is no great expense connected to paper, say, though paper ought to count to people who make a living writing on it. But while my father's work takes place on the kind of temporary yellowish crud that turns to powder almost at a touch, my mother's, even when it's stacked to manuscript length, always seems to be on the backs of some watermarked bond with a hotel or office logo. Nobody was using it, probably.

It's amazing how much nobody is using when you come down to it. Soap and sugar, for instance: Mummy never has to stoop to buying those. Then there is the free sample if you can think of an angle for the magazine. Mummy gets kitchen stuff and all her cosmetics that way. She couldn't forgive some hugely famous French perfume maker who sent her a dummy bottle of colored water "to photograph" when she worked for the *New York Times Magazine,* so "I had to pan their scent without, of course, having smelt it."

Once, pressed in a book, I found not money but a tiny shrunken V-mail letter she had sent to Daddy during the war (they gave you a copy when the original was photographed to go overseas).

Jan 5 1945

Little sweet dear—I was so touched with your anniversary present and most of all with the message that went with it. I am glad you are glad. Sometimes I don't feel you have had anything much out of the deal, yet, maybe someday you will. I liked it so much, especially when I used to feel as if it would be for ever. Perhaps it will be after all. But perhaps it is better not to let yourself believe in things being durable. Maybe that is the way you get to take things for granted. Actually nothing makes me feel more happy and wonderful than to be able to take things for granted and not always have to struggle and fight, but I know you are not like that; you like to do things the hard way, and I will try to remember to make life a little difficult for you if I can. Anyway I sometimes think I am becoming almost as volatile as you. I just looked it up: "of gay temperament, mercurial; evaporating rapidly." Well, most of the time you are pretty gay and you certainly have a habit of rapidly evaporating, so that must be right.

Gaiety is certainly the word for her, if not for him. It is what makes her so irresistible, I think—Mummy sure has no trouble finding men, and apart from Daddy she doesn't lose them. She *embraces* gaiety, becomes it, exudes it. In her state of rapturous joy and good humor, she can captivate everyone. Without it, she is like a missing person. The double entendre in her party joke—"He said, 'Do join the party!' and it all sounded such fun. . . ."—only really works when she does the telling.

Gaiety implies an edge of hysteria. "High-strung" is maybe the right description for my mother, like the perfect purebred horses in the books I've spent years reading. Except the horses usually go through helpless torture in the wrong hands, and with me and my mother the torture is pretty evenly distributed. One April Fools' Day in Croton, I crept downstairs early with Nicky and put salt in the sugar bowl. At breakfast, puffed up in expectation, we peeked at each other, suppressing our titters as she groped for her special large mug and stirred the ingredients. What a joke!

She took a sip and screamed. It was a crazed scream, terrified and terrifying, a scream audible for years. She flung the coffee in a sweeping arc around the room. Its stain striped the walls, an irregular dado.

Mummy's favorite beau is Louis Fischer, who wrote part of *The God That Failed* and later ended up with Svetlana Stalin but now comes into town regularly from Princeton, where he is some kind of a Thinker, to see my mother and load her up with ammo to fight my father. I can see that Louis has a certain sexiness, even at his age, with his furtive, hooded eyes. He never tries to play up to me and Nicky like the others do. Besides, I had to read a book he'd written about Gandhi for a school report and was forced to admit it was pretty good. But he is still not forgivable, because when Mummy quotes Louis at Daddy the row is deafening. Why does she have to do that? She knows perfectly well that the one thing a leftist can't stand is an ex-leftist. They call each other names like running dog, fascist hyena, capitalist swine—four-legged things, for some reason. Not that Daddy sinks so low, but show him a turncoat comrade who becomes an anticommunist socialist and he can spit *social democrat* with more venom than a Mexican pit-viper.

Word reached the FBI too about Louis entering our lives: he had "been in frequent contact with MOLLY BEL-FRAGE, according to XXXXXXX." In fact, "from all indications"—whoever or whatever they were—the FBI got the idea that "Fischer and Molly Belfrage are presently in the relationship of master and mistress without the knowledge of the latter's husband." To plump out the dossier, they collected various background snippets about Louis, like "The files of the New York Field Division revealed that STEVE NELSON wrote to LILLIAN HELLMAN and stated that he met her in Valencia in 1937 with LOUIS FISHER [*sic*]." There was a list of Louis's books—mainly about the Soviet Union, where he'd lived on and off for fifteen years starting in 1922—and the observation that he had "made an ideological break with them following the Moscow Purge Trials in 1937 and 1938." Now, he is quoted as saying (to the FBI or in their hearing), he is "anti-Soviet because I think the Soviet Government is doing more harm than good" and "Stalin made a fatal blunder by aligning himself with Hitler."

Louis is the only beau with politics. When Daddy left he took all that with him. Mummy is pretty well indifferent to such matters except as they adhere to whatever man she's interested in; but it's the man who counts, not his philosophy. Before the politics had been punched out of her, she'd been enthusiastic enough. In one novel, she wrote of a character in Hollywood not unlike herself:

We looked at the world and saw how it was in those countries where . . . all the decencies of life, all the freedom and democracy, had vanished. And that's where we began to do something about Fascism while there was still time.

Committees! You should see the committees that started shooting up like devil-grass in your pet lawn. Committees for peace, for civil liberties and against anti-semitism, committees for the consumer, committees for the Spanish Loyalists. And I'm up to my neck in all of them. . . .

She was, too. Not anymore.

It's all so messy, this politics business. She has no stake in it now, and with her reason for living here gone and her mind more and more on old friends and glories, why can't she just go home to England, where one is left alone? There, eccentricity is celebrated, if only to provide others with interest and amusement. That's her view of it too; America still leaves her baffled. "You see," she has her character explaining to her children in one novel, "I'm not even half American. I don't really live here at all. I'm just . . . well, visiting." Even in the novel this "visit" had already lasted more than a decade. When they start investigating my father and talk about deporting him she almost hopes they'll deport her too—though what for is a problem—if only she wasn't frightened half to death of what they might do first.

Without provocation the FBI decides to get her. One day in 1952, out of the blue, they send two men to *McCall's,* and the next thing you know she's fired. Because she isn't informed of their visit and the magazine gives no explanation (she only hears later by chance), she is in shock, assuming some awful personal deficiency. And we're broke, as usual. What to do? She's got a second-string job writing radio scripts for Carlton Fredericks (all tried out on me first even though I'm not eleven anymore); the government hasn't bothered to pounce on that one yet, but it may not be worth their trouble. There's something she can do better than anyone alive: home in, with uncanny speed, on the only four-leaf clover in a whole field of threes, and the only typo on a page. But just one of these skills is marketable, and she's never had to stoop to copy editing. Even the lowliest employ on a big-time slick would attract a visitation from the Feds, anyway. She can fill in ghosting a medical book, but it doesn't pay. There are brainstorming sessions with me and Nicky along the lines of: "Let's think of a name for a new perfume!" This funny game, played with oddly gritted teeth, is going to make our fortune, and she is assured of access to the appropriate ear because the boss of Fabergé lives in Croton and his daughter used to baby-sit for us. Somehow we never come up with it.

In no time, though, she has rallied and found work, editing a magazine called *Health Digest*. The people who own it are lefties who don't care about calls from the FBI. Besides, they can get her cheap because she's desperate. And she does such a good job. This is her idea: she reads all the medical journals and writes to the doctor authors, flattering them that their stuff is too significant for such a limited audience and that ordinary other people ought to read it too (what a credit it would be to them in their waiting room . . .), if only it were rewritten in plain English— which she offers to do for them, for nothing! The doctors are so thrilled they don't ask to be paid; plus they subscribe for the waiting room.

The next time I go to dinner with Daddy and Jo we talk about the situation. Washington seems to be closing in on us, he says, via the weakest link: Mummy. He is full of admiration for the way she's handling everything. Making salad while Jo mixes ingredients for a meat loaf, he says how guilty he feels about her fate, and how inadequate to protect us from deportation or any other ghastliness that might intervene. He only prays that since I enjoyed my summer in Britain so much last year, I can adjust to life there. After all, unless they change the laws I'll always have dual nationality, and eventually will be free to choose where I live. This sounds about as realistic as the "choice" I am one day supposed to make among my names—Sally and Mary and Caroline, which represented to them the spectrum of female possibility, one of which would be revealed as me.

While the meat loaf bakes Daddy launches into a speech about the imminence of American fascism. This is the signal for my mind to glaze over, as if he were talking Italian or Zulu, and instead to contemplate what really bothers me. It occurs to me that now I have a new D-word to write everywhere and try out my magic on: D– – – – – – – – –. But the fact is, I no longer believe in the efficacy of such a charm, not least because it accomplished nothing last time. Besides, chance, luck, magic—the way my mother stacks the deck, she's taken all the sport out of wishing.

Instead of wishing, I've taken to tampering with the evidence, working hard in my diary and photo album inventing our perfect sham family. I keep the records, so why shouldn't they say what I want them to? It's not as if I'm the only one. Last Christmas, 1951, to fool their families and friends in England, Mummy and Daddy arranged for us to pose for pictures all dressed up and sitting around together, Nicky fiddling around with a baseball bat while we three "related" for the camera—as if we actually had something to do with each other, almost the genuine article if you didn't look too close. None of *that* was my idea. But if I'm sticking them in the book with cozy captions about "Mother and Dad" (the way real American children call their parents), it's for the same cosmetic reason, so when people see it they'll think we're just like the pictures, always dressed up and hanging around together like that.

Of course my mother has done enough picture layouts in women's magazines to know how we are supposed to look. She has also read all the psychology books, she even ghostwrote some of them, so she is aware of how we are supposed to act. She can kid strangers, but not me. She goes through the motions of loving me equally; it's just that I don't get that feeling. She thinks I shrink from her because of some allergy to kisses. "Don't kiss my!" she's always telling people was my first sentence; they have a good chuckle. God, is she embarrassing. "I think I shall go and fetch my little pink beads," she says I said when her mother Piggy tried to kiss me. I didn't like Piggy to kiss me because she had a mouth like a ventriloquist's dummy's, deep lines separating jowls from a little claptrap rubbery hole in the middle. But now that don't-kiss-my and the pink beads and the whole shebang is carved in stone in Mummy's latest novel: "Sheila [that's me in this one] didn't like demonstrations of affection . . . it was like kissing a poker. . . . Jonny [that's Nicky] loved to be loved and petted and hugged and to feel the warmth of affectionate, loving contact." This anti-kissing mythology is some big deal. Maybe her kisses do mean something like love at that moment to her, but it's a queer love I feel, all about her loving herself for making me, not about loving *me*. I wipe them off when she's not looking. Keep them. I am not here to be a gift to you from yourself. All I want is for you to care about me the way you really care about Nicky, not cover up with smooching.

For instance. I haven't got anything decent to wear and even though we're the same size she won't let me borrow her clothes. She says if I wear her black dress to go out with Bob the acolyte on Saturday night she'll jump out the window. This dress is heavy grosgrain silk with a ballerina skirt, it cost $34.95, a fortune, I never stop hearing how she slaved for it, and once she did let me wear it in a play. This time she opens the window and sticks her leg out. "Don't worry about me," she says. "I'll be better off dead. *You'll* certainly be."

It's my first real date alone with Bob, and he's taking me downtown to a real nightclub, the Latin Quarter or El Morocco or the Copacabana. The thrill of it! I am so in love I haven't eaten in a week. Why can't my mother and I just talk like regular people? Transact a little this and some of that, be nice or angry or anything, why crazy? I could say, "Oh please, just let me wear it this once, I promise I'll never ask again," to which she might reply selfishly, "Listen, I can't let you, it's my one good dress and I need it too badly," or esthetically, "Don't you think black is a bit old for you?" or even, if there were miracles, maternally, "Let's find something else that looks wonderful on you." This insanity of hers is so *mean*. I don't think you should threaten to kill yourself over a dress, but she always outmaneuvers me with madness. I say go ahead see if I care.

I know it's strange, but I don't feel guilty about any of the things I do to hurt her. None of them can possibly be as bad as her original sin in not loving me, even though the last emotion she is ever likely to feel for me, considering how I hurt her, is love. But it's too late; it doesn't matter. Most oddly, the whole thing mirrors her problem with Daddy, and I am his surrogate. "What did I ever see in her?" I heard him mutter once. I am aware too that she is in many ways admirable—plucky, brave, and clever.

The annoying thing is that I'm really in the mood to jump off the roof myself this time, just to show her. I read the psychology books too, after all; they help me figure out things about life, since she's no use. In one book a child victim says, "I didn't *ask* to be born." That's a good one, I thought, I'll save that one. And now this is exactly the moment for it, her with her leg out the window. When she hears me, my mother thinks I am so amusing that she comes back inside; any minute now the remark joins "Don't kiss my" and the whole darling collection of Kiddies' Kute Sayings she exhibits to her friends to make my flesh crawl. Oh god. Now I'm going to throw myself off the roof out of sheer frustration. But if I do, what about Bob? What if he's The One?

We don't talk. I spend all Saturday cleaning the apartment so it passes in a dim light, then I take a bath and *to hell with it,* I put on Mummy's black dress. When she sees what I'm doing she starts to scream and look completely wild, then slams out the door. I don't care, she'll only wreck the impression I'm trying to make on Bob if she's around anyhow. She's always humiliating me with boys.

I've bribed Nicky to answer the doorbell when it rings and give Bob a beer while I pretend I'm not quite ready. I am so starving and terrified with love that I can hardly face him. When I come out I cover up with the sort of chat they say is expected, how my mother regretted not seeing him, how are things going with the Knights. My heart is talking louder than my voice: I could faint just looking at him. As we're getting ready to leave and everything has gone as smoothly as a story in *Seventeen,* the door bursts open and my mother plunges in, all wet and completely black with soot, moaning and wailing. She's been rolling around on the roof. There are white tear streaks runneling down her face among the soot.

I am appalled. Fifteen years old and my life is over. Freeze. No, die. Leave. Get out, pretend it didn't happen. Bob helps, he doesn't mention it. We drive downtown and take in a show, then the big event: he has actually got us a table at the Stork Club! The band and the celebrities and the glamour—FLASH! The club photographer captures us forever. Who cares about my mother? Maybe it really didn't happen.

But something worse is saved up for the end. Bob is kissing me good night, and I forget about my mother—my insides have entirely dissolved with groveling, helpless passion when, as I reach my arms up around his neck, I hear the sickening sound of ripping cloth: I have torn the black dress under both arms and ruined it forever.

We have a lot to forgive each other, my mother and I.

6

CATCHING COMMIES

You had to have been there in the golden age of Red-baiting to appreciate how strong the anti-Communist fever was in the United States. All you needed to do was paint someone with the Communist label and that person never worked again.

—ART BUCHWALD

Just as trains in the Old West needed cowcatchers, our society, speeding along, needs spycatchers. Toot to-o-oot! It is vital to get those foreign bodies off the track before they derail us. The difference is that while a cow gives itself away by going *moo,* a spy doesn't always wear a trench coat and talk with a Russian accent. All true-blue red-blooded Americans have to sleuth him out. It's our first duty.

So how do you tell a commie when you see one? There are many signs. Commies, cryptocommunists, comsymps, parlor pinks, and all their fellow travelers—even misguided liberal dupes—try to fool you by hiding behind words like "peace" and "brotherhood." Therefore, one way to expose these people is to call their bluff by not using those words anymore. If that means forgetting about things like unions and workers, tough. "Comrade," "solidarity," "militancy"—

we'll call them *jargon*. Giving up the ideas behind them? Small price to pay. What about we just say everybody's middle-class? Shazam! We're all the same! So how can we be class enemies? If I exploit you, it's just because I'm a ruggeder individual! How come nobody thought of that before?

Of course, commies are big on "revolution." Well, we had one of those once, but it was in the olden days, and besides, ours had those nice Founding Fathers, large homey figures carved on a mountain, none of that raggedy bomb-throwing anarchist stuff that foreigners go in for. And certain songs and emblems we'll just pass on for now, thanks. They can keep their "This Land Is Your Land," their peace doves. May Day, who needs it? Let's have an I Am an American Day—that's more like it.

One surefire pinko pointer is their constant harping about "civil liberties." Some people actually think our freedoms should extend even to those who disagree with us. What a crackpot idea! Another dead giveaway is the argument that just the other day the Russians were our allies, so cooperation with them at the time could hardly have constituted treachery. Some smart alecks allege they were only being "antifascist" ahead of the rest of us. Well, if they're in trouble now it serves them right for stepping out of line.

A tip-off and a half is the screwball notion that there is no "secret" connected to our Bomb. It's ours, isn't it? *We* know if it has a secret or not.

Then there are the malcontents. They do not agree with Ike that we are "the greatest force that God has ever allowed to exist on his footstool." Those people should go back to Russia. Kill a commie for Christ!

And furthermore: If you don't want to be called a traitor, don't act weird. Toe that line. No oddballs! Introverts are oddballs, they're not one of the gang. Therefore, introversion is un-American.

Yessirreebob!

The *Guardian* is full of causes. The minute anybody becomes a truly unspeakable pariah, you can bet my father's in there sticking up for them. There are the Smith Act defendants, a dozen Communist Party leaders jailed for "conspiracy to advocate the overthrow of the government by force and violence," their convictions upheld by the Supreme Court. Harry Bridges, the West Coast longshoremen's union leader fighting deportation to Australia. Steve Nelson, the Pittsburgh Communist who had fought for the Spanish Republic and couldn't get a single one of the fourteen hundred qualified Pennsylvania lawyers to defend him, so had to do it himself and was sentenced to twenty years for sedition. The Hollywood Ten. The Trenton Six. Alger Hiss. Carl Braden, jailed for "state sedition" after he and his wife sold a house in a white neighborhood of Louisville to a Negro family. Charlie Chaplin, who'd gone to Europe in September 1952 and couldn't come back again. Anyone who won't sign a loyalty oath or is on some blacklist or takes the Fifth Amendment. At one point the paper took on the fight for both CP leader Elizabeth Gurley Flynn and former CP leader Earl Browder, who was expelled by the party. This eclectic policy annoys the orthodox, who don't get the point: it's being a victim that counts.

But my father's persecutors, people like Harold Velde, chairman of HUAC, who calls the *Guardian* "a propaganda arm of the Kremlin"—can they really be unaware of the paper's problems with the Communist Party? Fomenting behind-the-scenes unrest in the staff, the CP might not, as my father said, "want to kill us if they could help it, rather they wanted to push us into the background or take us over; although just what purpose another party-line organ could serve, only they knew." The CP's fury peaked in 1949–50 when the *Guardian* defended Anna Louise Strong, an American radical journalist, after the Russians accused her of spying; and until Stalin's death in 1953 there was party animosity over the paper's siding with Tito against the Soviet Union. Sometimes it went beyond animosity. "Their [the CP's] private war against us . . . was waged vigorously," my father wrote later. "The going was rough with the political group that we had resolved to defend as a mat-

ter of principle, but we were surer than ever of the principle: keeping our eye on the real enemy."

The biggest victims of all are the Rosenbergs; nobody
else in America, including the CP, will speak up for them.
Julius and Ethel are awaiting execution for "conspiracy to
commit espionage." They are accused of giving the bomb to
the Russians, and the judge in their 1951 trial said their
crime was "worse than murder" because they had supposedly caused the war in Korea and were responsible for its
fifty thousand American fatalities. For two years they've
been in line for the electric chair, and their appeals keep
being rejected. What happens to them happens to the American left.

On Saturdays Daddy takes the train to the death house
at Sing Sing with the Rosenbergs' lawyer and their two little
boys. The *Guardian* tries to publicize the case with stories
of the Europeans who are on their side, from forty British
MPs to the pope. Jean-Paul Sartre, quoted in the *Guardian,*
writes that people may feel the Rosenbergs did something,
"perhaps not much, but something," yet "when one has
read the 1,715 pages of the trial record, doubt is no longer
possible: Julius and Ethel Rosenberg are innocent." But it's
hard to drum up much U.S. interest in the trial record.

In 1944 Julius Rosenberg, a twenty-six-year-old electrical engineer, was said to have passed on to the Russians,
our allies, a sketch of a lens mold that he supposedly got
from Ethel's brother, David Greenglass, a machinist at Los
Alamos. Julius said, "Our case is being used as a camou-
flage to paralyze outspoken progressives and stifle criticism
of the drive to atomic war." That's my father's kind of language; they're his kind of people. But even if they're out-
and-out Reds instead of just "progressives," it's impossible
to believe that any of them, least of all David Greenglass,
had the competence in physics to do what they're charged
with. Why would they need to anyway, when the Russians
had already recruited their own top physicist, German
refugee Klaus Fuchs, who'd been on the spot in Los Alamos
and had already revealed in England that he *did* do it?

It isn't really about that, Daddy says. It's about terroriz-
ing left-wing Americans, who are overwhelmingly young,
Jewish, and urban, like the Rosenbergs. It's about humbling
yourself to these bastards by abandoning your principles.
Greenglass got off in exchange for his sister's life, and she
and Julius could get off too if they would only "confess"
and name names.

But real Americans don't worry about this kind of thing
and what am I supposed to say to them? To people like the
Giglios, I can't talk about my father's motives, they're not
interested. Nobody wants to think about it at all. Your regular guy and gal are having their version of the good life,
getting richer by the day, praying and staying together, and
they want to keep it that way. They have no reason to
doubt the existence of what the Rosenberg judge called "a
crime worse than treason" and a "diabolical conspiracy to
destroy a God-fearing nation." And the irregulars are too
busy ducking blacklists, loyalty oaths, and the fantasies of
salaried stool pigeons to risk speaking up now.

The activity around the *Guardian,* the Rosenberg Defense
Committee, and all the fund-raising and fight-back groups
on the left keep Daddy busier than he's ever been. He still
manages to come to Kappock Street occasionally, but it's
usually more convenient and less tense for Nicky and me to
visit him downtown. There's no more question than there
ever has been of his taking time off to have fun with us—
though last summer he and Jo went to stay with friends on
Shelter Island for the odd weekend, and once I got to go
too. It's not because he's depriving us, just that he doesn't
have time for fun himself. That weekend at the beach is the
first occasion I can remember when he went away to relax.
However, if the logistics aren't too complicated, you can
always tag along with him on his normal ports of call.

Once in a while Daddy takes me downtown to visit his
friends. Mostly they live around Greenwich Village among
the arty bohemians. Many of them *are* arty bohemians. The
idea that they might want to overthrow the government by

force and violence is just silly. This is borne out by the fact that "at none of these trials was it ever proved or even alleged that anyone had engaged in any actual conduct which might result in the overthrow of the government," according to Victor Rabinowitz, one of the few courageous lawyers who defended them. The supposed overthrowers are in fact just gentle, nice, and scared. They stuck their necks out on behalf of the Spanish Republicans or too early against the Nazis, and they have a lot of naive (it seems to me) ideas about peace, justice, and the brotherhood of man. They get dewy-eyed at the sound of Woody Guthrie and pretend to hark back to some American "folk" tradition, as if American folk had ever done much besides grub for gold and kill Indians. But their own souls are pure. "The Communists are the *good people*," Laura, a friend of Daddy and Jo's, says to me, sensitive to my strange state of mind: confusion tinged with pride and shame. She herself isn't in the party, so far as I know—the whole point is that she respects party people for being braver than she is. But she and those like her are pretty brave themselves, because they're losing everything by sticking to their guns.

All of them are in a cocoon. As long as they're in there together they feel snug and strong and free to make wisecracks and pretend everything is okay. Their places are like Jo's, cheap and rent-controlled with bumpy walls, but full of books, bright folk art, Weavers records, and bottomless pots of chili, curry, bolognese sauce. Like the folks at Finney Farm, they resemble one another in their nonconformity. The oddballs among them are all oddball in the same way. The fathers have beards over their turtlenecks, and the mothers wear leotards and Capezios, black or beige, with natural leather bags and sandals, their hair straight and long and smoothed back into buns and ponytails, and no lipstick, only mascara. The kids, Red-diaper babies, make me nervous: goody-goody and unrevolting at home, they are naturals at the jargon, in on everything politically, and up on all ten stanzas to the Red version of "Green Grow the Rushes-Ho."

> *10 for the days that shook the world,*
> *9 for the nine Scottsboro boys,*
> *8 for the Eighth Route army,*
> *7 for the Seventh World Congress,*
> *6 for the Haymarket Martyrs,*
> *5 for the years of the Five-Year-Plan,*
> *4 for the four great teachers,*
> *3, 3, the Comintern,*
> *2, 2, the opposites, interpenetrating-ho,*
> ONE IS WORKERS' UNITY AND EVER MORE
>   SHALL BE SO.

They even know what all ten things *mean*, and they don't think it's funny. Mostly they go to "Little Red" or some private school in the cocoon where they don't get into trouble. If they're in public school, they have to lead double lives like me, but inevitably their names blend in, nice Jewish names like everybody else's. They don't have to worry about being called *Belfrage*.

But just like the kids in my neighborhood, the second they're home from school these kids leap into blue denim. It makes me think a lot more about how much alike we all are, or want to be. Jeans have made it as the uniform of youth only in the last two or three years, but already it's as if they're God's greatest gift to the world in the history of America, as if people have been waiting forever for the chance, finally, to look *exactly alike*. Yet at the same time you hear constant dumping on "Red China" for making everyone wear navy blue, and on communists in general for their supposed uniformity. "Uniformity," their thing, is for some reason not the same as "conformity," ours. Maybe the trouble with the Chinese is that they're just lousy salesmen and can't get people to want whatever it is badly enough. Americans don't mind being navy blue from sea to shining sea as long as they think it's their own idea.

One part of the cocoon Daddy takes me to is Paul Robeson's, one day while he is practicing with his accompanist, Larry Brown. This Paul Robeson is the biggest man I've ever seen. I seem to come up to his knees. When he shakes my hand he engulfs it in his, and then he engulfs the room with his deep dark voice. Even when he speaks, he throbs. It's my own private concert, he says. But he has nobody else to sing to anyway, because he can't get a booking, and his records have been removed from the stores. That he was an all-American end for Rutgers has been erased from the Hall of Fame in Canton, Ohio, leaving the only ten-man team in football history. He can't get a passport to go where he is invited to sing or act because, as for so many others, his "travel abroad would be contrary to the best interests of the United States." So his only big concert since the war was for twenty-five thousand Canadians who massed at their border, which he was not allowed to cross.

People are locked in, locked out. The European, Canadian, Asian, and Latin American friends who used to visit us can't come anymore: they are in "the Black Book," as we call it ("the look-out book" to the Immigration Service), which contains the names of all suspected subversives, and if they get as far as a border they are turned back. But for foreign pinkos, U.S. visas are impossible to come by anyway. How you get on the list of the forbidden is not revealed; but to get off you have to prove you are untainted, by supplying affidavits from five people (who are then fingerprinted and investigated themselves) that you have been "an active anti-communist."

One of the most telling songs Paul Robeson sings is "Which Side Are You On?" Everything is about sides; there is no room in the middle any longer for simple, decent people. One of the very few to reach a position of some power is Clifford Durr, FCC commissioner. He's had his say, warning that "we are going to elevate to a new level of dignity informers, stool pigeons, and gossips, a class which since the days of Leviticus we have been taught to regard with suspicion and scorn. We are going to fight communism by employing the methods upon which we profess to base our abhorrence of communism." Durr is soon on the way back to where he came from, Alabama, there to try to practice law with no paying clients.

Going to the *Guardian* office is as nice as being in the kitchen with Daddy and Jo. There's a warm feeling, everybody part of a team doing what they call "togetherwork." The staff are all paid the same wage—when they can afford the payroll in the first place, which isn't every week—and they seem to enjoy themselves. Also in common with Daddy and Jo's place is an atmosphere of live-for-today excitement and alertness, as if J. Edgar Hoover and his G-men might march in the door any minute yelling, "The jig is up! Gotcha red-handed!" It's true, they might.

Of course the whole staff indulges the editor's children. Ever since the paper started, when I was eleven and Nicky seven, we've been allowed to play with the presses (they let me work the linotype and ink the block and print a sign, the one yearned-for sign missing from my childish collection: PLEASE DO NOT SPIT ON THE FLOOR); and we're given candy by the compositors and caricatures by the cartoonist and told nice things about our father, whom they all love. After a while you can forget about purges and oaths and blacklists and all the gruesome things happening outside; you can even forget about fear and believe the world might work their way as you get caught in the momentum of activity and smell the printer's ink and hear the machinery rolling and listen to the stories mocking the whole show out there.

A favorite of Daddy's, which sums up his attitude, is the one about the guy from the local paper in Madison, Wisconsin (Joe McCarthy's state), who stood on a corner and tried to get signatures on the Declaration of Independence; 111 of 112 people polled thought it was subversive and wouldn't have any part of it. After looking up "subvert" in the *OED* one day, Daddy reports, "First used in John Wyclif's 1382 translation of the Old Testament," which says, "Whan forsothe God had subuertid the cities of that regioun." If subverting is a good enough activity for God . . .

A Harvard professor, Zachariah Chafee, has figured out that according to J. Edgar Hoover's estimate, $\frac{1}{20}$ of 1 percent of the population are Communists. This means "the odds are 1,999 to 1 in favor of free institutions. . . . What can we do to prevent them from harming the other 99.95% of us who have on our side only city and state police, almost every newspaper and schoolteacher and professor and preacher, FBI, Army, Air Force and Navy, never forgetting the Marines?" Daddy says the professor is bending over backwards on those figures, as everybody knows that not only is Communist Party membership going down continually, from fifty-four thousand in 1949 to fewer than twenty-five thousand at latest count, but a large number of the remaining card carriers are FBI agents. However, since none of them know who they are, they're mostly reporting on the other agents. Lest anybody think he was joking, Robert Kennedy commented (much later, but nothing had changed), "It is such nonsense to have to waste time prosecuting the Communist Party. It couldn't be more feeble and less of a threat, and besides its membership consists largely of FBI agents."

At the *Guardian*'s peak there were seventy-five thousand subscribers—how many FBI agents?—but that's about it. And Daddy talks only to them these days. The world is so black and white and scared of crossing boundaries that he rarely has the chance to see anyone who doesn't agree with him. Some of them go a lot further than agreement; they worship him. I think this distorts your perceptions. It's nice for him to have that moral support, fans laughing at his witticisms and bowing down when he comes their way, but I've got to go out into the world where the normal people live, and they think other thoughts entirely. Daddy scoffs at them, the great American public; he is fooled into thinking that the "bad" ones behave as they do not out of ignorance (since if "the truth" were not available how could it be so clearly understood by his friends?) but out of cynicism or perversity or greed. I know that's wrong, or anyway it's not right. But actually I have internalized his reactions so well that I wouldn't dream of bringing up anything touchy like that to him.

A lot of this stuff leaves me out, honestly. I don't get it, or I don't care enough maybe. Whatever the reason, I know when to keep my mouth shut. I remember a day several summers ago when my father's friend Jack McManus took me up in his seaplane from the Hudson River and we flew all over Croton and up to Peekskill—where, it so happened, Paul Robeson was singing at a "Summer Musicale" for the Civil Rights Congress, and among the stick figures we could see far down below a five-hour riot broke out. Jack had taken his plane up specially that day to view the concert from above. But to me it counted far more to be flying over Finney Farm and photographing our house. Later it counted more that the pictures—the proof of a unique vantage point—were printed backwards, making no sense of the landscape, than that scores of my father's friends, caught in the Peekskill fighting, had been wounded and frightened out of their wits by American superpatriots shouting: "Go back to Russia, you niggers!"

The worst of it is that Daddy has stopped trying to make sense of things to me. Maybe he thinks someone of fifteen or sixteen can understand on her own, or maybe it's all so loony it doesn't make sense anymore to him either. In any case, with his back to the wall he has too much else to worry about. There is a growing gap of incomprehension between us, which I attribute to his being so out of touch with American reality—even though it's not entirely his fault; but just as he only sees friends in the cocoon, he only reads what allies write, hears one side of the story. When Whittaker Chambers's *Witness,* about how he fingered Alger Hiss, was a 1952 Book of the Month, for instance, I thought Daddy would have been better off reading and rebutting it than just jeering about pumpkins. If he can't explain his reactions to me, what chance has he got to beat this rap?

He's not comfortable talking about the Soviet Union,

either. He suspects that Stalin has loused up his end of the dream but thinks the official U.S. version of events is wildly exaggerated and the West is out to destroy socialism anyway so what are the Russians supposed to do? After all, goes the speech, fourteen countries, including the United States and Britain, invaded the USSR when it was born (they don't tell you that in school), and obviously they're still trying to overthrow it, a job made easier by the destruction of so much of the country and the loss of more than twenty-five million people in the war—a war that the Russians, no matter what the Americans say, were instrumental in winning. Even Churchill admitted it was the Soviet Union that "tore the guts out of the Nazi war machine." As for Stalin's excesses, to my father they are aberrations, and there are successes in Asia to offset them. China has shown that the people themselves can choose socialism, and the Indochinese under Ho Chi Minh and General Giap, in taking on the French, are trying for the same thing.

Since Daddy believes "the Red menace" is a lot of malarkey, nothing will persuade him to take seriously the basic axiom of Western policy—that the Russians are bent on war. Washington never seems to take into account the extent of Soviet suffering in World War II: how could they be willing or even able to go to war again now? Thus he rejects everything Americans have to say on the subject. He won't believe a word of any Luce publication, for instance. Nomenclature tells you whom you can believe and whom you can't. Anyone who refers to "Peiping" in "Red China" and calls the USSR "Russia" is automatically identified as foe (the *New York Times* occasionally even says "the Soviet," which is like calling the United States "the United"). And those who stick up for the idea that Chiang Kai-shek still rules "China" and not just the island of Formosa, and that he should keep the Chinese seat in the Security Council that by rights is Mao's, are in Daddy's book lunatics. (U.S. passports are even stamped NOT VALID FOR TRAVEL TO OR IN COMMUNIST CONTROLLED PORTIONS OF CHINA, as if there's anything much else, or indeed as if anyone who got there might immediately "go over" to the Reds.) On matters of relative sanity, he may be right: Secretary of State John Foster Dulles makes Daddy look like the most reasonable man in the world. Not that that's saying much. Maybe both of them overdo the old defense about the enemy's enemy is my friend.

Wishful thinking is Daddy's flaw, rather than excessive adherence to dogma—the perceptible pause between exposure to, and acceptance of, any truth about the Soviet Union that might happen to be disagreeable. He takes too long, for my taste, but he accepts the truth in the end. Because the one thing you can say for him is that whatever hyperbole he goes in for, he is never less than absolutely true to his principles. Soviet betrayals may secretly break his heart, but he is more immediately concerned with the Western left's constant infighting. His big idea is to get them to quit dividing up into smaller and smaller name-calling factions by attempting to create in the *Guardian* the one place where all kinds of radicals can concentrate on what they have in common, not what divides them. He never ignores the truth when he sees it for the sake of some doctrine or discipline. He can dish it out, but he can also take it. He is an honest man.

That's why they're after him.

Daddy's turn to be victim comes in May 1953. He tells HUAC, "I have no confidence in this committee and I believe, on its past record, that whatever answers I would give would be used to crucify me and other innocent persons." To a congressman who says that my father "ought to go back to another country" he replies, "I think just as much of this country as you do." He won't answer their questions.

Soon afterwards he and his best friend, Jim Aronson, who started the *Guardian* with him, are summoned to appear before the Permanent Sub-Committee on Investigations of the Senate Committee on Government Operations (the McCarthy Committee for short), where chief counsel Roy Cohn puts it to him: "Now, between 1937 and 1953, that is, today, have you continuously been a member of the Communist Party?" Daddy has the nerve to throw Christ at him: "Mr. Cohn, 'Thou sayest it' is a famous answer to a similar trick question." It seems likely his reference is lost on members of the committee, who haven't had the benefit of Bible sessions with Reverend Claude.

By what right, asks Senator Stuart Symington, has he invoked the Fifth Amendment?

"I cherish the Bill of Rights," my father says. "Its Fifth Amendment was adopted for the protection of the innocent as well as the guilty. I am invoking it as such."

"Do you think you are completely innocent?" asks the senator.

"That is correct," says Daddy.

Or thus it's reported in the *New York Times,* which goes on:

> Mr. Belfrage's testimony was heard not only by the subcommittee, but by Mario T. Noto, chief of the Subversive Activities Division of the Immigration and Naturalization Service. Mr. Noto had been called in by Senator Joseph R. McCarthy, Republican of Wisconsin, the subcommittee chairman.
>
> Last week, when Mr. Belfrage testified before the House Committee on Un-American Activities, Representative Bernard W. Kearney, Republican of upstate New York, called for his deportation. Senator McCarthy told Mr. Noto today that he hoped "prompt consideration" would be given the Belfrage case, already under study, and that his subcommittee would expect reports on progress made.

Roy Cohn, too, demanded "prompt action to eliminate this man from the shores of this country."

My father said, "Until these charges are proved in a proper way, in a proper court, I do not regard anybody as having the right to take any such action."

What do they care what he thinks of their rights? Cohn left the room and phoned the FBI then and there. "Roy

Cohn called," reveals a memo to Hoover's sidekick Clyde Tolson, and said that Belfrage had appeared and refused "to state whether he was a Communist." The very next day, May 15, 1953—as the FBI put it in another interoffice memo:

> SUBJECT: _____ BELFRAGE, Subversive
> Deportation proceedings.
>
> #### CEDRIC BELFRAGE
>
> XXXXXXXXX of the Department called today to advise that the Immigration Service at 11:15 this morning arrested the above-named subject, and he is being taken to Ellis Island and being held without bond.

Pretty prompt.

This is interesting. No evidence, no charge, no bail. Coincidentally, his arrest happens just as we're learning in social studies about U.S. constitutional safeguards against vicious Old World laws and customs. We've just heard all about the evils of ex post facto and bills of attainder, and the practically religious sanctity of the right to habeas corpus. But here's the mystery. Since my old man isn't accused of anything, just put away without a charge, what happened to habeas corpus? If arrested, this one goes, "the individual must be presented with a statement of the charges against him, and provision must be made for bail and for a speedy trial." With no statement of charges the lawyer can't apply for bail. And since all they have in mind, presumably, is that he is a Communist and everyone knows he isn't, even if he might have been once when it wasn't a crime, so much for ex post facto—a law that "seeks to declare a person guilty of a crime for a former action, although the action was not criminal at the time committed." A bill of attainder removes the civil rights of traitors. Suspected Communists are routinely called traitors on the Senate floor—you could say this is what the Red menace is supposedly about. And you could certainly say that anybody arrested and locked up without a charge has a certain civil rights problem, especially when there's no "regular judicial trial," constitutionally guaranteed or not. But in any case the original point of congressional committees was to develop material for legislation, not to persecute and punish people for what they think. What to make of it?

None of these refinements mattered to the FBI. They just wanted to get rid of him. After years of researching the subject, they got no nearer to Daddy's politics than they did to the color of his eyes. A couple of paid perjurers said he was a Communist, and that was that. The truth was rather blurred: he didn't want anyone to know precisely, in case they were forced to speak, but he certainly had joined the party in 1937, and quit again within three months. Couldn't take the line, the discipline. As he later wrote, "Some hundreds of thousands of Americans of my complexion, temperamentally argumentative yet accepting that socialism stems from discipline, had tried joining the party at one time or another. We had decided that 'fellow traveling' (as the non-Communist, non-anti-Communist role was known to inquisitors) suited us better." Even *Time*, not generally known for its accuracy in this department, got it right about Daddy: he wasn't "the Red" but "the deep pink Cedric Belfrage." But the nuances counted little and the shade of pink was academic. All you had to be was "progressive" (which could almost give a bad name to progress, god forbid) to get a summons to Washington.

In any case, he and his coeditor, Jim, wouldn't answer anything, responding over and over that they sought the protection of the Fifth Amendment to the Constitution to avoid replies that "might tend to incriminate" them. The *New York Times* printed Daddy's photograph—a face in pain, dejected, rejected—with this underneath:

WILL NOT ANSWER: Cedric Belfrage, British editor of an American magazine, who refused to tell Senators whether he had ever been a spy working against the U.S.

My pity and sorrow at the sadness in the father's face were overcome by my shame. How I hoped nobody was buying the newspaper that day. What would any reader infer from such a caption? Everyone knew that those who took the Fifth were guilty. There was no difficulty seeing this point of view. In the world of "The FBI in Peace and War," we had the innocent and the guilty. Which side are you on? The guilty were those the FBI was after: the pursued, the caged, anybody who wouldn't own up, all the way to those on Death Row. "I am getting rather weary," said Senator McCarthy during Daddy's hearing, "of these Communists"—it was all one to him—"coming before this committee and claiming the privilege when they are not entitled to it."

What people didn't know about this "privilege" was that invoking it was the only way to avoid being a stool pigeon. Daddy has explained it to me, and I sort of get it, it's just that I don't see how to convince anyone else. At one time my father's friends had tried the First Amendment, because after all, wasn't it all about being free to believe and say what you thought? But they went to jail for contempt of Congress. The way *Time* saw it, "For years, squatting behind the rock of the First Amendment (free speech), and insisting blithely that they were a danger to no one, U.S. Communists had screamed their denunciations and thumbed their noses at U.S. democracy." This could not be allowed to continue! As for the Fifth, if you answered only their questions about yourself, you waived your "right to privacy" and could not constitutionally refuse to name other people, thus subjecting them in turn to the blacklist and possible prosecution. In other words, you *could not* simply deny that you were a Communist spy, because answering the accusers at all gave them the right to demand the names of your friends, and in Daddy's case, the *Guardian* subscription list. In fact, as he wrote, Hoover's men already knew who was who, and the object was not "the extraction of names as such, but the public self-defilement of the victim in giving them." At this stage, a refusal to name names meant risking a prison term for contempt. "Of course, contempt is a mild word for what one feels toward these committees, but offering oneself for a period of enforced impotence behind bars is not necessarily the best way of showing it." So even though it made them look like fools and cowards, as well as Communists, no other formula was legally available.

I. F. Stone—the uniquely honorable journalist who put out his own newsletter, beholden to nobody—wrote in a 1953 issue about how

> the committees regard the invocation of the Fifth Amendment with equanimity. To invoke the Fifth is to brand oneself in the eyes of the public as guilty of any offense implied by the dirty questions these committees put. Those who plead the Fifth in most cases lose their jobs and reputations. This satisfies the committees, for their purpose is nothing less than an ideological purge of radicals and liberals from all positions of influence in American life and the demonstration to others that nonconformity is dangerous.

In a history of the *Guardian* that my father wrote with Jim Aronson, *Something to Guard,* he said:

> When Jim, Jack [McManus, the managing editor], and I were hauled into the inquisitorial labyrinth in the *Guardian*'s fifth to seventh years, we responded with incantations of the Fifth Amendment to the U.S. Constitution. Our readers well understood our reasons for this performance and might have disapproved any other. Yet how easily it could be interpreted as at worst conspiratorial, at best ignoble, by those who did not, or pretended not to, know the nature of the labyrinth! The trap was artfully baited. If we represented high journalistic principles, why didn't we take the opportunity to proclaim them before America?
>
> The short answer is that we could only do so at the peril of jail for "contempt" or "perjury," and that, in our case, would mean the paper's death. But even so we would only

have been feeding our own egos, for there was no opportunity to proclaim anything beyond the inquisitorial chamber's walls. The only forum we had was the *Guardian*. The media were themselves in the witch-hunting vanguard. They even rejected paid advertising for radical causes and, until the signal came from above to turn and rend Joe McCarthy, almost all ate from his hand. They could be trusted to distort anything we said that they didn't suppress.

Under the inquisitors' ground rules, the "witness" answering any one question in an "area" must answer all others. Thus to identify ourselves as publishers of the paper was to open the trapdoor for questions about anyone or anything connected with it, so we didn't admit even that "on the grounds [no other was acceptable] that it might tend to incriminate us." We shared the shame of this with America.

So since the committees could seldom prove anything, and since the one thing their victims refused to do was squeal, the Reds took the Fifth, which made them look so bad they were ruined anyway. All the questions had to be handled the same way. Daddy couldn't even say, when he was accused of being a Soviet courier by Elizabeth Bentley (the "Red Spy Queen"), that he had never seen the woman in his life. Not that she had much on him—according to FBI files, she testified that he had given the Russians "a carbon copy of an article" containing

a contribution by some prominent burglars in England, who apparently made the following information available as a patriotic gesture. This contribution concerned the technique of surreptitiously opening safes, doors, locks, and gaining admittance to most any type of building or office equipment.

For an authentic feel, she—whose FBI code-name was "Gregory"—revealed that Daddy's Russian code-name was "Benjamin."

Elizabeth Bentley, who made a living as a professional witness, testifying against everyone she'd ever known and many she hadn't, had been the roommate, back in the thirties, of a Communist friend of ours, Lini de Vries. According to Lini, she was an insecure, less than lovely nymphomaniac who had a collection of fantastic hats and had joined the Communist Party after getting a look at how many attractive CP men Lini knew. She cut them down like a thresher through a wheatfield, but failed to hold on to anyone for long until she met Jacob Golos, a Russian who gave new meaning to the term "double agent," as he was (a) a travel agent, and (b) a KGB agent. The two had a romance for a couple of years during the war until Golos's death, with Bentley helping him (she later confessed) in his spying chores. At that point came her political turnaround, which Lini attributed less to any political principle than to the recognition that there were no more party members left to seduce, and to the serendipity of having encountered just then a likely-looking FBI man. In any event, she became a salaried informer for the Washington committees, managing over time, with her phenomenal powers of recall, to dredge up the names of hundreds of party members. Some of them didn't come back to her for years.

The thrilling claim about Daddy's transmission to the Russians of British burgling techniques was never brought out at the hearings, where matters stalled on a much more tedious level: the Fifth Amendment. Much later he could joke about it—"you had to feel dirty afterwards although you weren't the one who really needed a bath"—but nearer the time, he wrote in *The Frightened Giant*, "The only personal regret I have is my indifferent performance in defying the inquisitors. . . . The fact is that I was extremely nervous about possible harm to the paper which was the apple of my eye."

His performance was far from indifferent, but you could tell he was badly scared, and his fear was infectious. I longed for them all to be like Lionel Stander, the big, gravelly-voiced actor who growled that he wasn't "a dupe or a dope or a moe or a schmoe." But Stander was almost unique. Although in their homes many lefties laughed at the sheer silliness of the committees, hardly anybody overcame their terror enough to mock at the scene; even if they started, the instant they were recognized to be "uncooperative witnesses" they were drowned out by gavels or hauled away by bailiffs. But I still wished Daddy had tried. After all, as an alien, he was obviously going to get the boot sooner or later anyway, and meanwhile, though Jim stayed free, Daddy *was* locked up.

Lots of my friends' families had experience of Ellis Island, seldom as they alluded to it. But they had been stopped on the way *in,* to be deloused, tagged, named, inspected, and sometimes detained as suspected syphilitics, psychos, or subversives. As usual, in my family it's the other way around. Naturally nobody would have stopped two highfalutin Brits from entering in the thirties, and naturally such Brits couldn't be expected to humble themselves to become citizens like mere immigrants and other swarthy foreigners who arrived by steerage. Unlike any other national group, the English were quite uninterested in blending in: they were citizens of the world. They grew up learning they owned it. They did own it.

My father had never had that problem. It was carelessness, not arrogance, that landed both my parents in a jam and him in the clink—because while she couldn't be bothered, he did take out first naturalization papers. But during the waiting period the war came, and technically, since he then worked for the British (being unable, naturally, to work as an American), he had, it seemed, "disqualified himself" and was told he would have to start over—which was impossible for an already suspect alien. Whatever the color of his passport, his central passion was America; if only he'd begun the whole process earlier we wouldn't be in this mess. Another mess, maybe, but not this one.

But this mess is our very own, the only mess we've got, and here we go, Nicky and I, together with Jo and Jim, to visit our Daddy in the lockup. We have to take a boat. The view from Ellis Island is of the Statue of Liberty's ass, which does not escape my father's ironic interest. We visit in a big room that's like an institutional dining room, with one unwanted alien and his family per table. Kids are in big demand because if you don't have any you have to visit in a prisonish set-up where visitors and deportees are separated by a screen. One woman, Mikki Doyle, whose husband is also about to be shipped to Britain, has cottoned on to the kiddy gimmick; she recruits mobs of stray brats from her Lower East Side neighborhood with the promise of a boat outing, and then she doles them out to the childless so that everybody gets one and can visit in the big room. The brats, of course, have no good reason to behave themselves, and so it's sort of a madhouse. The guards must think that Reds can't even bring up their own kids.

Daddy tells us they've put him in a dormitory for undesirables. One of them snores and keeps the others awake. Nicky is induced to smuggle a water pistol in next visiting day. He hands it to Daddy under the table, and Daddy is delighted, we don't quite get why. The pistol is for shooting the snoring undesirable.

Speaking of my brother, he's having a rough time. The publicity about Daddy has reached the eyes of the people at P.S. 7. Miss Coyne hauls Nicky up in front of the class one day and says, "Who you gonna kill today, Belfrage?" How does a kid defend himself against these maniacs? He's only twelve years old. Nobody has explained anything to him, so he feels ashamed for no reason. All Nicky wants is to be back in Croton, swimming and playing softball and prowling around the countryside with Frankie the dog. He's a nice person, a little like Daddy, cheerful, gentle, smart— why pick on him? Of course *I* pick on him, but that's different. It only seems just, in the cause of equally distributing the agony, that Nicky should get some too, since he's so perfect and everybody loves him. Anyway, I do it not to get at him but to get at my mother. Does he understand that? Why should he, from his position pinioned to the ground, where I can always so easily wrestle him—until one day he is

strong enough to stop me (just sitting straight up, the nerve
of him!) and wheel on me to get his own licks in. Then I
wither him by saying, unforgivably, "Oh, Nicky, don't be so
childish!"

I feel sorry for him in another way too: just as a boy.
I've always thought how badly designed they are with those
messy-looking things between their legs, compared to my
smooth, neat line. And once, pinning Nicky to the floor, I
poked him there with a knee and the howls were horrifying.
"Don't do that! You mustn't do that *ever again!*" my
mother shouted at me as she comforted him. How sad for
them, boys, how impractical, to be so vulnerable.

Even when I do Nicky a favor it goes wrong. Debbi
taught me this really neat way to faint by holding your
breath and ducking your head down quick between your
knees three times, and Nicky was dying to learn, so we
taught him. Wouldn't you know he tries it in the hall and
ends up out cold on the stone floor. "Boy, are you in for it,"
says Debbi, taking off. I really am. My mother has a fit.
Does she ever scream!

One day at school, someone in my geometry class hands me
a clipping from the *Daily News*. It says my parents are
divorced. What with Daddy in his island incarceration,
nobody's even bothered to mention it.

It doesn't really matter anymore. Other things have
taken over at this point and all I can feel is numb to it. The
two principals are, as well—at any rate it isn't talked about.
Even my mother, I realize, has for some time now given up
playing patience for that particular result—the object of her
passion having become such an obsessed person that he's
not the same man as the one who once obsessed *her;* the
two of them have even started to construct a more polite
and friendly modus vivendi. Now if her game comes out it
means "the *New Yorker* will take my story." It does come
out as often as usual, thanks to some deft dealing of bad
cards, though the *New Yorker* never takes her story.

By now the divorce was a formality, but to achieve it an

adulterous farce had been staged, it seemed, with a friend of each parent pretending to catch my father in flagrante while also pretending—what a nerve—to have been on the way to church. The paper said:

LEFTIST EDITOR, ON ELLIS IS., DIVORCED

As if Cedric Henning Belfrage, now on Ellis Island awaiting deportation back to Britain as a leftie, hasn't enough woe, his wife won a divorce yesterday on testimony by two friends that her husband played cozy with a cuddly girl companion in his bachelor apartment.

Supreme Court Justice McNally signed an interlocutory decree, which will become final in 90 days, for attractive Mrs. Mary Beatrice Belfrage, 500 Kappock St., Bronx. In addition, he awarded her custody of their two children, Sallie, 16, and John, 12, plus $125 a month for their support. She did not ask alimony. Belfrage has been paying the support money since the couple separated. They were wed in London in 1936.

Mrs. Lettie Grierson, also of 500 Kappock St., and Theodora Peck, of 50 E. 34th St., put the left-wing editor of the National Guardian on the spot with testimony of the events one Sunday morning in September, 1952.

Mrs. Grierson said she and Theodora were driving downtown to attend church when, finding themselves ahead of schedule, they decided to pop in and visit Belfrage in the bachelor flat in which he'd been living since he and his writer-wife split up in 1950. They went upstairs at 310 W. 99th St., she said, and rang the bell.

What followed might best be described as an awkward pause.

Finally, she testified, Belfrage answered the door, garbed in robe and slippers. From where they stood, they could see a cuddly little damsel in the apartment's one and only bed.

What did they do? They beat a hasty retreat—back to the Bronx, where they spilled the beans to Mrs. Belfrage.

Theodora told Referee Peter Schmuck [*sic*], who took

the testimony March 23 and then reported to McNally, that she'd give the same answers to the same questions that were asked of Mrs. Grierson.

He was arrested May 15 after twice refusing to tell the McCarthy committee whether he was a Communist, and taken to Ellis Island to await deportation. His lawyer, Nathan Dambroff, 38 Park Row, will appear today before U.S. Judge Weinfeld to plead for Belfrage's release.

7

UP TO A POINT

To make us love our country, our country ought to be lovely.
—EDMUND BURKE

Nineteen fifty-three, some year. An inauguration for Ike, a funeral for Stalin, a coronation for Elizabeth. An armistice signed in Korea, the French heating up at Dien Bien Phu. The war is dead, long live the war. Two men finally climb Mt. Everest; another pair crack the code of DNA; the Russians explode an H-bomb. Meanwhile my father, though behind bars, can still be useful: he helps me get a summer job. What kind of a job can you get at sixteen? Daddy drafts a bright, charming, witty ad for the Sunday *Times* help-wanted section.

Whining all the way, I end up on Fire Island living with a vacationing family in their beach home as baby-sitter for George, age 1½. I have baby-sat in the evenings to support myself since my allowance lapsed at thirteen. It's all right, better than home in some ways—a way to think about another life, all furnished in its neat clean stage set, and the kids are often nice; you get some peace after they go to bed, and if you look behind the other stuff on the top shelves there are interesting sex books and appliances.

This is different. It seems like some kind of sentence. Naturally the family, with nothing but the ad to go on, have planned on my being bright, charming, and witty. How were they to guess I am sullen, bigoted, and lazy? I hate them for unspecified reasons, aggravated by the way the week goes by with the husband at work in Manhattan while the wife slouches around in curlers and a bikini getting her tan in order for the big event: waiting on the pier for the Bayshore ferry on Friday night with a martini shaker and a secret smile on her ratty face. I hate George, because if not for him I could stay out late like the other girls who are on vacation with their families and go to parties every night and lie around on the beach all day making out with the lifeguards and resting up before getting rigged out in new toreador pants for the next party. What George does is, he runs away. He's so good at it he sometimes gets lost, and if I can't catch him his mother punishes me by not letting me go out at all. Punishes *me*. It isn't as if I've ever been punished before.

There is very little to redeem this situation but mail from the family, who write brilliant letters, even Mummy— we can be quite affectionate at a distance, on paper—and from various pals. One day there is a postcard from Lee, a girlfriend from the next term up at Science, about her date with a real West Point cadet called Dan King,* who used to go to Science too. Lucky stiff. After the summer, she writes, she'll get me a blind date at the Point. Debbi never writes but I hear regularly from Rick. Poor Rick, who's been in the Coast Guard since graduation from Farragut and loathes it just as much as the academy, has taken to sending three-by-five index cards with not always scrutable quotations from what he's been reading about the awful side of life, carefully copied in emerald ink in his strange, square handwriting. I put them in my pocket to think about in my spare time. George vanishes while I'm pondering this one from *The Good Soldier* by Ford Madox Ford:

Is there any terrestrial paradise where, amidst the whispering of the olive-leaves, people can be with whom they like

and have what they like and take their ease in shadows and
in coolness? Or are all men's lives . . . broken, tumultuous,
agonized, and unromantic lives, periods punctuated by
screams, by imbecilities, by deaths, by agonies? Who the
devil knows?

Who the devil knows?

One day comes a letter from Daddy to say that he has
finally got bail and is hoping to take a little holiday with Jo
on Shelter Island. He encloses a clipping from a paper he seldom reads but which in this case, unlike the "respectable"
press, reports the facts.

Daily Worker, July 2, 1953

Judge Edward Weinfeld ruled yesterday that Cedric Belfrage,
editor of the National Guardian, was entitled to bail pending deportation proceedings. Belfrage has been held on Ellis
Island since May 15, where he was taken 24 hours after he
refused to knuckle down to Sen. Joe McCarthy at a witch-
hunt hearing in Washington.

A native of England, Belfrage has been a resident in the
U.S. since the early 1930's. He applied for citizenship in
July, 1937, but was forced to interrupt the five-year resi-
dence requirement in order to undertake a World War II
assignment in Europe with the Supreme Headquarters Allied
Expeditionary Forces.

On May 14, McCarthy subpoenaed Belfrage and James
Aronson, executive editor of the Guardian, and subjected
them to the usual treatment accorded by the committee to
journalists whose views do not coincide with McCarthyism.
Belfrage and Aronson refused to answer McCarthy's questions, invoking their rights under the Fifth Amendment.

Under a printed line, the text continued:

More than 700 persons, at a Cedric Belfrage fight-back meeting Friday night in the Palm Gardens, affirmed their determi-

nation to work for the freedom of the National Guardian's
English-born editor now held without bond on Ellis Island.

Speakers included Dorothy Parker and Albert Kahn, writers; Russ Nixon, legislative representative of the United Electrical Workers, and Thelma Dale, of the Progressive Party.

Six other speakers enlivened the meeting with accounts
of their recent appearances before congressional committees.
They were Nathan Witt, labor lawyer; William Mandel,
writer; Arnaud D'Usseau, playwright; Victor Perlo, and Joe
Joseph, economists, and David Flacks, teacher.

Prof. Henry Pratt Fairchild and John T. McManus of
the Guardian co-chaired the meeting.

I knew that Daddy's lawyers had deliberately dawdled
with the case in order to wait for the notoriously principled
Judge Weinfeld's turn on the bench. He was their one hope.
His opinion in the bail case is worth quoting.

If for the long period of seven years [since his last entry to
the U.S.] . . . the immigration and other government officials
did not consider Belfrage's presence and activities inimical to
the nation's welfare and a threat to its security, it is difficult
to understand how, overnight, because of his assertion of a
constitutional privilege, he has become such a menace to the
nation's safety that it is now necessary to jail him without
bail pending the determination of the charges as to which
the government has the burden of proof. . . . The privilege is
for the innocent as well as the guilty and no inference can be
drawn against the person claiming it.

But five days later the government, disagreeing, appeals
Judge Weinfeld's decision. In any case the Shelter Island holiday is out. Even with bail, Daddy isn't allowed off Manhattan—like the Soviet UN delegates. Still, he's luckier by
far than most of the victims: he can't lose his job.

September is the start of my junior year, and of all wonders
I am picked for the cheerleading squad. Both halves of this

two-track life seem to be doing all right for once. Daddy is free, my new best friend is Fran, I am in love with Mr. Berger, my chemistry teacher, having somehow survived the mad marker of social studies. I am no longer going to church every Sunday, which immediately provides a nice, clean feeling: could it be honesty? This means less social life in the neighborhood, and less Debbi, with all the feelings of inadequacy she has always provided. Everything is looking up. Then, to top it all, Lee comes through with the West Point weekend. She gets Dan to fix me up with his room-mate, who has some name like Horace D. Shoulderpad III.

If I didn't live in this total split I wouldn't consider going anywhere near West Point. My mother, of course, is thrilled; but what do they do at West Point, after all, but train my father's foes? Such thoughts never darken my door, however: I am simply entranced by the romance of it all. But why worry? There is no possible future in it anyway. Horace and I have a pretty bad chemical problem from the first. He obviously has a huge crush on Lee, who's dark, petite, and soft. I guess he was planning on her friend being like that too. I, on the other hand, want him to be like Dan, who's perfect. He's a sort of Gary Cooper type, only his mouth is sexier. He's even Jewish. He seems to like me a little too—anyway, at the hop on Saturday night we switch partners for a while and I get that feeling. It's hard not to hope, even after he tells me that for the last two years he's been going with a girl from Taft called Shirley.*

Is he thinking about me too? I write in my diary when I get home.

Did I look alright? Was I too fat? Did he notice my black-heads in the sun? What about Shirley, two *years* they've been going together, what am I crazy? So how come he's dating? Oh shit, wait till he hears about my father. Did I talk about the right things? Was I funny? Was I *too* funny? Did he notice that fellow at the game saying I was cute? What if he thought I was leading him on? Did he hear me tell Horace we're in the phonebook? Oh God does he even know my last name? What about those times we turned out to be thinking the same thing? What if he was incredibly brilliant & forgot to tell me something so he'd have to phone me up. What crap. What's to forget? He probably hasn't given me another thought. What a nudnik I am, he must go through this everywhere, ten times before lunch. He's gorgeous. Did he even know I liked him? How could he notice I was looking at him in a special way when he doesn't know how I usually look at people? What about the way we fit when we were dancing? Is he thinking about me right now?

Back at school on Monday, telling no one, not even Fran, certainly not Lee, and feeling like a real idiot, I skulk into the room where they keep the graduate records, and steal every piece of paper with Dan's name on it. After having it all photostated I return it the next day. His grades had been neither as good nor as bad as mine (but then, he lacked the weird paternal name that brought my teachers out in funny marks); in fact, his Science career was nothing special (among all the star students who made Arista, the honor society, or held office, or joined scientific clubs, his extracurricular activities amounted to "intramural basketball, intramural softball, lunchroom squad"). His address is nothing special either (nearby: ideal). I know it's meshugah, I don't care, I have to go there.

Casing the apartment house: oh, his luck, it's one of those really ordinary six-story brick tenements just a few streets down off the Grand Concourse, coated in soot and fringed in fire escapes, with neighborhood life on the loose in all directions. Women schmooz on the stoop, little girls play potsy on the sidewalk, there's a stickball game on the empty lot, the street bustles with men delivering this and selling that, half the talk in Yiddish and everyone communicating in the complicated dance they've rehearsed all their lives. I wonder about Dan, what floor he lives on, is that woman his mother, is that man his father, did he used to have a dog, did he play stickball when he was a kid? Just breathing his exhaled air is magic. I go back again the next day. For this reason I'm late getting home to find his letter.

Asking me back up to the Point.

Inviting me to come back.

Horace writes to Lee and invites her too, but she is stricken. We exchange this information monosyllabically before school the next morning, when I encounter her waiting for me, looking exactly the opposite of how I feel. Neither of us has eaten or slept since we got our letters the day before. I feel really sorry about Lee but not sorry enough to stay home from the Point.

Oct. 31

Well, I'm back! And I'm so happy I could scream and yell. Where did the time go? I can't remember doing anything except walking and sitting—mostly down Flirty where you're supposed to guess-what under Kissing Rock & he won't. He will not. Catch him a few feet further on though! Wow! (I'm afraid he really affects me physically.)

Things he SAID:

1) He's through with Shirley. He doesn't even want to *talk* about Shirley. So who wants to talk about Shirley?

2) He's invited me up again in 3 weeks!

3) Then, he's coming home for TWO WEEKS over Xmas!

4) He likes me. He said it! He said I was "different" and didn't fit a "pattern" as most girls do.

How's that for understatement of the month. Different? Try this one on, Dan: my old man's out on bail! (No, I didn't tell him, are you crazy?) Different? Any minute now we might be deported to England. Phooey, I'm not going to think about it. Just keep shout-n-singing . . .

Visiting Dan every weekend becomes a habit long before I have to make a choice between going to West Point or West Street Jail, the compass points of my different lives. But I have been so successful in keeping myself apart from myself that most of the time they simply do not overlap. At the

moment, I have found the necessary ingredients for the invisibility scheme, and it's full steam ahead. I'm going to pretend
away everything else and be an all-American girl. An AAG.

The United States Military Academy itself is no problem:
the very pinnacle of institutionalized anonymity. The men
accepted there have had to prove a deluxe degree of individual merit to qualify for the process of losing it in a conformity so total that the slightest eccentricity in word or deed
is grounds for the sternest retribution, and even the exposure of the peccadillos of others a matter of honor. "A cadet
will not lie, cheat or steal, nor tolerate those who do."
Nobody else like me has anything to do with the place.

True, for once they *look* like me. Every Saturday morning at ten o'clock we pile into the bus at Port Authority for
the two-hour journey up the Hudson Valley: fifty freckled,
snub-nosed females, a whole freightload of Miss Rhein-
golds. We remind me of the special talent Mrs. Giglio has
with pound cake: she takes identical slices and one time she
puts icing on them, the next whipped cream, or butterscotch, ice cream, maple syrup, canned peaches. That's
what we're like, us on the bus. But while any diversity
among us might seem to be a matter for a microscope,
amounting to no more than the varying colors of our kiss-
curls, the others, unlike me, are what they seem: underneath
the icing, same nice, wholesome pound cake. The others are
complete, consistent; they do not have Bronx accents and
they do have very straight teeth and a terrific AAG aura.
They are called things like Biddy and Bunny and Boo, and
they always look tickled to death. I'll bet they were born
demure, deodorized and depilated, with their pearls and circle pins presupplied. Hair by Breck, lips by Revlon (Fire
and Ice), shirt by Ship 'n Shore. They wear flatties, ponytails, and sweaters buttoned down the back, and their
smooth slim limbs are always tanned. A lot of them are army
brats who've been around, though always to the same place;
or they are being finished at some prep school in New York
en route to the Ivy League. I live in fear that they will find me

out: the foreign Jewish-hearted pinko schizophrenic impostor
behind the mask. I try to learn the language and the rules.

You soon detect that the AAG hierarchy of importance
is based on their men, rather than on themselves, and mirrors the men's position in the pecking order. Recognizably
the most important people on the bus are the pinned
(engaged-to-be-engaged) drags—WooPoo (West Point) slang
for dates, male or female, of firsties (seniors). A girlfriend of
a plebe, a fourth-year man, is beneath contempt, because
plebes are slaves, and what could be lower than a slave's
woman? The girls of "yearlings"—sophomores—don't
count for much; by the time you're dragging a "cow"—
junior—you're getting somewhere. Within this ranking system the biggest deals are the drags of cadets in companies
A-1 or L-2, while A-2s and L-1s are literally lesser, because
the former companies are the tallest and the latter are the
shortest. This is to get the Long Grey Line to line up right:
when the cadets stand in their appointed ranks upon the
Plain (which is imperceptibly graded to compensate for
human diversity), you could use them for a vast cosmic
spirit-level, so perfectly straight are the tops of their tar-
bucket hats, straighter than the surface of the earth. (Dare
you deviate from the norm? We will normalize your devia-
tion. Our Plain is a *plane*.) Therefore, when I reveal that
Dan is in company C-2, I am in fact disclosing in
WooPoo/AAGish that he is a mere 5'10", a measly matter
to a seatmate dragging, say, a C-1. But while size counts at
the Point, there is no status attached to high marks or even
military prowess: as long as you're not a complete dullard,
mediocrity and ineptitude are considered endearing, and too
much academic success is suspect because it's conspicuous.

Garment bags stuffed with gowns of tulle and taffeta
for the Saturday night hop overflow the luggage racks. Pairs
of scarved heads in pincurls. Moans at rain: rain reveals you
as you really are. Straight-haired, your curls will collapse;
curly-haired, your straightening will frizz. The idea is for all
hair to look just the same, straight on top, then curly around
the edges. Like Doris Day. She might be singing the ride's

accompaniment as well, so relentlessly grinny is its whole tone. Breathless dazed excitement, impossibly overpowering after weeks and months and years of getting used to it—any impulse toward the blasé or the cynical suffers instant suffocation in the bliss-and-terror-laden bus. (That's the way it's supposed to be, anyway. I have a little problem because there lurks, under the nearly perfect AAGish exterior, the not-quite-conquerable waggish voice of my father.) Romance on wheels: the dream of expectation of the dream come true. (That's better.) One day you too can pass beneath a canopy of swords leaning on the arm of all the glamour of the Western world. (And spend the rest of your life traipsing after it from base to base: bowling, bridge, and bingo with the lucky lady who's landed the C-1.) Bear Mountain is the only landmark I remember on the ride. All the rest is spent in the heavenly enterprise of trying not to choke on joy. Some of us are in love with our cadets. All of us are in love with ourselves for being on the West Point bus, the envy, in our opinion, of every American girl who is not.

The Hotel Thayer is where the AAGs are billeted, five each in dormitory rooms off-limits to cadets. (An awful lot is off-limits to cadets, mostly disguising what in this case is really off-limits to cadets: our bodies. Sorting his way through the regulations could qualify a guy to run a minor war.) After we've checked in and unpacked our crinolines there's the "Pee-rade," the Saturday morning tourist show, an exercise in symmetry that makes the Rockettes look like spastics. There they go, breathing as one, the extraordinary youths of the United States Military Academy Cadet Corps marching brass-banded, unconquerably proud and upright in their dress gray uniforms, plumed, patented, and brass-buttoned, white belts criss-crossing their splendid tail coats, shoes shined to mirrors: each like every other, excellent, together a theatrical spectacle that after a century and a half of rehearsal is flawless. One measure of this is the impossibility of spotting the singular. I never can see Dan out there. He's just another tin toy man, precision machine-tooled as the gun propped on his shoulder at just the tilt of every other gun on every other shoulder, his trouser legs indistinguishable from 4,798 other trouser legs, down to the very creases. And yet he's not diminished by the numbers: my pride in him swells to include them all, I see humanity en masse but *neat,* hundreds of Dans in rows, all moving perfectly to the very soul of the music. That military beat: its soaring sense of purpose could march me to hell. The pain in my breast I attribute to patriotism, God, and first love.

After the parade the soldiers change to their regular uniforms, limbs and torsos in tight tubes of gray and black, and we meet in Grant Hall. O love! Requited, perfect love—distanced by not only miles but rules, and infinitely structured. Impossible to eat each other up. Maximum outside interference keeps your priorities straight. Everything is longing, yearning for the day when we'll be free, aware that the taboos are what actually keep us going. Precious man, with all his privileged privations and prestige, he *loves* me. Beautiful full-lipped eager-eyed Dan, my very own apprentice hero, with shining face and black hair still wet from the shower: here he comes, smiling at *me*. He's only eighteen, but this place has made him a man.

And me? What has it made me? Nothing different, really. It's just that half of me is in mothballs up here. After I have finally gotten around to mentioning the unmentionable, this other half and Dan do not refer to it. He understands instantly that we have to ignore all that, forget about it completely, and anyway is probably too horrified to do anything else. Cleaning up my politics by brushing them under the rug is easy: school teaches the regular kind, with help from the media. Anyway, AAGs aren't political. And I am playing my role all the way, complete with costume and accessories, every last item borrowed from friends for the occasion to help me get in character. He understands perfectly: it wouldn't do to find ourselves in the wrong play, some chintzy horror show or tawdry melodrama.

We have a weekend ahead of us. Well, sort of a weekend. Only a few hours, actually. He still has duties to perform. We're not permitted any comfort or solitude; he is a prisoner of the Point and must respect its rituals. He's not even allowed to unhook the stiff black band that's choking his adorable neck except when he is deep in the woods. Duty Honor Country, after all, and he must tell on anybody seen to deviate, as others must inform on him. But within this elaborate construction of his life we have a little nest we've made, a place we can be still. It isn't a physical place, although we have some hide-outs around the post; it is the part of ourselves that we have pooled together, the promises and dreams that we augment with daily letters, weekly visits.

The weekends whirl away. Let others rave and wave *Go Army!* pennants at the football game, we have better things to do. First a walk alone above the river where the wind whips in the seasons with tremendous drama and where behind a rock or bush we can at long last *touch*. PDAs— public displays of affection—are absolutely out, of course, on pain of who-knows-what unspeakable reckoning. (How similar this one sounds to the lesson drilled into my father as a child and in his case never successfully discarded: "Through all my life," he wrote of the astonishing sight of people going mad with joy and hugging one another in London on Armistice Day, 1918, "I had learned that such public display of emotion was 'not done.'") But we have no trouble with the prohibitions, obedience to. You soon learn the thrill in a restraint that so immeasurably adds to the consummation—even if the consummation is nothing more than holding hands. Or the marvel of walking everywhere in perfect step, one body. We fit. We are in tune. To feel the length of him in motion next to me is to feel hooked into some huge harmony. I am so impressed with us!

Ignoring the hop with its dumb, time-wasting discomforts—gowns, dress uniforms, all the business of the formal transformation to begin with—we choose to get lost in each other's eyes as we sit in a booth in the Weapons Room sipping chocolate malts stiff with French ice cream and munching at cheeseburgers made of Grade-A steak—junk food dejunked, appropriate to the nourishment of the cream of the country's fighting youth. But who tastes food? The tiny cleft at the end of his nose fixates me. Nothing else ever has been or ever shall be.

Overpowered by magnetism, we fall into each other's arms, and in our catalepsy still remember to shuffle our feet around occasionally so that it is "a dance" and it is permitted. *There was a boy,* sings Nat King Cole from the jukebox, and the couples are plastered together so seamlessly that the finest blade could not be slid between them, each pair in its own smoky halo, *a very strange enchanted boy....* Melting with hope, in the nearest place to paradise ever known, I think I have found some new level of consciousness. (My old man thinks this song, "Nature Boy," is a real hoot, and mercilessly mimics it, but I suppress his subversive echo.) Late, in the dark, in the woods, we kiss and murmur and giggle and kiss. Sunday, after chapel, with the end in view, the time is harder to bear. *And when I hear you call ... so softly to me....* And finding new distances to cross, however minute, still we cross them to sink into one another: *I don't hear a call at all ... I hear a rhapsody....* Doesn't that just say it all? Anyhow, there is nothing left to say.

At 1800 Sunday night the men march in to supper, and their drags wistfully board the bus for the long ride home down Route 9W. At first the atmosphere is so subdued that no one says a word, so soft with sighing, reliving all the pain and sweetness in our bodies, in this two-hour decompression chamber where we try to find the way back to real life until heaven resumes next weekend.

How'd it go? one finally asks another, and little bursts of AAGish crowd out the darkness as the girls, stirring, adjust the little scarves around their necks to hide the hickeys: *Gee, was it terrif! We hit it off real swell, per usual. I was scared I'd botch it up this time and I was kinda shaky, but he's so adorable and sincere, he said I'm his OAO, his one-and-only, and I am falling, but good. Only he's on CCQ next weekend: I know I'll die.*

The agony will be relieved for me, I'm certain, by a letter from Dan waiting at home, and another when I get back with my schoolbooks tomorrow. There are letters every day: yesterday's and tomorrow's had to be mailed before our weekend together. It is one of our inventions. We are devising love for the very first time. Forever afterwards what we make here will be the pattern, the original. I will be in love for the first time over and over. It's always the first time. But the only real first time is Dan.

Every night after washing my hair and setting it in pincurls, I keep the bathroom door locked and Nicky has a catfit while I confide in my diary. "He is my only thought, my only dear, my only hope," I write, bewitched by my own drama. Between weekends "I am suspended in longing, caught stranded, strung up between the magic and the fear, terrified that Saturday will come or that it won't." "He kissed me. I thought I would die, right there on the spot. Words cannot do justice." "We have been together for all of the past three weekends—and, if it's possible, our love has increased by the second." "The weekend blew past like a tornedo [sic], catching my heart and flinging it down again, a wreckage." What is all this? There is no question of ever having committed to paper a genuine feeling. The diary is like an extension of last year's conversations with Debbi— we don't have many now—the effluence of a misunderstood movie heroine (Debbie Reynolds? Natalie Wood?) who, if she comes to grief, will be seen to have done so for pure, romantic, all-American reasons; meanwhile she is leaving last words strewn around for her fans like Hansel and Gretel breadcrumbs.

Reversals there had certainly been at first. After the brief interference of Dan's ex-girlfriend Shirley I had a lot to tell my diary:

Jan 13

Okay, that's it, I'm finished. Four months and it's all over. Dan's been two-timing me from the beginning and now this bitch Shirley just called to tell me. I can't stand to write it

down even. That she's just been to the Point this weekend
&. I can't I can't I can't. He pinned her! The bastard, he
pinned her! I don't give a good God damn about Shirley, but
how could he lie to me like that! All my hopes are shattered.
Boy, has he led me over the rocks. He's been just as cheap
and insincere as a person can get. My love. I spit on it now!
It was once such a beautiful, shiny thing. Now it is but a
scarred, battered remnant of the past.

Not only that, I have to MEET her tomorrow. Beat
that! Our schools have a game. Unless I can get out of it. Fat
chance.

Jan 14

It's really hard to believe when you think about Xmas vacation & how much time we spent together, all the ups &
downs and swoony scenes. I haven't stopped crying since
Shirley called me yesterday and already I've lost 5 pounds, 2
in tears I'll bet, & today I actually had to STAND there and
shake HANDS with her yet. The squad even had to pose for a
cheerleader picture for the yearbook before the game & Fran
was holding me up, I mean literally. How I was supposed to
come on with the wim & wigor I'll never know. It was all
Fran. I was just a big hollow pain in a short green dress. She
kept begging me not to give in & try & look cheerful: "The
worst thing you can do is show her how you feel."

The second I laid eyes on her I knew her out of hundreds. Even before she came near me or I saw the pin. Story
of my life: she's the one who walks like a winner. She's as
gorgeous as he is. Look at those bazooms, as Dan calls
them. Luckily I didn't have to say anything right away
because the squad was on and I can do that stuff like a
machine. Fran's kicking me: "Smile!" Who could smile?
"You know what cheerleading's about? *Cheer.*" I'm trying.
"Hey," Fran's helping, "at least she's not a cheerleader." Big
deal. She's got everything else. "You're crazy," Fran says,
"& he's even crazier. You both need a *head* shrinker." She's
not kidding. I need one for getting into this in the first place.

Meanwhile our boys were making clowns of themselves as per usual, and me trying not to look at Shirley. At half-time she makes this bee-line for me and Fran pushes me up. We shake hands and say "Hi," her smile half-real and mine half-tears. (She must have noticed how swollen my eyes were anyway.) I saw the pin sticking out at me off the point of the left bazoom and told her "Congratulations." I meant it. Anyone who could pull that off deserves congratulating. She was very gracious, smirking like the queen at her coronation, a cut above the rest of us you bet.

Why go on? I must deserve this. I always knew it would be a disaster, I just didn't know what kind.

One thing. I am not going to act jealous. First of all I'm not jealous—if that's what he wants, he certainly knows what he's doing. Second of all if he's that kind of a frigging jerk I don't need him. Third of all I have a theory: it's like if you say you're not ticklish, people stop tickling you.

Later the same day:

It's going to take a few lifetimes to figure this one out. Like crazy, man, dig? I mean, am I flipping? Dan just called. It seems Shirley called him & he's FURIOUS. She set this whole thing up, he said. She *did* go up to the Point (obviously) but she got the pin off him on some bet. Am I supposed to believe this? That big lug. He's getting it back off her he said. He even said the whole reason he *got* the pin was for me. Then there's this great line for him to live up to: "It's *you* all the way. You're my OAO." OAO = One And Only. Hot spit!

I'm going to take it, too. But I better watch out for this guy.

Two days later:

For the 4th time (?) in my life I heard the most wonderful words anyone can hear: "I love you." This is the first time the feeling has been reciprocle [*sic*], however. This is the first time they have awakened something wonderful.

With my true love, my own Cadet Charming, I am *The Sleeping Beauty* by Walt Disney. I am condensed and anthologized by *Reader's Digest*, at least the most unforgettable character I have ever met.

I have enough to think about without Rick and his darn cards, which keep on coming. Now I've written to tell him I'm pinned, engaged-to-be-engaged, spoken for, *taken*. So what does he send? It's one of his little three-by-fives, and all it says is:

> As a rule, we may say that while short-term prostitutes are generally looked down upon, long-term prostitutes are treated with respect.
>
> —Tolstoi, *The Kreutzer Sonata*

Sometimes I wonder about Rick.

As someone seeking AAG-hood more feverishly than ever, one day I realize I have reached the summit of the dream, and without even climbing. Seventeen and pinned to a West Pointer. This dreamboat has attached a teeny double gold pin, with a little chain and a ruby-studded "A" for Army, approximately one inch above the center of my left tit— which, however, he will not get to touch for some months yet—where it must be placed every day, puncturing every garment in my wardrobe and conferring unbelievable prestige on me with everybody but my father's friends, who think I am at best berserk, at worst seditious. Naturally, I could take the pin off when I'm around them, but that would be like wiping off the Ash Wednesday smudges on my forehead. Whatever was wrong with taking the ashes or the pin in the first place, if you do it you might as well do it.

And somehow I am still suspicious that the whole thing has only happened as part of life's plot to make me more conspicuous.

8

TWO MEN

Everywhere men assume that they have a right to kill other men in defense of what they consider to be their vital interests. Since one man's vital interest is often another man's hurt, the carnage is difficult to equate with any morality. This universal complacency about killing, rather than communism, capitalism, colonialism or what have you, is the heart of the peace problem.

—I. F. STONE

Who is he anyway, this Dan? When I try to reconstruct him I come up with something adamantly middling, so successfully has he become uniform in his uniform. And yet he won't play ball with my invisibility scheme, which doesn't interest him at all for its own sake. When he came home for Christmas I took him to a carol service at the old Riverdale church, since he'd never seen anything like it. I told him to kneel when the others did, as in: This is the form, this is what you do here; but really meaning: Don't be conspicuous. And he said, from his rigid upright posture on the pew, poking up among the whole congregation, in a voice loud enough for several rows to hear, "Jews don't kneel."

On the other hand, rocking boats and making waves are definitely not Dan's shtick. Out of the Bronx just over a

year when we met, he'd already abolished its traces. He had
a big head start with his name: changed from Kuntz to King
by his father (otherwise absent from the scene), who was
tired of being teased. The one time Dan's background still
shows is when he gets dressed up: his idea of a fancy outfit
is a flashy suit that makes him look like Nathan Detroit.
My father wears drab tweeds, and anything livelier is an
offense to me. I am embarrassed to be seen with Dan in
mufti; also by his presents. On my birthday he gave me a
necklace and earring set of fluted gilt cornucopias stuffed
with pink rhinestones, all laid out in a pearly plastic snap-
ping-turtle gift box padded with imitation Chinese silk. I
haven't had the grace to wear it once. He never mentions it.
He does tell me his mother got a discount on it from one of
her clients. I can't figure out whether she actually likes that
stuff or is trying to tell me something.

Mrs. King is an accountant. There is no Mr. King anymore, or he is not mentioned, but his widow or his ex-wife
has authority enough for any family. She has terrific personal power, and the physique to back it up. Let's face it,
she's fat. It's a good thing my mother never runs into Mrs.
King in the Grand Union, because she'd just go ahead and
tell her how fat she is, and probably get a smack on the head
with a handbag for her pains. All year round Mrs. King
wears flimsy print or polka-dot dresses with the flesh hanging out. In her little apartment no room is big enough to
contain her, their relative sizes are so mismatched, never
mind the furniture. She doesn't look quite safe on a regular
kitchen stool, for instance, but in her big tilt-back swivel
leather armchair behind the institutional brown desk she
finds her scale: massive and momentous together. She always
sits there whenever she has something significant to say.

Dan's mother is very nice to me, even though I am a
shiksa. She seems to understand that I have the right veneer
for a West Point girlfriend but at the same time can catch
on to her way of thinking without an interpreter—an
unusual combination. I love the deli food she gets in, the
chopped liver and gefilte fish, tongue and potato salad and

pickles, black bread and rye and challah, and she loves feeding me. Not only that, we really get along. On weekends
when Dan has leave we spend a lot of time together, driving
around in her Plymouth or going to the movies or out for a
meal. But also I drop in on my own after school, and she's
starting to treat me almost like a daughter. We sit and nosh
and gab about the man we love. I watch her at her desk
gobbling up columns of numbers faster than any machine.
She sees them as wholes and she sees their relationships:
having learned to add with fingers, I've overlooked the fact
that there might be some better way to do it. Like her, you
can see numbers as friends. What a novel idea. Thus she
teaches me arithmetic, after all this time. How about that.

Mrs. King cultivates a realistic atmosphere. I can learn
about Dan from her too, from the way she is as well as
what she says.

Mrs. King is not superstitious. She doesn't give a hoot
about black cats and ladders and she doesn't knock on
wood. Nor does Dan. I am the same, now more emphati-
cally than ever.

Mrs. King doesn't make small talk. Nor does Dan. It's
something I like about him even more than his looks. Small
talk is not something I can do either. For one thing, it's hard
to find things to say that are the right size. Most people
make cute wisecracks about the familiar, things they have in
common. I don't have much in common. They talk about
the pitfalls of existence and everybody shares them and
laughs. My pitfalls are all wrong because they are more like
abysses, not very funny ha-ha. Dan, though, just seems to
accept me in spite of everything. He doesn't react as if I'm
especially fascinating, outlandish, exotic, or weird. Me,
with a father like that, a mother like that, and my very own
split personality: he makes me feel like the girl next door. It
isn't that I love Dan because he understands me. I love him
because he doesn't.

That never stops me from trying to understand him. I
want so badly to be enveloped by him, to shake free from
this outsider's identity and be absorbed in his, to belong, to

see with his eyes and hear with his ears, to be a vicarious person: his wife. I'm pretty good at pretending, but sometimes it isn't easy. For instance, it's obvious that he digests what they feed him at West Point. He takes seriously their efforts to instill (it says in the catalogue) "a sense of duty and the qualities of character, leadership, integrity, loyalty, and discipline." Notice what they leave out? Tolerance. How can you kill people for a living if you're tolerant? Dan is very brave and strong and resolute, and merciless to anyone who isn't. Not that he's gratuitously mean the way some of them are (as they're expected to be), like those who pause on their way around the post to have a little fun, persecute a plebe—"Rack that neck in, smack!"—and then indulge in a little imaginative sadism. Dan would never do that, any more than he'd go out of his way to be nice. Although he can display both in an almost accidental way, cruelty and kindness don't come into life's equation for him. In the behavior stakes, my father has him beaten hands down.

But just as there is no charm in him, neither is there artifice. Doesn't go in for imaginative flights, our Dan, not at all. You get *the truth*. Irony, too, is foreign to him. What good is it? Can you eat it? Beat the Russkies with it? Nah. He is just who he is, and you always know where you are with him because he never moves, like the North Star or the North Pole, something to steer by. Here I am trying to be so many different people at the same time, forgetting who is where, liable to mislay the one I need, wobbling and weak and despicably indecisive, and there he is sticking straight up in the same place helping me get my bearings. I can't stand to think what I'd do without him.

One funny thing. When you ask him what he'd like to be if he wasn't in the army, he says: a cartoonist. A cartoonist! True, he draws a cute li'l Kilroy peeking over his fence or whatever it is he peeks over; but Kilroy wasn't exactly Dan's idea, and while it's perfectly possible that he could draw other things too, he doesn't. Anyway, shouldn't a cartoonist have a sort of satiric, not to say jaundiced, view of official goings-on? Dan certainly doesn't have that. Dan approves of all possible goings-on, official or otherwise, a state of mind alien to me. I know I'd be happier like that. Maybe when I'm his wife I'll learn to be like that.

Dan is safety. I am drowning; he is the raft. I mean, take Rick. Rick seems to think *I* can help *him*. His latest index card is from *Macbeth*.

> Canst thou not minister to a mind diseas'd;
> Pluck from the memory a rooted sorrow;
> Raze out the written troubles of the brain;
> And, with some sweet oblivious antidote,
> Cleanse the stuff'd bosom of that perilous stuff,
> Which weighs upon the heart?

Who does he think I am? Why does he have to be so gloomy?

It sure must be neat to be *one thing*. It's quite interesting leading all these separate lives, but tiring as all get-out. At home with my mother I am the mean rebellious brat. At Daddy's on 65th Street I'm the silent, enthralled yet slightly cynical worshiper. At West Point I am the AAG-initiate. Only at Science do I feel like me. But who is that?

Dan doesn't need to ask himself such a question. He is a winner. He smokes Chesterfields, the winners' cigarette. And he's a Yankee fan, the winners' team. Nicky and Debbi are naturally both Yankee fans. They're all-white, those boys. Every year they clobber the Brooklyn Dodgers, my team, in the World Series. Underdogs unite around the Dodgers, and we almost seem to need to lose somehow. We get all the way up there in '52 and '53, we win the National League pennant, and then I have to prepare my heart to be strong enough not to break again when those Yanks give us one more shellacking.

In my mind Dan has his own special corner on winning. I've never known anyone like that before, and I suspect it but respect it too. (Will it rub off on me?) In his winning way, he is serving his country, and there is no room for subtleties. It's not so much My-country-right-or-wrong with

Dan, more My-country-right. In some ways it's comforting to find the country in the person, because a country is not a manageable entity to reason with or make much sense of; whereas on this subject Dan is willing, if I can stand it, to discuss his whole collection of convictions, loves, and limits.

Pretty easy to tell what they are, too: the exact opposite of my father's.

Daddy has a good laugh on schedule once a week when that mean *New York Times* reprints transcripts of Eisenhower's press conference. Usually news about Ike is limited to reports on his golf swing from the putting green on the White House south lawn, but once a week our president bravely confronts the media, an event my father anticipates with all the relish and mental salivation that some men reserve for pornography. He tries to read out the presidential thoughts with a straight face. "In our efforts throughout the world," says Ike typically one week, "on outpost positions, I mean positions that are exposed to immediate Communist threat, physical threat, if we will help those people hold out and get ourselves back where we belong as reserves to move into any threatened danger point if they carry it to that point, carry it to that level, then what we will be doing it will be taking these 22 million South Koreans, pushing programs for getting them ready to hold their own front line." There you have the Korean situation.

In general, though, since Ellis Island, my father's state of mind is pretty embattled. He's gone way past any discussion of how the world should be organized or of the principles he once felt compelled to defend. Now the fight is negative: against the witch hunters and stoolies and the superpatriots like the American Legion with their new National Americanism Commission, set up to gauge and assure "100% Americanism." The left's specific fight is now against the McCarran-Walter Act. According to this law, enacted in 1952, all members of "Communist front" groups (as listed by the attorney general) who don't register (with the attorney general) are subject to a $10,000 fine and five years in jail for every day of not doing it. Another section of the act has to do with the incarceration of all suspected subversives in the event of a national emergency. They're setting up concentration camps for us.

Such matters are not subjects of debate in the world at large; you don't hear them talked about on television. That's because everybody already agrees that enemy saboteurs, spies, and subversives have a Master Plan for Conquest, and thus, in our struggle to root out Reds, all methods are fair, even the abrogation of the Constitution in order to defend the Constitution. Of course nobody talks either about old-fashioned personal loyalty to those who have lost their friends and jobs after the FBI has paid a call—better cut them adrift, or they'll pull you under too.

Daddy has his work cut out dealing with the witch hunt's by-products, with little energy to spare for presenting his case to daughters, or doubters—if such creatures still exist in this black-and-white world. But he'd probably only say that these laws are evil and mad and if they don't watch out the next step is fascism; and how are they supposed to credit that when they are obviously prosperous and thriving in the Land of the Free?

Daddy loves to heckle his antagonists, but his jests mean awfully little to the man in the street. Besides, most of what he has to say is about our all being participants in mass madness, a notion apt to make people feel even more insecure than an H-bomb drill. Not that he can't always come up with the evidence. For the impending Russian invasion, for instance, he found an ad for the ATOMICAPE: "Protect yourself against atomic radiation. Be shielded from contamination and flash burns. Satisfaction guaranteed or money refunded." It's illustrated with a picture of an ATOMI-CAPED Superman type.

Or there's the old routine about "conspiracy to advocate the overthrow of the government of the United States by force and violence"—the official sin of which my father and all the others stand accused. "Well, I can see, certainly, what's meant by *overthrowing* the government . . . " (puffs on pipe to light it) ". . . and I can see how one might *advocate* the overthrow . . . " (puff, puffa-puff-puff) ". . . but for the life of me I cannot see" (blows out match) "quite how you'd go about *conspiring*—at some unspecified future date—to *advocate* the *overthrow* . . . ?" (pipe going comfortably now, steady small puffs). He felt pretty good the day Mr. Justice Black on the Supreme Court gave him some back-up on this (in a dissenting opinion, naturally, so as not to matter much) when he said he thought people should be punished for actually doing something, not for "agreeing to assemble and to talk and publish certain ideas at a later date." Isn't that nice, a Supreme Court judge agrees with Daddy that the witch hunters are *crazy*.

But this is all sophistry. So what? What kind of a hill of beans does it make to Joe Shmoe? The only thing that's laughable to Mr. Shmoe is the idea that the Red scare could actually have been conjured up to justify the continuation of a war economy. No one is going to persuade a reasonable, smart guy like Joe that there aren't any witches. For anybody to insinuate that, or suggest that the upright fellows who run our show could come up with such a thing— that's *crazy*. For Joe Shmoe, you might read: Dan. Only Dan takes it further. Try discussing the Fifth Amendment with a West Point cadet who is having it drummed into him daily that honor requires you to rat on your friends.

The odd thing is that it's only their ideas that are different, not my two men. The ideas spring out of very similar instincts. At heart they are Boy Scouts, decent guys who take basic principles like honor and truth and justice much too far. They each have standards of rectitude you could cut with a knife. You would never catch either one of them being sneaky or petty or hypocritical; nor, unfortunately, would either ever dilute the purity of his principles in some low act of compromise.

I feel at home with Dan because, like Daddy and most of the English of my parents' class, he's not really comfortable about expressing his emotions directly. You have to pick up what you know by radar. Feelings that go unac-

knowledged soon droop and die out. My English relatives—
the males among them, anyway—perform great feats of
stony stoicism when the occasion demands. Just as the public schools mold men this way in England, West Point has
done the same to Dan, or at least perfected a natural tendency. After all, it's the attitude you need in a winner.

Being able to see these kinds of basics about my men sure
doesn't mean that they can see them about each other, though.
Who people really are behind their labels doesn't seem to matter in the world at all, to them or anyone else, and these
two—for all that they have hardly met for more than a stiff
"hello"—have the most terrible kind of contempt for *the idea*
of each other, for the very reason that they are so interested in
honor and truth and justice and don't seem to be able to focus
too well on the human beings the principles are supposed to
apply to. Everything seems to be a matter of interpretation.
But at the bottom of the pot, after boiling, this is what's left:
ideas may separate them, but ideals are the nub of the matter.
And to be an idea*list*, like my old man, is definitely to be on
the far side of lunacy, suggesting as it does that we in God's
country may not, after all, have arrived—that there may be
further to go before we reach the gates of the seventh heaven.
Dan wouldn't hold with any such fantasy.

It's soon obvious that there is nothing very poetic or
even bearable about being stuck loving two dedicated ideological enemies. Since defending any sort of position does
such obvious damage, I take no positions. I avoid con-
frontations between the two, not only for fear of political
battles but because I feel Dan's uniform to be an affront to
my father and his choice of civvies no less so. On the rare
occasions that they do bump into each other they are identi-
cally, uncharacteristically stilted and stupid. They share the
knack of the deadpan. Dan insists on calling Daddy "Sir,"
which gives my father grounds for some totally diversionary
opposition (can't stand being called Sir) on the basis of
which he can disapprove without making overt trouble.
Dan doesn't need grounds. "Out on Bail" will do.

Anyway, they can't seem to think of much to say.

* * *

Despite his by-the-book behavior, even Cadet King slips up, and our weekends are often enough disrupted so that he can be punished. There is a certain muddle in my mind between Duty Honor Country and that other three-word motto, recently made so famous by photos of liberated Auschwitz, *Arbeit Macht Frei*. The thing about the rules at West Point is that they seem to exist entirely for the purpose of instilling obedience to them. Any lapse is measured in demerits. Demerits are also earned by a cadet's failure to maintain a weekly 2.0 (out of 3.0) average in his academic subjects. If you get enough demerits you get "slugged" and have to give up your free time to "walk the area"—march up and down in "full dress gray under arms." Or you get CCQ, Cadet Confined to Quarters, and you're out of action in your room for the weekend or even longer. All Dan's ingenuity is as inadequate as everybody else's in avoiding punishment. Somebody is always walking that area: it's obviously part of the plan. Trudging back and forth in full dress uniform with your rifle, after all, gives you lots of time to think about what has to give, you or the system. In the cause of indoctrinating discipline, if no other, the system seems very sensitive to the frailties of its participants: there is no way of outwitting it, there's bound to be something about you that merits demerits. It works, it has worked since 1802. You probably wouldn't find a lot of academy graduates with any questioning, let alone rebellious, inclinations left.

Dan certainly doesn't question the system, though he gripes at its excesses often enough. He's supposed to, you have to show a little spunk. It's part of the good sportsmanship of taking it—with the token groans due a punishment, or how could it punish?—but of taking it like a man, seeing the funny side. (Since I am only a girl, I don't have to see anything funny in it.) Thus some of our weekends are entirely forfeited and others cut short while he walks and I hang around waiting. He's very tired and irritable afterwards.

So many rules! But they aren't enough for us. We have to make our own as well: chastity until marriage.

Marriage? Marriage is confusing. Life for a female is confusing. Neither of my men, no man, is any help with this. They think they know, they spout their spiel. Of course, so does my mother, the one about girls not needing to go to college, falling in love with a rich man, blah blah blah, suggesting that she thinks women shouldn't work—as of course they shouldn't, because it's their job to stay home with the kids—but on the other hand it's obvious that Mummy despises women who stay home with the kids. She gets satisfaction out of her work and doesn't *only* do it because she needs to. Ditto Mrs. King. So why are the girls at Science, who are as smart as the boys at Science, deciding on careers and learning all this chemistry that won't help them with the cooking? What are we really supposed to want to end up doing? And with whom?

There are lots of subjects besides politics, including marriage, that I don't want to talk to Dan about until I've worked out the confusions. Luckily we don't need to talk much. We're not too good at words anyway. He is the strong silent type. And somehow all that Giglio lemonade and pimple-picking have yet to produce in me the intended results of banter mastery. When you come down to it, the words we use are ready-made, lifted straight from songs, which say everything so much better than we can. Just as we have dancing to substitute for sex, we have lyrics for our feelings. The miracle about the songs is you don't even have to be together to get that feeling. All you need is a jukebox, and there's one of those at every corner drugstore and diner table with your shake and burger. Anytime you're feelin' lonely . . . music! music! music!

I am the happy wanderer—Mr. Sandman, bring me a dream: I'm in the mood for love. When I fall in love, it will be forever—but who knows where or when? Once I had a secret love, sh-boom, sh-boom: somewhere there's music (but not for me?). They tried to tell us we're too young, but fools rush in where angels fear to tread. Hey there, you with the stars in your eyes, the more I see of you, I'm beginning to see the light. Hey, good lookin'! Whatcha got cookin'? If

I knew you were comin' I'd'a baked a cake! I'm falling under your spell—what have you done to my heart? Because of you there's a song in my heart—you fill my eager heart with such desire, I just long for you only, here in my heart, my one and only heart. Bewitched, bothered and bewildered, now I shouted from the highest hill: You are my Destiny.

Tunes invade us, pursue us, speak for us. Maybe it's the tunes we love? Maybe it's the love we love? Life, power, ecstasy: hearing the music, all at once I am everything, my schisms have healed, I am a blessed unity. I hover just above the ground on a cloud of affirmation: the man I love loves me. If I can just keep my mind on the one thing.

9

COLD WAR

Freedom for the supporters of the government only, for the members of one party only—no matter how big its membership may be—is no freedom at all. Freedom is always freedom for the man who thinks differently.... Freedom loses all its virtue when it becomes a privilege.

—Rosa Luxemburg

I tell Fran everything. Do you realize, I say to Fran, that if it wasn't for my cat Callie, it might have occurred to me, when my mother moved us to Spuyten Duyvil, to get sore instead about her having left behind my collection of autographed movie star photographs ("Yours truly, Tallulah Bankhead," "Best wishes, Robert Donat," "Sincerely, Hedy Lamarr")? If I'd taken the aptitude test with *that* for a grudge, who knows—maybe I'd have gone to the High School for Performing Arts. Or I could have had a fit about my forgotten oil paints and easel, and ended up at Music and Art. Or about her not packing anything of mine, as a matter of fact, that didn't happen to fit into the turquoise jewelry box that has turned out to be my whole luggage whenever we move. If I'd given a thought to the full picture instead of only part of it, I might even be stuck in some godawful ordinary school, like Walton with Debbi, flunking Home Ec, bottom in the batting order, rejected by the Junior Debs, pretending I didn't care. I'd never have come to Science! I'd never have known you! Motto: Forget God, thank Callie.

In the counting-of-blessings department, Fran is right at the top. My Fren Fran I call her, and she calls me My Pal Sal. The only trouble with Fran is that she lives in the farthest reaches of the East Bronx, so I can't see her except in school. Even then I don't really catch on to her until junior year. She's in the cheerleaders with me and is otherwise unlike me entirely. She has curly black hair and a sweet heart-shaped face, behind which hides the brainbox of a mathematical genius. She hauls me single-handed through trigonometry, lends me her clothes to take to West Point, and keeps my secrets: she is loyal, devoted, and gentle, with a personality of perfect selflessness. Because of her, I find out that another human being can be trusted.

Before Fran and as well as Fran, there is a small mob of insubordinates at Science, others as satisfied as I am to let the closed books of calculus and higher physics remain closed, who jam pencils in the one-way locks of the doors at lunch and sneak out to Nuts 'n' Butts, the local knish-and-egg-cream bar, or take an occasional afternoon off to go to a movie at Loew's Paradise or shoplifting at Alexander's or downtown to a TV quiz show. If "Black Sam" Levinson, the big ape of a school disciplinarian, gets you (Cheezit!), it's detention, which means you have to show up at dawn, but somehow he's always checking the back door when I'm slipping in the front. What are wits for? Anyway, in a world where I'm graded according to my father's politics and scorned at dances for reasons of pigmentation, the rational and irrational, the Done and the Not Done, the obedient and the delinquent, are all of equal value, or none.

There are a stunning lot of great kids at Science. What isn't apparent for ages is how many are not American kids at all. Their families came out of Europe one step ahead of the Nazis. This may explain how original, hilarious, and

nice they are. Steve Vinaver's first language is German, so is
Joey Neugroschel's; Marie Winn speaks perfect Czech;
Mike Kaufman, Polish; Anna Kisselgoff and Natalie Bien-
stock, Russian. There's a Romanian girl who was named
"Lourdes" to fool the fascists that she wasn't Jewish. Their
families came here to save their own lives, not because they
had any advance yearning to melt into the American pot.
Far from it: they still treasure their lost European culture
and have salvaged something important—another, parallel
set of values. Many of my friends don't have parents who
play the American game or know or care about producing
standard-model American teenagers; so the kids are prod-
ucts of their own imaginations, plus what they can pick up
here and there, as I am. The irony is that when they do
decide to conform to the American Way, at least on the surface, the girls take me—with my hoked-up performance
rehearsed in the wings in Croton, coached by Debbi, and
fortified with those telling little extras picked up on the
West Point bus—for a genuine AAG. They copy my socks?
What a scream.

It's true I get the socks right, thanks to the Giglios; Mrs.
G keeps me abreast of the latest fads when she corners them
for her girls. But by junior and senior years all the Science
girls look AAGish as anything. Like others girls, we yack
about calories and lipstick colors and "Where'd you get
that *adorable top?*" and "I *love* your *shoes*," and we dress
to kill in different outfits daily, a shirt or short-sleeved
sweater with a little scarf or bow or dickey at the neck, and
incredibly cinched-in waists. Some iron their hair; I set
mine. Aside from color, the results (please God the weather
should be dry) are identical.

But there's more to life here than hair and socks, and it's
not just the unflagging intellectual energy. The recent past
of some of these kids and their near escape from the death
camps gave every moment of survival a vast significance.
One boy, whose parents had brought him from Poland on
one of the last trains out, told me that it seemed to him
almost a lottery, and that he owed it to those who hadn't

held the winning tickets to live and learn and do things for all of them. But it was not just a solemn enterprise: he was also funny for all of them. For my part, in a virtually all-Jewish school, I could never get out of my head the remark my father had made years before about the refugee child we'd passed in the street: "Hitler doesn't like little girls who look like that. He likes little girls who look like you."

These kids have frightened parents who on no account want anybody rocking boats in too radical a direction, but there are those among them who follow the lead of some second-generation kids organizing silence in the auditorium when Washington decrees that "under God" be stuck into the Pledge of Allegiance. "How childish you are!" one teacher berates a student who is arguing that the new words contradict the principle of separation of church and state. Dr. Meister, the principal, is in a terrible snit about it, but what can he do? He can have the words, all of them, projected up on a screen as in a community singsong, which makes more kids than ever ostentatiously ignore those two.

For me, school is probably the opposite of what most American kids experience. Instead of a place where a lot of bored people serve time with a lot of boring time servers, my school is more interesting than television, movies, or hanging around. Not more *fun* necessarily, but more consistently absorbing. It sure beats religion, with all those exhortations and longueurs. The only thing more interesting than school is love, but you can't think about that the entire time. True, I sneak peeks at my beloved's snapshot during explanations of the less lively sections of the periodic table, and I illuminate the margins of notebooks with his name in a variety of calligraphies and typefaces, not to mention languages (Roi, Rex, Re, Rey, Tsar, Krol, Kralj, Konig, Koning). Still, there are limits to the entertainment to be wrung from this; underneath I know it's more engrossing to work out a new orthographic projection.

The special brilliance of this school depends on the excitement generated by—of all things—what we're learning. I still can't get over the fact that at Science, a new piece of information is met not with a dull thud of resistance and resentment but with a blotting-paper eagerness, and the enthusiasm is epidemic. And to think of our part in *progress*—the rat-a-tat-tat, inexorable forward motion that is America's given since the war. The sun doesn't set without some new invention, development, or cure to show for the day: all problems are being solved. Know how! Can do! Science, the discipline, not the school, is our religion. The body is what interests me: someone's just come up with antihistamines, and now that they're knocking out TB, VD, diphtheria, and polio, we'll have a cure for cancer soon. The other day they even put one person's kidney into another person! We'll be able to get a replacement anything! We could live forever! With its perfect order and clarity, science is figuring everything out: there is no hitch it can't overcome. Science, the school, not the discipline, is the shrine, and we all worship there. Working on the mysteries of metastasis with the others in the Cancer Club is a far more transcendental experience than anything that ever happened to me in church.

But Science is holy for real reasons, not sentimental ones, and nobody takes its symbols seriously, least of all us on the cheerleading squad, whose team *never wins*. The building is dilapidated and supposedly they're building a new one, but who cares about a building. And nothing gets the whole school sniggering like the song, which is about as sapheaded as the rousing victory chants that we bray in our teeny greeny-yellow dresslets at our lost-cause basketball games. "Science High, you school whose towers reach for truth and li-ight, all for thee our hearts and powers solemnly unite." I mean, really. "Hearken how the chorus heightens as our praises soa-oar . . . " Can you believe it? "Through the years thy glory brightens. . . . Science evermore!"

The thing is, it's true.

There are problems even at Science, though, and I don't know which is worse: what Mr. Kisch* is doing to me or what the Washington inquisition is doing to the school. Of course, Mr. Kisch is just a pathetic sex maniac picking on one person; how can he be comparable to the devastation brought on the faculty by fear? But *he* is what *I* fear.

It's possible—sort of—to see him as an object of ridicule or pity, and occasionally I can work up the generosity or backbone to render him harmless, but on the whole and pretty constantly I feel just terrified. He isn't bad-looking. It's something to do with what looking at me does to his face. Otherwise he's broad and athletic, with hair so thick and fibrous it's stiff, as if the only way each hair can find room is to jut straight out. That hair has gone from mostly reddish-brown when he was my tenth-grade algebra teacher to pure white by my senior year. As my teacher, he paid me no extra attention. It was some craziness that overtook him soon after, and from then on he has never let me alone.

He knows where all my classes are and stations himself nearby when I'm coming or going, or failing that, he resorts to the old corridor-interception routine. While the student body is changing classes, he comes at me through the relentless tide of moving crowd making our meeting inevitable, and I feel such disgust, loathing, horror, shame, that I would be paralyzed if the mass surge wasn't carrying me along. There is something about that look of his that is a violation in itself. Aimed exclusively at me, yet entirely depersonalized: *I* have done nothing to arouse or sustain it, who I am doesn't count. He just *looks,* with those wide-open pop-eyes magnified by steel-rimmed lenses, electric blue with white all around, eyes starving like mouths that could swallow me whole with a glance. When we pass he pants my name, breathing it more than speaking it, and then a note lands on the books clutched to my chest. The notes are clammy: he's been holding them in his sweaty palm for this moment, and they make me feel as contaminated as his seething looks. "God you gorgeous thing how I want you!" they say, or "You adorable creature I'm going to *eat you up.*" Sometimes he comments on my choice of clothes that day, how nice I look in blue, or wonders why I

seem particularly happy or downcast. What business is it of
his? I crumple them and throw them away, if possible without even reading them, except for the very last communica-
tion, which is preserved forever because it is written in my
yearbook. "Remember that song you were singing with the
jukebox when I asked you about college? . . . From the first
moment . . . Goodbye, you touch of Venus. . . ."

I remembered. He had taken to accosting me even in
Nuts 'n' Butts after school, leaning on the jukebox with his
stare all set. *That song* sticks too, "Once in a While" . . .

> *won't you try to give one little thought to me?*
> *though someone else may be*
> *nearer your heart . . .*

He knew perfectly well who was nearer my heart. He had
sleuthed out almost everything there was to know about
me, and he knew who was responsible for the A-pin on my
blouse. Dan was not only his ex-student, Mrs. King was his
neighbor.

He didn't even bother to disguise his handwriting:
immune to harm? or relying on the idea that the daughter
of a man who believed the greatest act of moral cowardice
was informing would not report him anyway? It was true, I
wouldn't. I did tell Dan—anecdotally, never suspecting their
connection—and Dan went to see him in a rage next time
he was down from West Point to tell him to knock it off.
But how can something so irrational—which after all boiled
down to little more than looks—be knocked off?

The notes stopped briefly; and the next time his corridor-
prowling paid off and we met alone, for once he didn't
press me to the wall—pinning me there, not touching, his
arms like a cage—and *breathe* while I made small bleating
noises, rigid with terror. His temporarily modified behavior
brought home what really mattered. It was the looks that
got me, the way he seemed charged, like Tom when Jerry
sticks his tail in the socket.

Between encounters I actually managed to forget him. It was an unconscious defense—as long as he wasn't there, I had the edge on him. Reaching the stage of plotting out evasions, routes around the school designed to foil him, would have meant giving him as much thought as he was giving me. But then I'd see him coming. Cornered, stunned with fear and shame again, unprepared as usual and with no way out of a collision, I'd resolve to take precautions next time, go another way. And then he'd slip from my mind, I'd forget, until he was upon me with another note.

Maybe panic is simply panic, whoever feels it and whatever fuels it. While Mr. Kisch was stalking me in the halls, officialdom was engaged in a general hunt for witches among the faculty. But while I was never really hurt, these people's lives were at stake, and more: they had the imagination to worry about the entire country following them down the drain. The Second World War was fresh in all minds. The teachers were virtually all Jewish. "First they came for the Jews"—they had taught us Pastor Niemoller's words—"and I did not speak out, because I was not a Jew." Maybe it was the Reds to go first this time, but it just so happened that the Board of Education's citywide purge since the beginning of the decade had resulted in the dismissal of hardly any but Jewish teachers. Nearly five hundred were relieved of their duties in New York City's schools and colleges.

No one said out loud or in any official way that all teachers were under investigation as to whether "There is/There is not/evidence . . . of subversive friends and ideas." It was not mentioned at assemblies by Dr. Meister nor lamented in class by colleagues nor written up in the school paper, *Science Survey*—but when a biology teacher vanishes suddenly, that's no rumor. Who would speak up? The risks were clear. Then one day in April 1953, Dr. Julius Hlavaty, chairman of the math department, was gone. Dr. Hlavaty was not just respected, he was revered; he was considered the best mathematics teacher in the country. But the previous week he had taken the Fifth Amendment before the

McCarthy Committee, and according to Section 903 of the New York City Charter, teachers who refused to cooperate with congressional committees were automatically dismissed.

The first details about Dr. Hlavaty had come from I. F. Stone, who attended the hearing in Washington and wrote about it in his *Weekly*. "A committee sated with victims took him apart indifferently, like a small boy taking the wings off a beetle. Dr. Hlavaty has been in this country 32 years. He has been a teacher for 24. He has a national reputation as a teacher of mathematics. He is one of the best loved teachers on the faculty of the Bronx High School of Science. His chances to avoid dismissal are slight unless students and parents organize to support him."

No hope of that. It had become so popular to think of radicalism as a kind of pestilence to be stamped out for fear of contagion that the idea of anybody organizing anything was laughable. In a national survey, 78 percent of Americans said they thought it was a good idea to report relatives or acquaintances suspected of being Communists. Over half thought that known Communists should be jailed. As for the schools, "a network of professors and teachers taking orders from Moscow want to corrupt the minds of youth," said Senator McCarthy. The fear was palpable if you had the antennae for it.

Far from organizing, nobody even really knew the facts. Over the next weeks there was a virtual conspiracy to suppress information and let rumors run wild. Where was Dr. Hlavaty? Some mentioned suicide. Some said he had been sighted running one of the new laundromats—a popular occupation for those the witch hunt threw out of work. You got a lot of tut-tutting, isn't it awful. In "normal" times, in the kind of ideal society we were drilled by some of our teachers to believe we inhabited already, people surely would have protested. They would have taken the *really liberal* position: Dr. H is a most distinguished scholar, a fine teacher, a decent man, a conscientious citizen, and if the accusations about his political opinions have any basis in fact, so what? What does that have to do with his ability to teach calculus and run a department? The school misses him a lot, such a man cannot be replaced, and isn't it a waste?

But he was not the only one, went the thinking, and you couldn't be too careful. To coddle Commies was almost as bad as to be one. This was the new wisdom: the exclusion of Communists from teaching was the very essence of academic freedom since Communists, forbidden by their enslavement to teach objectively, were the ones who violated it.

Few stopped to think that even the *really liberal* position didn't go far enough, since to say, "So what if Dr. H is a Communist" accepted the possibility that he might be— i.e., might be a plague-bearing rat—based on nothing but the accusation itself, thus acknowledging the right of the accusers to limit free thought; sure, okay, but in this case what harm could a math teacher do? (My father et al. would of course go further: What if Communists were not plague-bearing rats? What if they were the good people, poor devils who wanted the best for humankind?) It was back to the witch on the ducking stool: if she lived, it was because of her magic powers, and therefore she must be crushed between heavy stones; if she drowned, it turned out she was innocent. After all, running a laundromat wasn't as bad as being dead.

The Rosenbergs looked as if they'd soon be pretty dead, and it was hard to think of them as anything except the first of many. And the ducking-stool was exactly where they— lefties who wouldn't recant—found themselves. How did you prove you weren't a witch? Especially if you didn't think witches were so awful anyway, so you couldn't as a matter of principle join the Down-with-Witches crowd. After the failure of their last appeals and the refusal of the Supreme Court to review the case, with the electric chair waiting, they were offered one last chance of salvation: confess. *What if they had nothing to confess?* Too bad no one believed them. How to combat the universal conviction of your guilt based on the universal conviction of your guilt?

There was a mass frisson throughout liberal Jewish New York. It wasn't hard to feel. Who was next? Some who had disguised themselves as Adlai Stevenson campaigners in the last election were already fighting the next: cover your tracks, look mainstream. Of course there was nothing-doing on this score at 65th Street. My father was standing up to be counted for all he was worth, looking taller than ever in the flattened landscape. Jo cleaned out closets a lot. In school there was the history teacher who self-consciously distanced himself from the whole Red plot by objectifying it into a "subject of study"—well, he had to prepare us, didn't he: the subject was included in the syllabus for the New York State Regents exam. (They provided old questions to practice with. Sample essay question from June 1952: "In the struggle between the Communist and non-Communist worlds, there are three fronts on which battles are being waged—military, political and economic. Show what the United States is doing in this struggle on *each* of these three fronts.") This only incidentally involved reading out another scurrilous front-page story about my father—its truth blended with innuendo so skillfully that I was unable to refute a word and could only hotly hang my head. I was incensed about the unfairness of it: he didn't read out stories about another classmate's father, John Williamson, also about to be deported to England (*Daily News* headline on the day he was shipped out: RED SAILS IN THE SUNSET), because with a name like Williamson you had a free invisibility ticket. Just wait till I'm Sally King, you bastards.

Teachers sympathizing with my father continued to give me higher marks than I deserved, it seemed to me—is it still paranoia when "they" are doing you a favor?—enough for me to make Arista. But there were oddities. One of my teachers, Mr. Q, had called me up after the first day of his class, trembling inexplicably, to say out of nowhere, "Just because I've been a *Guardian* subscriber doesn't mean I'll give you a break: you'll have to be *ten* times as good as the others!" He seemed deranged. Nothing would help him one bit if some canary sang that Mr. Q had once, say, belonged to a group now on the attorney general's blacklist of subversive organizations, or God forbid had perjured himself by signing a loyalty oath. *Tainted with Communism.* If he then didn't finger his friends, he couldn't clear himself and at the very least would lose his job. So maybe the Bronx could use another laundromat?

The time came when it looked as if the whole thing was falling apart. When the Rosenbergs really were electrocuted—June 19, 1953—people went past a frisson; they were in shock. After the volts went through her, the papers reported, *a plume of smoke rose out of Ethel Rosenberg's head.* Two sets of charges had been necessary to kill her, said a television journalist standing outside Sing Sing just afterwards: the executioner had had to reconnect the straps and electrodes when the first shock—the same strength as the one that had killed Julius—left her still alive. "After two more jolts, Ethel Rosenberg had met her maker," he ended, adding, lest anyone accuse him of sympathy for her, "She'll have a lot of explaining to do."

W. E. B. Du Bois said, "These people were killed because they would not lie." Jean-Paul Sartre said, "If we can have some hope, it is because your country gave birth to this man and this woman whom you have killed." Up to the last minute, demonstrators outside the White House screamed, "Fry the Jews, Burn the Rats!" My father wrote, "By arranging that all those who sent them to death should be Jewish, justice was seen to be done."

The state of shock lasted until the following spring and the Army-McCarthy hearings. The senator had finally overdone it: Reds in the Department of Defense, Reds in the weapons plants, and now he claimed that even the Pentagon was riddled with Soviet agents. He constantly interrupted the proceedings with his insistent low whine: "Point of order, Mr. Chairman, point of order." Each day a bunch of teachers, playing hookey like me, crowded into the school library, which held the school's one tiny gray TV, to watch the hearings. It was my senior year by then, so I hadn't much left to lose from minor disciplinary infractions. I didn't know how much any of them had to lose. Students and teachers craned to see from the back of the room, sat on tables, stood on chairs. Nobody revealed an interest beyond the academic, the historic. But there was such tension in the packed room the atmosphere had white knuckles.

When Joseph Welch, the army's counsel, wearily confronted McCarthy with the question we all wanted asked—"Sir, will you not stop? Have you no sense of decency, Senator, at last?"—something palpable happened, some release of the anxiety began. When it was over, the perfect power of that special persecutor, the myth of "Tail-Gunner Joe," was finally punctured. He was subsequently condemned in the Senate.

My father said not to believe it was finished, though: to call the whole system of inquisition "McCarthyism" gave everyone the wrong idea. He quoted in support one of the latest victims, a newspaper publisher in Ohio named Edward Lamb, who'd said, "To blame it all on McCarthy is like blaming the temperature on the thermometer." If they had to call this nightmare after somebody, J. Edgar Hoover was a better bet. Hooverism? J. Edgar Hooverama? To keep the ball rolling Hoover had just contributed an editorial to the *Journal of the American Medical Association* entitled "Let's Keep America Healthy," in which he pointed out that the physicians of America, like other citizens, could best fulfill their responsibilities regarding internal security by reporting to the FBI any subversive information coming their way.

While Dan would never have known it, nor anyone at all who was linked to my AAG project, I—the other I—was still sick over the Rosenbergs. The effort was not to think about it, because the thoughts felt like stones in the stomach. In one way there was no doubt about their guilt, but they were only guilty of believing the same kinds of ideas as my father, the fired teachers, the readers of the *Guardian*.

"We were obviously criminal agents of a foreign power," my father put it later, "because our only explanation of why we took the position we did was that we believed it; and the very concept that any one could act on such motives, materially 'for nothing,' was foreign to the ascendant America." It was exactly the kind of honorable cynicism that got him nowhere. If the Rosenbergs did anything, I knew they'd done it from the same motives that animated my father and the others: to make a better world. For this they should die? They were scapegoats for all the left-wingers around: *Get in line, the rest of you.*

Come to think of it, whoever did give the Russians any atom tips—though as far as I could see from what came out of the trial, it sure wasn't Julius and Ethel—ought to get a medal. This way, wasn't each side less likely to start something?

My father, awaiting the worst, has a growing tendency to make speeches. Cornered in his kitchen by the force of one-sided sound, I skulk by the barred window and the broken dumbwaiter, trying to distract myself with the view of the airshaft, waiting. On and on he goes. Every kind of mishmash gets thrown in, like one of Jo's risottos. It's obviously a case of godawful pressure combined with the English difficulty of coping with stress, but such is the contrast with his normal mode that you wonder if he's the same person. In a rant, he suddenly loses his delicate, wry wit and all subtlety. Understatement becomes overstatement, irony turns to sarcasm. Disapproval comes out in wildly exaggerated ridicule. If he were an epileptic you could stuff a handkerchief in his mouth to save him biting his tongue, but as it is all you can do is wait for it to go away.

The speeches are never personal or particular, except insofar as the savaging-by-scorn of some public figure can be called either. They aren't about him, me, or you. They're not dishonest—he doesn't pretend to speak for the oppressed proletarians, since it's pretty obvious he doesn't really know any. Even that would have been about flesh and blood. This is abstract, full of oversimplified complaint about the threat to, or the absence/withdrawal of, various concepts like equality, justice, brotherhood, faith, trust, *hope*. The whole lot is sprinkled with such images of horror that the words lose impact, become clichés; like a sauce reduced over too high a flame, they curdle. Once he clipped from the paper an "all-purpose headline," SITUATION WORSE, which has been yellowing on his bulletin board for years. It sums up everything. Doom is as foreordained in his view of things as in any end-of-the-world millenarian's. Fascism looms. It's all much too far-fetched to teach me anything, which is his presumed intention.

What he doesn't understand is that it's his example, not his precept, that wins him such esteem. It's the person inside, whom he thinks irrelevant, that we all love so helplessly. He's so charming that you can forgive the mistakes. It's perfectly understandable that he would have explained the war to his little girl by telling her about Hitler loving the Aryans like her and killing the other little girls—because at six years old, what could she be expected to comprehend of *world war* or *death camps*? How could he have had the imagination to realize that as a consequence she would feel an accomplice in genocide?

10

SITUATION WORSE

Communism is a way of life, an evil and malignant way of life. It reveals a condition akin to disease that spreads like an epidemic and like an epidemic a quarantine is necessary to keep it from infecting this nation.

—J. EDGAR HOOVER

The word peace might get you on the Attorney General's blacklist provided you're not yet on it.

—THOMAS MANN

Mrs. King is starting to get nervous: this thing with me and Dan is going on too long. At first she didn't care about my father, or maybe she was showing her big heart by sympathizing over what *tsuris* such a family must cause me. Her first serious case of objections gathers force behind my goyishness. It starts right after Passover, when she made a big seder for me, which Dan says is the first one he can remember. It's so unfair, because on top of everything else I can think of to fit into my chosen role and endear myself to her, I've been going to the Jewish chapel at West Point with Dan and have decided to convert.

Religion is no trivial matter. Faith is an article of faith.

This, after all, is the year they go so far as to list the Bible on the best-seller list and put God in the Pledge of Allegiance. The good citizen's mission is to *smite the Communist anti-Christ atheistic subversion undermining America*. Nobody dares call themselves atheist, even *agnostic* sounds extremist. I have decided to reconsider. Jewish is what I feel.

In the quest for anonymity, Dan has further to go than most. Only 1 percent of the Long Gray Line is Jewish, and he is certainly the only one from the Bronx. At the Point, Jewish cadets have compulsory religious services like everybody else, but on Sundays, so as not to mess up the routine with their weirdo sabbath, and the rabbi doesn't live in like the chaplain or the priest, he just turns up for the service, which is held in the Old Cadet Chapel, a hand-me-down from the early, solely Protestant days of the academy. It's a Puritan atmosphere there still, albeit with the cross removed from the altar and Jesus deleted from the agenda; with the student-soldiers I too can mumble *Baruch ata adonai elohainu* and various incantations as strange to many of them as to me (since naturally if they were anywhere approaching Orthodox and took it seriously, they couldn't attend West Point, not least since it forbids them their own sabbath), and I find nothing queer about learning the history and meaning of the words. What's one more philosophy to add to the collection? Besides, it's a wife's duty for the sake of the children to promote religion and religious harmony in the home. I *am* Jewish anyway, it's just this damn disguise. In fact, mostly what I pray for is to be reborn with a Jewish mother, a nice ambiguous name (Wolfe comes to mind, like Debbi's old boyfriend), a skinny body, and thick black hair.

But after a year of Sh'ma Yisroels, Dan's mother turns around and says it won't work, I won't ever be really Jewish, I don't have the tradition, we're talking five thousand years here, how could I keep the holidays? *Her grandchildren wouldn't be Jewish*. Soon afterwards the attack veers toward my father and gathers force behind the politics; then she gets a stomach disorder and starts telephoning me with health reports, crying and threatening. I understand her point of view, which makes it worse.

Of course her life might have been livable if she hadn't given up the whole thing for Dan, she explains, talking about how she slaved for him in the same tone my mother talks of slaving for her black dress. Well, it's true in a way, I guess: both were bought on credit for repayment out of the riches they will produce. Dan is certainly his mother's stake in life; there are few others—a two-tone green-green Plymouth for visiting him in, and Max,* her best friend and business partner, who drives her around and absorbs abuse like a blotter. But Dan is her real investment, and who should know better than Mrs. King, an accountant, about investments?

"Look, I'm telling you gal to gal, let's not talk to him about it 'cause it's for his own good. What are you, sixteen, seventeen? You're a kid yet, by you it's all roses, you'll find somebody nice. But I'm telling you, you should leave my boy alone. You with your father in jail, you think they don't know about it? You think it won't affect his career? He should go with the daughter of a Commie, get himself a traitor for a father-in-law? You want I should wish you mazel tov? After all I've suffered, how do you think he got where he is today? And you think you love him, you call that love? Wrecking his life? Listen, you don't know from love. And never mind what you're doing to me, you're giving me such a stomach, I have to send Max out for toilet paper once, twice a day, is that a way to live? Eight rolls of toilet paper I used up this week already, it's not even the sabbath yet. This for you and what you call love. I'm sick, I'm a sick woman. And don't tell me I'm not patient, listen, I'm Mrs. Patient. How long is it already, a year? Enough! I know about life, that's all, you know bobkes about life. So what do you think, they're stupid? They can read too, you know. They see the papers, Belfrage this, Belfrage that, McCarthy Committee, Communist spy, Ellis Island, Fifth Amendment, deportation, they can read. So then what? They're gonna give my son a commission in the United

States Army, he's running around with who knows what divorced Red spy's daughter? Hah! Well, I got news for you, young lady, I've invested my life in that boy, *my life,* and I'm not gonna sit around while you take my life and turn it into garbage, me, a sick person. Number one, I'm cutting off his allowance till he comes to his senses. Let's see how you like that. I should let *him* spend *my* money on *you,* a shiksa Red spy's daughter? Finished, already. From now on, you wanna see him, you pay for it. And I don't mean just money, either. Let's see you handle a little aggravation for a change."

This fat queen accountant adding up columns in her plastic-and-linoleum living room on the Grand Concourse, taking credit: Who does she think she is? But wouldn't I feel the same as she does? Sure, but so what? How can she be so two-faced? She used to pretend to care about me. The big fat cow.

Somehow Dan manages to get along between us. His mother has buried him in guilt for all the privations she has endured to get him where he is today, so he's unlikely to take my side, but he can't take hers either. He probably finds us useful, finally, with our quarrels and complaints diverting the negative energy to leave him undefiled and adored by us both. Though really he shies away from emotional displays and usually lies low until the climate is temperate again. Who does that remind me of?

My own mother gets a subpoena. The injustice! With her new philosophy thanks to Louis Fischer, she's been playing it safe. Since 1952, when she rooted for Adlai Stevenson, she's been working on this public persona of *liberal.* It doesn't get her off the hook. They want her to testify against my father. Now that they are divorced, this is "legal." If she refuses, she cannot stay in the land of the free.

It is her finest hour. "But m'lud," she addresses the judge, who cocks an ear at this unusual appellation, "at home in England, one was taught *never* to snitch against one's chums."

The judge points his finger in a generally external direction. "Out!" he says.

Or so her somewhat abbreviated version of her immigration hearing has it. "He also said he'd charge me with contempt of court. I said, 'But m'lud, I have the greatest *respect* for this court.'"

When the "Out" will take place is as yet unknown. These things do not happen in a hurry. Somewhere certain wheels have to get grinding. In a matter of weeks or months the wheels will result in her expulsion from the country. Nicky says he won't go. She insists. He gives in. I say I won't go. I insist. She gives in. It is provisionally decided that I will live on 65th Street with my father and Jo. They haven't anything like enough room, and who knows how long they'll be around either, for that matter. But I feel welcome, if only to their living room couch.

Mummy is given bail—actually, they just help themselves to her bank account—on condition that she take the ferry to report once a week at Ellis Island. Suddenly she is under attack on all fronts. Even her one regular diversion and release is gone because like Daddy, she's not allowed off Manhattan, so no Wednesday square dancing in Connecticut. Basically of course she's overjoyed to be seeing the back of this barbarism. But the uncertainty! How to afford any of it? For such ejections are, if the means exist, at the expense of the ejectee. How to keep her mind on her work? How ever will she find a job in London? How to endure the suspense? What will they do to her? Jail? *He* won't help, with his *Won't you join the party?* and she's stuck with two kids who need schools, homes, upkeep.

She stops eating. Might as well, since whatever she swallows comes back up. Spasm of the esophagus, they call it, but naming doesn't help. She's getting emaciated, waiting. No one can tell how long it will go on.

One day while writing up a report I come across it in

Mummy's thesaurus. There, in the middle of the most terrible words ever known:

> friendless, unfriended, lorn, forlorn, desolate, god-forsaken;
> lonely, lonesome, solitary; on one's own, without company,
> alone; cold-shouldered, uninvited, without introductions;
> unpopular, avoided, unwanted; blacklisted, blackballed, ostra-
> cized, boycotted, sent to Coventry, excluded; expelled, dis-
> barred, *deported,* exiled; under embargo, banned, prohibited.

From the beginning Dan has convinced himself that my
own politics, as they don't exist, pose no threat to his
career, since "our democracy" obviously works as given or
else why would he be defending it? Stories about my teachers' unconventional grading strike him as hallucinatory. My
claims regarding aberrations in the system earn the same
comforting, if irrelevant, innocence of response that I myself
feel.

"They're deporting my mother just because she won't
testify against my father!"

"That's impossible, they can't do that," he reassures me
confidently, delivering a brief lecture about due process.

"Oh yeah? How about when they picked up my father
in the street without a warrant and they wouldn't tell the
lawyer the charge so she couldn't get a writ!"

"Well, there must be some mistake, they can't do that."

Funny, that's exactly what I'd said on hearing the news:
They can't do that, it must be a mistake, that's impossible;
and the answer was, *But they did,* and thus I answer Dan,
and there we are, satisfied in our knowledge of our constitutional rights.

It becomes overwhelmingly important at this stage to
blot out reality with any means available. Luckily there is
the future to consider. Here we have the all-American Girl
preparing to be an army wife. There is a good deal of
brooding to be done over her name- and signature-to-be,
doodling on every desk, practicing in varied scripts and

shaded biblical-epic-style caps. It's too good to be true, the beauty of this name, the anonymity of it: *No one will know who I am!* Yet what class! And a miracle: I won't ever again have to spell it to people and correct them because they always get it wrong! SK may not make such a great monogram, but I have two middle letters too, the M.C. for Mary Caroline, to fancy it up with. (Dan has no middle name. At first I thought he had three, when I saw him listed on some academy document as Daniel N.M.I. King. *Far* too dumb to figure out it was army lingo for "No Middle Initial.")

Research continues among the more experienced drags of the circle-pin and cashmere set encountered at WooPoo weekends. The army wife's future duties, our AAG is reliably informed, will include donning the hat and little white gloves to leave calling cards for the wives of higher-ranking officers. (She should certainly not assume that, having left the academy behind, she will escape the Company C-1/taller-man syndrome.) She'll move around a lot, but they give you a house to go straight into, left all spic-and-span by the last army wife in residence; and she owes it to her successor to stay up all night scrubbing it spotless again before leaving for the next posting. The kids get used to all the moving, and they often meet up again with old pals among the army brats; they'll go to special schools if the posting is abroad so as not to have to mix with the natives.

The whole affair is becoming less plausible by the minute, but our AAG *never thinks about that*. Not thinking about it is a little like digging a hole in dry sand. She gets rid of bad thoughts and then they go sliding right back in. Not, mind you, that she is anything but head-over-heels. Just ask her, she'll tell you. Absolutely head-over-heels. What else is there in life, after all?

To prove it, just now she is often engaged in a typical AAGish endeavor, trying to disentangle the blue, gray, red, and yellow spools and bobbins dangling from the four knitting needles on which are slowly taking shape an argyle sock for the beloved foot. Getting the other sock to match will be no cinch, but it's the least she can do to try. Also, there is a quite a lot of renewed hovering down at the Giglios, though with Debbi now away at college it's less to corner her (the get-your-man expert) than Mrs. G (the keep-your-man ditto). That is, if you can prize her head out of the oven, which she is scrubbing out with Bon Ami, long enough to get her tips and recipes, or for that matter learn how to scrub the oven. Who knew ovens got scrubbed?

Debbi, home on vacation, gets a hope chest for Christmas and moons over its contents a lot. My interest in flatware patterns and monogrammed doily sets is mainly manufactured in hopes that it will become genuine and meanwhile no one will point at me for my trousseaulessness; I'm baby-sitting frantically every night to save up for that stuff. Debbi treats me with more respect these days: Dan just about cancels out my parents to redeem me in her eyes. Being pinned to a West Pointer, after all, is pretty good going, even if he is Jewish. One weekend I took her up to the Point on a blind date with the roommate, Witter T. Elbowroom III, since after all she is little and cute and feminine like Lee: his type. She looked amazing in a terrific new topper and the most gorgeous feather cut. But WTE III hardly spoke to her all weekend and told Dan later she reminded him of a llama. What's that supposed to mean? Everybody knows Debbi's perfect.

So is Dan. Even not seeing him too often is perfect. An official steady boyfriend, especially one who is out of town, leaves you a lot more time for homework. To pass our New York State Regents exam in social studies we have to be able to define words like "jingoism," "chauvinism," "xenophobia," "totalitarianism," those follies and wickednesses committed in the world by foreigners and other people. The radio and TV and papers tell you what to think of *them*—"the mouthpieces of Soviet imperialism," "the sleeping dogs of war," "the great Red horde," "Kremlin cat's paws"—and it's no trouble really: turns out to be exactly the identical teeth-gritting, stomach-clenching, eye-squinching hatred so familiar from our having once felt it for the Nazis. You just switch over. When you see the hammer and sickle you go into the same push-button paroxysm you once got from the swastika. It's strange about the similarity of this to George Orwell's three-minute hate, but that's *their* bag; we only hate what's truly hateful. "By the iron curtain," says our textbook, "the communist peoples [are] deliberately cut off from all contacts with the democratic peoples." If you thought about it you might get muddled observing that among the democratic peoples are those who can't get passports and are also cut off, so it's just as well not to think about it.

I can't help feeling nostalgia for life during the war, when I could go along with everybody else without this awful confusion and ambiguity; but it's OK if I keep remembering that for most people (including ones I love, like Dan and Fran), it's just automatic, they're not really aware of all the complications, so they can't help themselves. It would be great if I could explain to them, though, or if there were anywhere to go between these antagonistic extremes.

In a talk he gave in New York, Daddy spoke about those who sought safety in a "middle-of-the-road position." He said it seemed a pretty cozy place, the middle of the road, he had searched all over for it "diligently for years." But: "There is none today, either in reason or morality. It is too late. The Nazarene did not find anyone to put in the middle between the sheep and the goats on the day of judgment. The atom and hydrogen bombs may have brought us pretty close to that day."

I refuse to think in terms of sheep and goats. Daddy makes everything so simplistic it's insulting. So what am I supposed to say to people? Throw the Nazarene at them? You can't tell them about any gospel of three square meals a day because they are too haunted by the fear of being smeared as subversive. Besides, American prosperity is pulling the rug out from under him. Look at all this progress! Know how! Can do! Naturally the populace parts company with him entirely when he says, "But if there is something that needs subverting, what is wrong with subverting it?"

Meanwhile he sure has a point about the middle of the road. It is simply an unacceptable position to both sides, to his as much as the other. When Adlai Stevenson lost the 1952 presidential race, the middle of the road lost its last credible exponent. A big rumpus is going on now with the Republicans saying the Democrats have been coddling Commies, even Governor Dewey of New York warning people to blame the Democrats whenever they thought of treason and "the blood of our boys in Korea." All this has toughened up some spines, and Sen. Hubert Humphrey, one of the erstwhile liberal leaders of Americans for Democratic Action, has hit back: "I am tired of reading headlines about being soft toward Communism. . . . I will not be lukewarm. I do not intend to be a half-patriot."

To show his stuff, Humphrey has drafted a new law, the Communist Control Act, which makes CP membership a criminal offense subject to five years in jail and a $10,000 fine. Since many victims of the witch hunt have already been fined this exact amount—a fortune in the early fifties—and been sentenced to more than five years for crimes like "sedition," the bill may be academic; yet putting it on the statute books bothers some people, even Republicans. Attorney General Brownell points out that proof in these cases would require witnesses and the FBI might have to sacrifice one undercover agent for each Communist they catch. Can that be worth it? In the end they decide it isn't, and the bill gets watered down: the party is outlawed, but membership per se is not a crime. There is chaos on the floor of the Senate for the vote, which is unanimously in favor as members rush to be counted, one Florida senator even showing up with shaving soap on his cheeks to shout "Yea!"

But in the House there are two negative votes, one from each party. A New York Democrat, Abraham Multer, says, "Putting any group out of business this way . . . is the way a Fascist would use," and North Dakota Republican Usher Burdick is against "any form of tyranny over the mind of man." Two for the middle of the road. But you don't even read about them except in the *Guardian*.

At school, like other American kids, we have studied and memorized chunks of the Declaration of Independence (that document which the citizens of Madison, Wisconsin, thought too subversive to sign), the Preamble to the Constitution, the Gettysburg Address. Every year but one, which is reserved for the history of the world starting with cave men, we are taught the same legends and mottoes of America's greatness. Don't shoot till you see the whites of their eyes! Liberty and Union, now and forever, one and inseparable! Fifty-four-forty or fight! Give me liberty or give me death! I have not yet begun to fight! Don't give up the ship! Go west, young man! The only thing we have to fear is fear itself!

Daddy thinks it's pretty goofy to reduce the whole of history to these relatively recent provincial matters, but you can see that his love for all the We-the-People stuff is as strong as anyone's. How the Red-baiters have twisted it all to use against him! I too am stirred by the stories and songs, for whatever reason, and have long ago stopped embarrassing teachers with questions involving contradictions. Even at Science they don't like that kind of question. I stop noticing contradictions. I am both us and them, and all the rest too. Everything is split, cracked apart. I absorb everyone's myths, believe them all. I am the personal embodiment of the Cold War, and if I can't keep it cold, I'll be destroyed. My mind feels like a zoo, full of savage animals clawing and shrieking to get at one another. They will eat each other up unless I keep on mending fences. But between Dan and my father, *I am the fence*. Whenever I am with one of them, I am ashamed of the other.

One day we are thrown out of paradise. That's what graduation feels like. Since the school auditorium isn't big enough

the ceremony takes place a couple of blocks up the Grand
Concourse in the local movie theater, fittingly called Loew's
Paradise, which is where we've spent quite a few afternoons
taking in a double feature after cutting class. If I had that to
do again I'd stay in class. For a final triumph, I even get
chosen runner-up for prom queen again. I get to wear the
white tulle tiers and the coming-second crown. Naturally
Dan can't get away from the Point that night. Herby Kohl
and the others still don't ask me to dance. Mr. Kisch sidles
up and asks, but I decline.

Since the FBI sequestered her bank account for bail money,
my mother's protestations of insufficient funds for me to go
to a decent college have at last become believable. It
wouldn't even occur to me to ask Daddy. I could try for a
scholarship somewhere, but what's the point? Since I have
to stay in New York near enough to Port Authority to catch
that fatal weekly bus, I figure I'll go to Hunter for a while.
It's free and will pass the time before Dan is ready to make
me Mrs. Second Lieutenant. When I think about the Cancer
Club and how much I wanted to do, there is a disappointment underneath that nearly fells me, so I don't think about
it. Who's better than me at not thinking about things? What
do I need an education for anyway? Let someone else find
the answer to cancer. I've got what I came for: first prize,
dreamstakes.

   The ante's upped and the stakes are higher too. Now
when Dan's mother calls it's no more with the reports on
her plumbing but how she's siccing the FBI on us if we don't
stop, how she's going to tell the press ("It'll get publicity!
It'll get newspapers! You think what your father is about is
newspapers? I'll show you newspapers!"). She says she's
hiring a private detective to follow me around—nobody has
trouble keeping track of Dan—so she'll know if we meet.
The vision of my own personal Humphrey Bogart in a
slouch hat has a certain appeal, but the press and FBI
threats are just cockamamie, it seems to me. Because the
fact of my existence in the life of one cadet seems to have

been overlooked by the media and the feds (maybe too hard to believe?), she'll just draw their attention to it? I say this is smart, like getting your heart removed so you won't have to worry anymore about cardiac arrest. She fires off a string of her normal retorts, like look who's talking, what do I know, I should get my head examined, me she needs like a hole in the head, oy ge*valt,* get out of my *life,* and hangs up.

Life is about waiting: waiting for the 10A bus, waiting for the mailman, waiting for the weekend, waiting for the next issue of *Mad* to come out, waiting for my parents to get sent back where they came from, waiting for my life to start. Waiting for Dan. Meanwhile there's another summer to kill, but this year forget about running after George. Just before school ends, someone—Charlotte or Fran or Bobbi or Janet or Marcia—sees a help-wanted ad for J.C. Penney: the head office needs lab assistants. We think we have the right qualifications, so we all troop in together, a giggling gaggle, for interviews.

Fran and I are hired. Thirty dollars a week! Fran is also going to Hunter, but we neglect to mention college; in fact, they specifically ask and we specifically deny we're going anywhere, as naturally they don't want to train us only for the summer. We put on our sophisticated going-to-work outfits, complete with stockings and girdles and little white gloves, and from opposite ends of the Bronx, plunge into hell each morning, converging via rush-hour subway and arising from its hellish tunnels dripping, bedraggled, to something even worse—a boiling midtown office all day. It's a new first in the torture line.

But the physical discomforts are as nothing compared to my discovery about life. What it's all about, it turns out, is this major affront of having to go somewhere and sell the best energies you possess to total strangers for the privilege of being able to eat (to renew the energies to sell to strangers to . . .). And after you've figured out the job, which takes maybe eight or twelve minutes, further observation provides a quick course in the natural order of

things. This is what office workers really do all day: watch
the second hand, have a smoke, work up a trance, drink
coffee, sneak a minute by the boss's fan, go to the bathroom, exchange jokes, steal a pencil, dawdle over lunch,
sink into catatonia, have coffee, pander to the boss, move
stuff around, move it back, have a smoke, go to the bathroom, sulk, get some water from the cooler, gossip with a
pal—anything to cheat them out of half a minute, anything
to demonstrate how little you can give for how much you
can get. How demeaning! Boring! Stupid! And that's the
real world they've been keeping from us all these years.
How do people ever grow up if they're kept in this kind of
pettiness?

And this is a *good* job. The lab is run by Mr. Finn and
employs around a dozen of what he calls "my girls," they're
all pretty nice, the work is not uninteresting and soon to be
over anyway. Fran and I are allocated lockers and sticky
white nylon uniforms and are taught to test fabrics for ten-
sile strength with a ferocious machine that rips samples
apart between its metal teeth; and also to perform tests for
color fastness to sunlight, sweat, soap. In the lab the best,
most senior jobs are in the sealed room containing those
whose lives are more precious than ours because they are
harder to replace, and are needed to taste-test the woolens
for insect repellency. Their room is *air-conditioned*—the
only place in the whole huge building, except maybe the
executive suite (wouldn't the bosses keep themselves as
comfy as the bugs?), that's under 90 degrees.

Luckily the other people in the lab don't seem very on
the ball newswise. Maybe if you ride in a rush-hour subway
too jammed for paper-reading, you give up bothering. None
of them seems to have the first idea about my father; nor do
they worry a lot about Washington politics. As a matter of
fact, you don't hear or overhear much about the world outside anywhere in the building. I become familiar with most
of the place because another of my duties as a new recruit is
to trot around in my dinky white dress pushing a cart of
test samples for return to the various buyers. Not that com-

munication with the other people goes much beyond an exchange of toothy smiles and the occasional "Good girl" pat on my backside. Corporate America, view from the bottom of the heap.

Several weeks go by before it dawns on me that not one of the hundreds of names on the doors I knock on or enter or pass with my trolley on any of the floors is Jewish. In New York City! Fran is a Catholic. Charlotte and Bobbi and Janet and Marcia are Jewish. So that's why we got the job.

Daddy and Dan think it stinks. But Dan is practical. Half the summer is gone, he reasons, I'll never find another job now, and much as he hates being beholden to me, we need the money to see each other since his mother cut off his allowance.

I always try to do what Dan says.

11

DOING IT

Young women, whose beauty was the pride of a parent's heart, have, by listening to the flatteries of a vile seducer, been bereft of their innocence and peace; scorned by the world, and rejected by their friends, they finish their career of vice and wretchedness, in misery too horrid for description. O that the young, when tempted to impurity, and when virtuous resolution is staggering, would call up to view their emaciated form once so lovely, their sunk eye once so sparkling, their broken heart once so gay, and it would be the preservative of their innocence!
—HENRY BELFRAGE, MINISTER OF THE GOSPEL, FALKIRK, 1817,
PRACTICAL DISCOURSES, INTENDED TO PROMOTE THE
IMPROVEMENT AND HAPPINESS OF THE YOUNG

He is very proud of my virginity. The torture this imposes so electrifies our time together that we're stiff with lust from first to last, paralyzed with longing for each other. In the Weapons Room we drink our chocolate malts and dance to Patti Page and Nat King Cole, deep purple, blue velvet, all the lovely lilts allowing virgins to rub their bodies together in an ecstasy of fantasy.

Stop!

Such mortification of the flesh produces a relationship that is as much a shared religious trance as a romance. We are in thrall to our promise. I feel shooting pains in my stomach just to look at him, the way the skin tightens over

his cheekbones, the blackness of his lashes: I can't breathe.
My bones melt and my eyes roll up into my skull at his
touch, just a finger on my palm or in my ear. When he actually holds me, dancing, I'm transported from my flesh and
made one with it, with him, with the universe. And yet
however helplessly carried away we become, we never
break our rule, for we understand its purpose.

We never break it until we break it. This is because
somehow or other I have got pregnant while I am still a
virgin.

He was very proud of my virginity. I understand I can only
keep him by denying him. Like all the other boys I've known,
he makes great drama of his suffering: but tales of agony and
aching balls are taken as the good girl's due, some mysterious
blue effect we've always wrought on male plumbing, testimony to our attractiveness. Girls of course aren't supposed to
have feelings like that; it's his unique suffering that drives us
on, on, on, until eventually my virginity becomes the cause of
an automatic shut-off, the No of fear—not of sex, but of losing him. Then on a hot weekend in my J.C. Penney summer
when we were for once on a *bed,* nearly (never wholly) naked
on my mother's bed, rubbing, stroking, tantalizing still
because not there, not quite . . . suddenly I felt the wet
between my legs. No penetration, as they put it later, one in a
million, but there you are: you're pregnant. I hadn't even
taken off my pants.

It swam in.

He was very proud of my virginity. It enhanced the illusion
that had become my life's work, to be the American wife for
him—unexceptional but unexceptionable, toothsome but
wholesome, sexy but not sexual. Clean. You can't erase a
bad reputation. Bad girls put out. They are *soiled merchandise:* easy, fast, and fickle. You can tell them by the mascara, dark lipstick, thick makeup, falsies, tight sweater, tight
belt, cleavage, perfume, anklet. Bad girls are too real: their
nipples or their asses show. They are too fake: their hair is

dyed and their eyelashes are false. Nice girls are *dainty* and *well-groomed*: they smell of soap and cold cream, they wear a slip and stockings with the seams straight, white cotton underwear, Jonathan Logan dresses and dickies with Peter Pan collars, sweater sets two sizes too big, dress shields, pearls (single strand); or dungarees with spotless saddle shoes and white wool socks. A hat for dress-up, suit with matching accessories, white shorty gloves. *Never* use profanity or smoke in the street or check your makeup in public. The worst thing in the world is to be seen with lipstick on your teeth, straps showing, slip showing, hem falling, seams crooked, heels run down, skirt seat shiny, hair in your armpits, *telltale outlines*.

In such a world, no question about virginity, none. Even "heavy petting" is shocking, though "soul kissing" is just permissible if you're really in love and if you don't call it that. There are other things that nice girls have heard of only in whispers, like "dry humping." The point is, you don't get to experiment, because once you've gone too far by going all the way you're gone forever. Losing your cherry is losing your soul: outcast, a tramp, you are doomed to the twilight world of dope fiends and promiscuity, VD, sin in back alleys, uncontrolled passion and depravity. You might as well turn in your charm bracelet and start wiggling your hips right away, buy slingback shoes and sweaters that fit—because you are branded, you have a reputation, it's all over. Imagine the shame of a girl swamped in such clichés to find herself pregnant.

My mother has enough troubles. The main trouble was covered in the morning newspaper—to her, less the substance of the piece than that it *reveals her age*.

N.Y. Herald Tribune, September 15, 1954:
Communism Charged

MRS. BELFRAGE GETS WISH:

WILL BE DEPORTED TO ENGLAND

The Immigration and Naturalization Service yesterday granted the wish of an alien to be deported and further ordered her exclusion on the grounds she became a Communist party member after coming here from England as a permanent resident in 1937.

The order was directed against Mrs. Mary Beatrice Belfrage, fifty-one, of 500 Kappock St., the Bronx, divorced wife of Cedric Belfrage, editor of the Leftist "National Guardian." It was handed down by William Fleigelman after a hearing at Immigration headquarters, 70 Columbus Ave.

Mr. Fleigelman said Mrs. Belfrage would be deported at government expense to England later this month or she might choose to pay her own passage back sooner. Mrs. Belfrage said she would take her son Nicolas, fourteen, but leave her daughter, Sally, seventeen, because she is attending college. Both children were born in the United States and enjoy dual citizenship. Mrs. Belfrage said she hoped to continue earning her living as a writer in England. She said she and her husband had been divorced eighteen months ago.

A deportation hearing against Mr. Belfrage is also under way.

Mummy at least starts eating a little again, now that the suspense is over—the date is set for October 6, two days after my eighteenth birthday. She has three weeks to move a life, no money, a future full of phantoms. She is making piles of stuff to pack, stuff to sell, stuff to throw out. The apartment doesn't look too different despite all this.

I have to tell her I am pregnant. Apart from an annoying tendency to flirt with them, she has never shown the least interest in my life with boys, even Dan, as if it's all too childish to concern her, but who else can I turn to? Daddy's out on bail at the moment, but he must never know. Debbi? I'd die first. Even Fran is too sweet and innocent for such a terrible revelation. I feel like that poor dumb cluck Shelley Winters, who loses out to Elizabeth Taylor in *A Place in the Sun,* this year's big movie, after Montgomery Clift gets her "in trouble" (heaven forbid they should once use the word *pregnant*: saying it is almost as shameful as being it). But whatever word you use there isn't much doubt left—not only two missed periods, but my breasts are swollen and I feel sick. What else could it be? I don't understand heroines in novels who claim not to know they are pregnant. Or stories in the papers about girls who never dream anything like that is going on except they seem to be gaining some weight, months go by, and all at once this baby pops out. I mean, you *know*. Even if you haven't actually done it and the whole thing is impossible, you still know.

Last weekend at the Point, Dan and I discussed the situation. After I got him to believe it, or at least to pretend to believe it, or maybe just to temporarily stop disbelieving it, he explained what I had already heard time and again, that cadets are not allowed to marry until after they graduate. Left unsaid is that if I go ahead and have a baby either he will have to quit or I can't visit him when the lump shows, plus it would put the fritz on his career for sure. Also unmentioned is the fact that abortions are so illegal you can't even find out where to get one, it's not as if he can help with such a thing, and if you can locate someone who doesn't use a coat-hanger then it's really expensive, but he can't help with that either since his mother stopped his allowance for continuing to see me. I have exactly $273 in the bank from years of baby-sitting and summer jobs. The money makes me sad: all that saving up, scrimping, resenting the quarter for a pack of cigarettes or the nickel for an orange, because of the years of taking care of other people's children who congealed in memory to an image of running after George.

The idea of telling my mother makes me sicker than I am already. After all my prissiness with her, it's sure going to be serves-you-right time. In fact, while she's supposed to be the naughty one and I'm supposed to be nice, if you scratch us I think we are just the same. In one of her novels she divides herself (an only child) into two sisters who talk about their sexual attitudes:

"Mother herself was a hangover from Victorianism when 'no lady liked sex,'" [she has the elder one say]. "She tried to instil the same noble ideal into us. Of course it's my opinion she's always had the sneaking idea she may have missed something—but instead of wanting us to make up for her lost time, she tried for just the opposite."

"Sour grapes?" [replies the younger sister.]

"Definitely. Bad luck for her she was a generation too late. We're not exactly free from all those old shibboleths because although we go ahead and do what we feel we have to do we still feel guilty about it."

"Then you don't think we're being thoroughly immoral?"

"By mother's standards of course we are."

"But are they the right standards?"

"Of course not. We both know that. Nevertheless training, education—whatever you call it—is pretty strong. . . ."

"D'you suppose mother never had any normal instincts?"

"If she had, social pressure against expressing them would have been too great. . . . At least I hope we'll have learned enough not to tie our own children into emotional knots."

It's hard to imagine how, despite her actual behavior, her (or Piggy's?) ideas of modesty and shame got through to me, since all Mummy ever did was deny them, but I know they did and what they are. Telling a child the opposite of what you mean or feel doesn't make the child believe it. Mummy's attitude was defiance, and who's a greater specialist in defiance than a child? Now, either she's going to agree I'm doomed or she's going to laugh at me. I can't stand it.

I decide to pick the one moment in the week when we're all in a pretty good mood: right after "You Bet Your Life" with Groucho Marx. That has the added advantage of delaying the disclosure for a few days while I try to reverse things by a lot of jumping off the elevator shaft on the roof, with no result but a twisted ankle.

*   *   *

The killer-diller is how nice she is. She stops everything and comes to me. When she hugs and kisses me it feels real for once. I see suddenly that for her I've joined the humans now, and that I can never again condemn her. Also, that if she'd been the pretend Mrs. G of my dreams she would be throwing tantrums; instead, she says to leave it to her.

She doesn't really believe I'm still a virgin, though. Well, who would? "Ask them to test you," she says. Test me? How are they supposed to test me? Besides, I don't plan to be a virgin anymore by the time "they" get to me.

I tell her how it happened, leaving out her bed for some reason—that it was a case of Everything But plus a good swimmer. "He wasn't inside me or anything." Oh God, it's so embarrassing.

"Bad luck," she commiserates. Easy to see she thinks it's idiotic to want to be a virgin anyway; she's just curious.

It's all so amazing that I'm almost sorry she's leaving—but then, it's partly because she's leaving that she's being so amazing. Close observation reveals in fact that she is feeling not so bad. Her repertoire of prewar songs has changed, or maybe it's the way she sings them. Where normally she'd be fogging up her glasses with "Smoke Gets in Your Eyes" or "September Song," now there's the odd jaunty rendition of "The Way You Look Tonight" or "Cheek to Cheek," and her own cheeks are dry. She and my father have become quite chumlike lately: she seems to have decided to cut her losses, and he is affectionate and supportive since her troubles—which derived, after all, entirely from him—began. Also, thanks to a brilliant idea she had, she has cheered up even more: getting back at America by using all her department store credit cards to buy herself and me and all her friends new clothes. The one surefire way to evade the bill collectors is to get yourself deported. One by one she's taken us on expeditions to Saks and Bergdorf's and Lord & Taylor, and everyone she knows looks terrific. She herself is absolutely stunning again.

Stunning, despite all my new skirts and sweaters, is not

what I feel. Stunned is more the word. At Hunter I'm sick all the time, constantly fleeing to the john and making everyone think I've taken up chain smoking, since there can't be any other reason.

Finally one day when I get home a strange woman calls. I'm not supposed to know her phone number or even her last name, but my mother has set some wheels rolling and word has reached her. She directs me to meet her at a certain station on the Long Island Railroad with $250 at 10 a.m. next Thursday, October 7. This gives you six days to think about it, she says. I have nothing to think about, I say. But how will I know you? *I'll know you*, she says knowingly.

Of course it's not true that I have nothing to think. I have nothing else. Think: why don't I have the baby? Because, dope, you have to choose between the baby and being with Dan. Think: Thursday is the day after my mother is leaving the country. I wish she could stay to be with me. Think: I wish she could help me a little with the money too. Don't be stupid, she'd get hysterical, and besides, if she won't pay for my education, why this? Although think how educational *this* is.

The first thing to get out of the way is my virginity. I'm sure I'll croak, because the only abortion stories I've ever heard have cautionary endings in the morgue. Why be a dead virgin? Dan is in agreement. "Though not a word was spoken. . . ." However, it's not the spirit with which to enter into these things. What's more, Saturday night at the Point is cold and drizzly, but when we get to the disused cadet lavatory where we've necked for a year, it's locked. So there we are: Flirty or nothing.

Famous Flirtation Walk. Plebes not allowed. Bad luck to pass beneath Kissing Rock without. A wooded path above the river, with here and there a bit of rock or thicket to be alone behind. On most dark Saturday nights the woods are alive with wriggling, giggling bodies under every bush, croons and cries, attacks and climaxes, admissions and rejections. Too bad about the rain this time, but that's how the cookie crumbles. The darkness is complete, and only maniacs would be at large on such a night. I for one am feeling so maniacal that I don't even care if my hair gets straight from the rain. And there among the damp leaves and pointy stones, after eighteen months of agonied and agonized refusals in which we learn each other's bodies like our own but never give them, hugging kissing feeling touching stroking in a thousand moods and times and places, there on the wet October earth with our coats failing to soften our resting place, two days before my eighteenth birthday and terrified, hating every minute of it, I

    let

        him

           do

              it.

That is the way it presents itself, *letting him do it*. It's ghastly. On a glacial slab my reversible coat is spread velvet side up with Dan's jacket on top, and then me and then him in his undone clothes, all of it chill and sodden. I can feel a point of stone beneath my back more vividly than Dan's flesh, or what there is of it poking out of his uniform. It's all finished in an instant, a dot, a meaninglessness of time. In no way does it resemble any of the momentous sensations I have felt from kissing and dancing. It feels like nothing, except maybe disgusting. I only want to get warm again.

Sunday is warm all right. It's a perfect Indian summer day, or a reprise of spring. We drag ourselves around the paths and in and out of rocky nooks and thickets trying not to think about this thing we've done. Everywhere you look the innocents are chirruping and scampering, playing baby animals, sensationally romantic. I feel sick. The only things we know how to say to each other don't sound right anymore when you consider all the entendres. *We'll make a life together*. We've made it. *I want you*. Not me, not like that. *I'll stick with you forever*. Okay, how about next Thursday?

But of course he can't come with me to Long Island. You can't just leave this place when you feel like it, even if we could afford it out of the $23 I have left after the bill for

the abortion, most of which is not left thanks to my bus
fare and hotel bill this weekend so we could have this glori-
ous experience together. Anyhow I'm going to be eighteen
tomorrow, and in some circles they consider that grown up,
so I'll make it somehow, bleak smile. I'll have to be grown
up, won't I, with my mother getting the heave-ho from our
great country on Wednesday, and who will look after me? I
might as well die anyway. What do I have to look forward
to? Being an *army wife?*

By now we've found an inlet in the bushes where no one
is playing Bambi and Thumper. The sun is heating up a
streak of rock. I collapse and melt. I sob at the destruction I
am causing. He stands above me, hands on hips and legs
apart, his luscious mouth set straight, squinting at me in the
sun. "Crying is a sign of weakness," he says.

I'm starting to figure these characters out on the bus ride
home. Take Dan, number one. He's never unsure of himself,
right? In his opinion he is A-OK. He doesn't ask for anyone's advice, consider the possibility of alternatives, or hesi-
tate. Maybe it comes from having a mother who is so thor-
ough and foolish in her devotion that you come to believe
her obsessions and then to live them. He really is arrogant
beyond belief. That's what I love about him. When he's
around I never have to wrestle with divisions of the brain.
This sort of thing sure endears itself to females, in fact to all
the halt and the lame. He tells me who I am! Men get mad,
though, and try to trip him up, all but the ones who also
need what he can supply: substitute spine. You'd think such
a type would make a good general, say, and he would. Just
his luck to land in the place where they appreciate and
know how to channel this kind of thing. But will it work?
Only 2 percent of these heroes ever make it as far as general, they say. And you've got to work your way up, after
all—but Dan's not cut out to be second, only first, so who
will help him get there? That's why I'm not too worried
about him staying a soldier. Maybe he'll figure it out and
quit after his four mandatory years of service. On the other

hand, what do I know? I'm just a girl, not an army.

It occurs to me that I have one of Rick's index cards on the subject in my bag. The ones he sends now from wherever the Coast Guard is taking him are unaccompanied by so much as a return address, let alone a letter, and seem to be in aid of erecting a military edifice against which he can square off. He is a man with a mission. This one is from *War and Peace:*

> A good leader need not be a genius, or have any superior characteristics; on the contrary, the loftiest and noblest qualities of man—love, poetry, tenderness, an inquiring and philosophical scepticism—must lie out of his ken. He must be narrow-minded, absolutely convinced of the importance of the task before him—this is indispensable, for otherwise he will lack patience; he must keep aloof from all affections, and know no ruth; never pause to reflect, never ask himself what is just or unjust. . . .

My father, on the other hand, is equally arrogant under the skin, maybe even more so. It's the style that fools you. He's so tender and giving. He too, though not his mother's only son, was her favorite. Some nerve it gives you all through life, once you've been Kid God. The trouble with my father, as with other gods, is that he can accept responsibility on levels both cosmic and commonplace—like deciding how the world or a bunch of flowers should be arranged—but he falls down on the job in between, where the lives of the people around him come into the picture.

I'd like to tell them both: you can't build love out of hatred, even if the hatred derives from love.

Meanwhile, lest we forget, something else has now happened. I am no longer a virgin. What does that make me, apart from fallen woman? I wish it felt different, being a bad girl. I still feel pregnant, but I wish I felt something *else* different. I didn't even bleed. Why? Did I ride too many horses? Why should he believe I even *was* a virgin? Was I already a bad girl at heart? What would have happened to me in one of those societies where family honor depends on the bloody sheet out the window the morning after?

One thing's sure. There isn't anyone to ask anymore, or talk to about what's on my mind. All at once I have secrets. My only confidant is Dan, and what can he be expected to understand? "Crying is a sign of weakness." But all my friends must never know about this dreadful thing I've done. The giggling is over. It's lonely.

When I get home that night they are dismantling it. Supposedly this is a good-bye party, but it's actually a division of spoils, populated by vultures pretending to be friends, all trying to buy our old oaken wonders at knock-down prices. Our heirlooms. I feel quite attached to them suddenly: brought from England in the prosperous days, hundreds of years old, witnesses to all my life. What else is there to hold on to? There is all the folklore: how they had two oak refectory tables when they met, and got one of them made into benches, all those lives ago when they still loved each other. There is the carved oak corner cupboard that came from some church, for the storage of communion wine. A framed seventeenth-century map of the world, showing California as an island. They carted the stuff six thousand miles to L.A. and polished the table and we had happy meals. Later, when these few bits and pieces got shipped east, the table was the scene of such awful, awesome battles. Finally, solitaire and board games. But still, the solidity of it! I feel like lying down on the table, both of me, to share our secrets. Of all of us and what we have, somehow the table alone survives with dignity. And here these *friends,* politely bidding and edging each other out of the way, are trying to suppress their greedy smiles. Daddy is there too. Inchoate feelings of rage boil up in me. *It is all his fault.*

12

KILROY WAS HERE

Moral decay weakens our resistance to the Communist masters of deceit.

—FROM A 1953 FILM SHOWN TO
U.S. HIGH SCHOOL HYGIENE CLASSES
ABOUT THE PRESERVATION OF VIRTUE

On Monday I am eighteen: old enough to fuck, buy a drink, and marry anybody but a West Pointer. I have morning sickness. Or is it mourning sickness? Mummy and Nicky creep around in whispers, being tactful. Has she told him? Some moving men arrive for what is left that was unsalable. Where it's going, I don't know. Who cares? My bed is carried past, then Nicky's. They leave Mummy's double bed till last, the one on which the dirty deed was done. I lie on it trying not to puke and watching the furniture pass by and out the door. The moving men ignore me. When everything is stripped I must get up. I don't feel capable of going to the roof to say good-bye, or even to the Giglios', but I do have to get down to the savings bank and take my money out before we leave the neighborhood forever. Happy birthday.

All my life I have been surrounded by people describing themselves as grownups. I won't be an official adult for three more years, but what do you call this double act now? This must involve membership in the *older generation,* whatever else it is, since I contain a representative of the next, however short-lived. It's more convincing than the numbers on a birth certificate. And look at Mummy's birth certificate: faked. No, by either reckoning I'm nothing like grown up, any more than most.

Mummy and Nicky go to a hotel and I move into Daddy's that afternoon. He and Jo put themselves out to make it cozy, though I can't believe they're overjoyed to have me. There's no question of an extra room: I have to sleep in a sort of corridor between the tiny living room and their bedroom, and it must cramp their style.

But actually they are too busy and preoccupied to worry about me, I learn soon. So many of their friends have gone to jail or into exile, lost their livelihoods or even their lives—you never know who's next. An air of menace lurks in the wings. Each new day you can see they feel the threat renewed: Is This It? Evening meals become celebrations that they've made it through another, still here, whew. Parallel to the draining sense of danger is the excitement of living with this intensity, keeping alert and determined to resist, sharing feelings, food, and friendship with the others in their boat. There isn't a television. They don't need it. So much to say, such precious time. Daddy sings a lot: "Oh, Freedom" is a favorite, and "Sometimes I Feel Like a Motherless Child." Occasionally he manages to sound as carefree as he intends.

The atmosphere around the neighborhood otherwise suits the mood—1954 is the year of the coming down. The Third Avenue el, which darkened and dappled the street below with stripes of light, is the first to go. Trains no longer roar along above us, and the tracks are being dismantled. Customers up and down the line hate losing it, but you have to make way for progress, and the city's top priority, says Mayor Wagner, is a new subway under Second Avenue. All the little neighborhood stores that have hidden in the el's shimmying shadows are going too—the fruit and vegetable market, the hardware store and shoe repair and corner grocery. These businesses are run mostly by immigrant families, shoestring places where they know your name and give you credit, or in our case warn Jo when the feds have been around asking questions. Now, enormous luxury apartment houses are coming up. They are made of sterner stuff and require bigger faster more efficient services. *That's* progress. One bright white gleamer, typical of the kind of building that is transforming Manhattan, is climbing up the air across from us on 65th Street. It is so white that it reflects sunlight everywhere in the neighborhood, even penetrating the corners of our deep dark rooms. White is what the city strives for, racially and architecturally. Plus, the new housing and shopping places are anonymous, just the way I want to be. Notice has been served that when the gleamer is complete and its tenants move in, they're not going to want to look at any rotten old tenements across the way, so our whole row will have to go.

Already they've started tearing down the brownstones at the far end from us at the corner of Third. An interesting consequence is that the cockroaches have begun to march. Since our building is at the other end of the row, and since the roach-march seems to work on a kind of inertia principle, they just keep walking till they can't walk any farther. That's our kitchen. When you turn the light on there at night the walls are moving, undulating in shiny brown waves of bugs all waggling their feelers, and you can't take a step without crunching some underfoot. I don't know where they go in the daytime.

One of the first things that happens after I move into 65th Street is a phone call from Dan to tell me his mother has gone ahead and hired some private detectives to see if we meet. She hasn't specified to him exactly what she's going to do about it when she finds out the worst. She hasn't, thank god, gotten my new phone number.

As for the flat-foot, what timing! Here I am, perfectly situated for sleuth-evasion, only six blocks from Bloomingdale's—since the one thing that sticks most vividly from Daddy's reports of British intelligence training is how to lose a tail: find a department store and run in and out and up and down the elevators and escalators. Not that I can be bothered. But it's funny to think how the private eye and Daddy's FBI tails will be falling over each other outside our modest little brownstone slum, getting their cloaks and daggers all in a tangle. My father calls his "the nuns" because they come in pairs. One will do for me, I suppose. No doubt the mail is opened and the phone here tapped as well, but Dan is perfectly impervious to warnings to watch what he says. *He* knows how innocent he is.

Jo is in on my secret and the plot I've hatched: on Thursday, I explain to Daddy, I've been invited to a party at Fran's in the northeastern Bronx, so I'll go straight from college and stay over, make a weekend of it. Not too believable really, when I've only just moved into their place, but I suppose I'm not terribly believable to him in general these days. He lets it pass. They have a little birthday cake with eighteen candles and we all congratulate me. Triumphantly, I do not choke.

I have to put on a hell of an act. I'm nearly crippled with nausea. Does species reproduction absolutely require this? But I try not to think about the cause. What's inside me bears no relation to a human, more like a bug that I have to go to the doctor about. I just wish she were a doctor. Who is this Long Island witch? Why can't she have a name? Do you bleed to death, or does everything just go black? Where does she stash the bodies? Who-where-when-what-how? WHY? There really must be something wrong with me that I'm so morbid. Millions of people have abortions, Dan says so. I take my first sleeping pill that night.

In the morning, waving merrily, I leave for uptown Hunter, my very own detective presumably in tow. After Science, Hunter is a deadly boring place to pass the days. Nobody asks good questions anymore. Everyone seems, like me, to be killing time. Boys evading the draft, girls on the lookout for boys. Worst of all, since half the students are Jewish and half Catholic, they instantly band together in sectarian mobs, join opposing clubs, mix not at all, and have no room for Protestants, even would-be-Jewish ex-Protestants. Thank God for My Fren Fran. She stays unattached, maybe for my sake. We scorn them even more than they scorn us, if anybody's noticing. They're such an unpromising bunch that we don't care much either way.

Today though, I care. I finished playing my part when I went out the door this morning, and there's no reason why I have to be sick at Hunter all day. I turn around again. Jo will have left for medical school and Daddy for the office by the time I get back, and Dan's letter may have arrived.

There it is in the box, my lifeline, the crisp cream oblong with the lined-up type; on the back flap, a cute little Kilroy. But of course it was written before the weekend. *My darling, I can't wait 'till tomorrow. Every time I think of what you're going thru I die a little. If only there was some way we could be together thru this time. I can hardly stand it when I think if what you must be going thru.* (Repeats himself a little, no? Just like he's dying a little. It's that "hardly" that counts, anyway. What's needed is for him not to be able to stand it *at all*.)

My reply is a form letter. I know how to concoct these things by now just as he does, how you mix up certain phrases, turn a new one, and make a promise of forever. Of course, it's not as if I don't *feel* it. My love is real, but I can see no point in going on about my fear. What can he do?

On Wednesday we're off to the *Queen Mary* to say good-bye to Mummy and Nicky. The space where all the aches should be is filled with bustle: finding cabins, disposing of bags, signing up for dinner sittings, hunting stewards to book deck chairs. Daddy is being gallant and helpful: in a crisis, you can rely on my parents' manners. I see my mother suddenly, so thin and frail, trying to work up a smile for the press photographers. But at least there's relief in it for her. It's over, after all: she's going home. For me, too, she's over. Maybe we can stand each other if we don't have to live together. Nicky beside her twists his mouth bravely. I feel so bad for him, and all I can remember from his eyes, which do not smile to match his mouth, are the years I beat him up, jealousy's tortures passed on. But it's nothing compared to exile at fourteen. He's such an *American* kid: Huck Finn, all skinniness, freckles, and tufts of red hair. His grin looks set in concrete. He never lived with Daddy long enough to make sense of it. It's not just understanding the ideas, either: what Mummy and I know and Nicky cannot is what you go through for love of this man.

I mean, what is this? I want to yell at my mother, who is surrounded with journalists asking her questions that are none of their business. You're letting them punish you for nothing! What's the crime supposed to be? Of course they had no right to ask you to testify, but you didn't do anything, not the remotest thing. You let them throw you out and do this crime to my brother. Why? Because you don't want to betray some principles? Maybe. You're not so big on principles. But I can see you and I know what it is: you didn't want to betray *him*. Why? Do you think he'll love you again for it? It's pathetic. Of course I'm the same, don't I have a mind? Can't I decide if I want a baby or not?

Keep the peace, keep cheerful, clam up. Bye-bye, kiss-kiss. Take care, bon voyage, write soon. I'll come visit you next summer. *Good luck, Nicky.*

Oct 6

Darling Moulie—Jim very graciously told me on the phone that the paper could get along without me today, so I am able to sit down at home and write to you. The log since we left you is that we drove back to 65th St with Blanch [Fried-man, their lawyer] and had turkey sandwiches; Blanch departed for her office and Sally after a while took off for school. Jo is now out having her hair washed. A good deal of the debris has been cleared away in the apartment and at least the beds are clear to be slept on tonight. When the clan reconvenes we are going up to Kappock St. to sort of inventory the situation there.

All this is very trivial. . . . I still find it a little hard to say anything sensible about this weird business in which I have involved you. Sally and I will find out in the course of the next little while how much of a real shake-up it is for us. I understand deeply how much you and she are going to miss each other. Anyway you will know that she is with people who love her and will make the best efforts to help her adjust to the new situation.

Just about the only thing I can think about at the moment is how magnificently you have handled a situation that called for a modern heroine (that's you). I have been very concerned about the effect that all this nonsense had on your health, but much more, filled with admiration for your mastery of it. It seems to me that the few days on the ship should do wonders to get you back in 100% trim—and that you will arrive in top form. I am sure you will get a warm and loving welcome from everyone in England who is worth two cents to you.

I already miss Nicky terribly. He looked so beautiful today that I was filled with pride. I am glad that he and I were able to be a team in rounding up luggage etc. We haven't often had "things to do" together. What could be more of a consolation than to know that you two are in each other's care?

We'll be thinking about you constantly. Write soon.

                                                             Love
                                                             Ced

P.S. Blanch's opinion, expressed to Sally on the way from the pier, is that there is very little if anything that she would not do to help you because you are what she admires most—a woman with guts.

All concur.

She kept this letter, as she kept all his letters. At the bottom of the second page, a note from me:

Dearest Mom—

I was so sad to see you leave today—you looked rather pitiful up there on the deck.

I know that everything will get better & better for you now—for 2 good reasons. One—you're going back home, where you've always wanted to be, & two—that magnificent wishing well result, which I know will come true (for once I believe in it).

I'll cable you as soon as I can about strategic you-know-whats—but I hope you're not worried.

I miss you terribly already.

Love & kisses,
Sally

This is a Gretel-breadcrumb note; evidence, like the faked albums, that the daughter knows how her performance ought to look to the outside world. Plus a dash of wishful thinking. If I really loved her, and called her Dearest Mom, or even Mom, the end of the world might be rescinded. Actually I probably do love her a little. But it's hard to know, now.

I go through a farce of trying on dresses to pack for the party and the "weekend with Fran." Am I overdoing it? Daddy, through all his preoccupations, seems convinced enough. On the Long Island train it occurs to me that the witch doctor has no means of recognizing me at the station. *I'll know you.* Maybe I should toss a few bucks around, see who picks them up? This wad of cash, reward for looking after all those other people's babies. It doesn't make sense to think those sacrifices were only to pay for a larger one. It doesn't make sense to think.

The train pulls in, but no women are waiting, only a solitary man who approaches me without hesitation. He drives me silently to an ostentatiously ordinary suburban house sitting in a yard with a fleabitten box hedge. The woman is waiting, gray-haired and aproned, anonymous and bored. "Ya bring the ergot?" she asks first thing. She had phoned me again to ask me to try to get ergot. I give her the ampules. It's supposed to expedite contractions.

Down to business. Pass the cash. Strip. Nightgown. She lays me out like meat on the living room sofa, its antimacassars peeping out from under rubber sheeting. The man who drove me, her husband, I suppose, doesn't even leave the room, but nor does he show the slightest interest in what is going on. He sits in an easy chair next to a radio, Doris Day chortling out, "You're not sick you're just in love," and reads the *Daily News*. The missus shoves some tubing inside me. "Relax, dear." Relax! Every muscle I am aware of I am aware of clenching. When the tube is in my womb, she injects some fluid into it. "There," she says. "You'll start contracting in a while, and it'll be all over by tomorrow. I'll just give you a shot of ergot." It's the longest speech she makes.

I have to keep the tube inside, and now and then she checks on me. "So what's happening?" she asks, and when I prove insufficiently responsive she takes to addressing the thing inside: "C'mon out, you critter!" I am shown a pile of old magazines, but I have brought my knitting and pick up where I left off on the second argyle sock. Between twinges I try to work out which comes next with my little bobbins and spindles, blue and gray for the triangles, red and yellow for the stripes. We are all compelled to listen to my mocked songs. "Love Walked In," one of my favorites. Did it ever. Love walked right in, or swam right up, uninvited and flaunting its tiny tail.

They have a turkey TV dinner each; I'm not hungry. After a while I can answer her question: "Bad cramps." She smiles in satisfaction. The worse the pains, the more satisfied she is. Soon I can't deal with the argyle sock anymore. By nightfall it's outlandish. Her husband turns the radio off in the middle of Perry Como claiming, "They say that falling in love is wonderful," and leaves the room with a grunt, "Night." The woman sets up a cot and beds down next to my couch. She says to wake her if clots come out.

No clots. Quite a lot of snoring. I can't sleep, of course. I am dying, and I am alone.

Friday, still no clots. "This little critter's hangin' on, darn it," she comments. "I should care, I should let it upset me," sings the radio. All day she potters around and her husband goes out and comes back and goes out and comes back while I lie on the couch, moaning, attracting no attention. This is at least instructive: it means, I suppose, that there are no grounds for alarm, this torture is absolutely normal, and therefore maybe not terminal. But by Friday night she is getting impatient. She has given me the last ampule of ergot, and still no critter. It occurs to me that I am in labor. I'm caught time and again unawares, thrown around, unhinged. Nobody said it would be anything like this.

By Saturday morning she is really fed up. "You're taking your darn time, ain't you?" Me or it? "Push!" Me. She has got me to squat over a dishpan so she can examine everything that comes out. "I don't get it," she says. "Maybe I missed it." This thing is never going to end. I can't stay in this position. The pains, the pains. "*Push!*" she says. If I don't get home by tomorrow what will I tell Daddy? "Do not forsake me, oh my darlin'," howls Frankie Laine. The woman keeps fishing around in the dishpan with her rubber-gloved fingers. She clucks to herself, half in disapproval of all this malingering, half in apparent dismay that something's wrong. At no point a word of solicitude or comfort. I gather this is my punishment and only mine.

Oh Jesus! I am being hollowed out. My whole insides are dripping into a dishpan, and soon I'll be my shell. How wonderful how wonderful to die and who on earth would care? The only thing between me and an overpowering death wish is sheer hatred: that man is working through his third *Daily News.* He has yet to look up. Nothing about any of this surprises him.

Then I feel it. A lump slithers out of me and splashes into the bloody pan. "Well, about time!" the woman says, at the end of her patience. Her rubber gloves seize the lump and she pulls it apart with some tweezers. As she leaves the room with it I see within the clotted mass a tiny leg. Kilroy Junior. The toilet flushes.

Oh, baby, I'm so sorry.

Sunday morning. The bleeding continues, and cramps still come sporadically. Whacked from so little sleep. But when I get to 65th Street I burst in with any energy left and shout out breezily to Jo and Daddy. *Hi!* How are *you?* They're in bed with the *Times.* I'm worn out, whew, what a great time! Funny, they aren't answering. Why does he look so fishy? I chatter on about the party I've invented, until my father gets up all at once and goes to the kitchen. There's something wrong. I look at Jo. "Don't bother," she says, "he knows."

That does it. You wait eighteen years to grow up, eighteen years of being everybody's toy and victim, and finally you arrive and what do you find? Why is everybody hurting me? What am I, a scab collector? This week is some endurance test. What's the prize? I'm waiting for the *prize.* "Don't bother, he knows." What a moron I am.

Daddy's washing dishes at the sink. I go in and watch his back. He says nothing. He has eliminated me from his consciousness, just as he has always done when I am bad. But this is different, because I'm not bad. Where is he? Where is he? Thank you, Daddy, you and your sermon-on-the-mount philosophy: where is that? In one week I'm cherryless, penniless, motherless, brotherless, childless. Now fatherless. What next? A nice amputation, maybe? I think I shall go and find my little pink beads.

Though of course I am little-pink-beadless too by now, since they got left behind in some move or other, along with everything else, but I'll get along, ho-ho. I'll just have to focus on something else. I am at the back of the room pressed flat against the long-defunct dumbwaiter with the Picasso print stuck to its ex-door, by the window, gazing at the woodwork, the outlines blurred by the accumulation of years of paint. Or is it my eyes? What am I doing here?

As a matter of fact, what I'm usually doing here is the opposite of what I'm now doing here. Usually it has to do with trying to evaporate in the face of one of Daddy's speeches. This time I'd settle for the works, the full-blown filibuster: *preach* at me, *tub*-thump, *speak!*

But he doesn't mention what is on our minds, and I know he never will. Oh well. Contemplate the airshaft. You couldn't call it a view. Walls on either side, another maybe a dozen feet away at the rear, and it's just as well the window doesn't open on that archaeological dig of garbage half a floor high. Then I notice, down among the ordure, a skinny sickly tree of heaven that has somehow planted itself and is struggling hard to grow. An accidental tree. Uninvited, braving life without a permit or the correct identity papers.

Everything's going to be all right really. "Sally's the practical one," my mother's saying in my ear—and, being practical, it is easy to see that if I were to tell him how furious I am, his reaction would be more of the same: no reaction. Or maybe he'd go hide in the bathroom, the way he used to when Mummy sounded off. I have to live here now. I just wish I could be more like him, and ignore the bad stuff. Maybe I have the gene someplace, if I could just locate it and water it like a little plant.

13

CLEAN BREAST

Desire for the future produces words which cannot be stood by. But love makes language exact, because one loves only what one knows. One cannot love the future or anything in it, for nothing is known there. And one cannot unselfishly make a future for someone else. Love for the future is self-love—love for the present self, projected and magnified into the future, and it is an irremediable loneliness.

—WENDELL BERRY

N.Y. *Daily News,* Sept. 8, 1954

PROUD TO BE INFORMER, WRITER TELLS HEARING

At a deportation hearing for British-born editor Cedric Belfrage, Hollywood writer Martin Berkeley said yesterday that he was proud to be called an informer by defense counsel.

Gesturing toward Belfrage and the latter's lawyer, Nathan Dambroff, Berkeley said to examiner Max Weinman, who had objected to the name-calling:

"May I say, sir, that I don't object to being called an informer by people such as these. It is for me next to the Congressional Medal of Honor."

Berkeley testified that he had known Belfrage in Hollywood as a member of the Communist Party. He was a member at the time himself, he said, but quit the party in 1944.

Berkeley said he worked for various studios in the film capital until 1949 when the "Communists wrecked my career and I didn't work for 19 months."

He testified that he had been introduced to Belfrage by movie actor Lionel Stander as "a trustworthy person," adding:

"To any Communist that phrase meant that both persons were members of the party."

The government has charged that Belfrage, who claims he was a British government agent in the employ of the British Security Coordination office at 63 Fifth Ave. from 1941 to 1943, was a member of the Communist Party after coming to this country in 1936 to seek permanent residence and therefore should be deported.

The hearing will resume at 9 A.M. today at the Immigration Service offices, 70 Columbus Ave.

Daily Worker, Sept. 9, 1954

STOOLIE CAUGHT IN LIE MAZE AT BELFRAGE TRIAL

Deportation hearings against Cedric Belfrage, editor of the National Guardian, continued yesterday, with Immigration Department stoolpigeon Martin Berkely [*sic*] finding himself enmeshed in a maze of contradictions.

Berkely, who the previous day claimed he had been a member of the Communist Party from 1937 to 1944, testified yesterday that Belfrage had written under the "Party name" of George Oakden, for a publication called "Black and White" in 1937.

Cross-examination by Belfrage's attorneys, Nathan Dambroff, Gloria Agrin and Blanch Freedman [*sic*] brought out that the byline "George Oakden" never appeared in the publication in 1937.

It was further brought out that at the same time that Belfrage wrote articles for the New Masses—under the name of Cedric Belfrage—articles appeared in that magazine under the double byline, George Oakden and Martin Porter.

The finger man had testified that Martin Porter was his own "party name," but denied ever collaborating with Belfrage or anyone named George Oakden, in writing for New Masses.

Berkely admitted that he himself had been fingered by another stoolpigeon, Richard Collins, in 1951, and had at that time denied being a member of the Communist Party. Under the threat of losing $1,000 a week job as a screen writer, Berkely admitted, he became an informer.

Of course a few other things happened in 1954, for those who were noticing. The TV dinner became the people's meal, Thoreau's *Walden* was banned in USIS libraries, and school libraries removed from their shelves Mark Twain's *A Connecticut Yankee in King Arthur's Court*. The four-minute-mile barrier fell, Marilyn Monroe married Joe DiMaggio, and the Bible was on the best-seller list for the second year running. Twenty thousand French troops were sent to Algeria. The most positive development from the point of view of the residents at 65th Street was the first Tom Lehrer record. The largest of domestic events, the *Brown* vs. *Board of Education* decision that school segregation was unconstitutional because "separate but equal" was "inherently unequal," passed most Americans by, and the smallest, the closure of the detention center at Ellis Island, passed everybody by but us.

Dan came to New York that winter and spring almost as often as I went to West Point. He came with the debating society, with the choir, to the screening of a movie about the academy. If they gave him time off afterwards, we had a quick spaghetti at Romeo's, a drink at the Rustic, or, for lack of funds, a ride in the two-tone Plymouth (if Mrs. King would let him have it) or night court for voyeuristic peeks at the bottom of the barrel.

One weekend there was a big holiday parade, and the whole cadet corps was bused to the city to march. Afterwards Dan turned up to meet me at 65th Street in his full dress uniform, complete with plumed patent hat. Daddy and Jo were home. They were convinced he was crazy. Probably we both were. Somebody poured him a drink, and we sat around the little living room in formal postures, Daddy as incapable of addressing the fellow as usual, only more so. Jo mentioned Dan's outfit in relation to the presence of the gumshoes outside. Oh well, he already knew about that, of course, he said fearlessly. He was thinking of his mother's detectives. When Jo explained that he was possibly implicating himself in something quite serious and dangerous, something that would certainly interfere with a future career in the army, he said:

"If there's a problem, then the thing to do is to go to the FBI and make a clean breast of it all."

"*All?*" said Jo, aghast. "*All what?*" Daddy looked as if someone had just punched him.

In the Bellevue psychiatric ward where she is working, Jo reports that among the patients who think they are Napoleon is one who claims the FBI is after him. "That's all right," she yearns to console him, "they're after me too." Through incredible work and concentration she has finished medical school, and now most of her internship, with the daily possibility of the FBI figuring it out and paying one of their fatal calls; but they never do. They really are slipshod, letting so much normal life go on. They didn't even seem to notice when, the day after Jo's medical school graduation, she and Daddy got married.

Sometimes I wonder: whatever happened to ecstasy? Neither the ecstatic misery nor the ecstatic happiness seems available these days. Most of the time I seem to be miserably happy.

Jo helped me get an appointment to be fitted for a diaphragm and Dan and I have sex now. Once it's happened you can't go back, can you? It's sneaky and quick and not much fun. I don't like it or anything to do with it. Am I frigid? The magazines say most American women are. It's sort of a cheat, though, to find that after years of denying yourself and anticipating this sublime reward, it turns out

to be so pointless. I miss the old days when we didn't have
to, because we couldn't, and everything was so much sexier.

But who can talk about it? If we did, it might come up
how much more comfortable we'd be on a mattress instead
of upright between urinals or outside on the ground, but
we're broke and that's that. And how sordid to register in a
motel—I'd have to wear a fake wedding ring: it would really
bring home to us both how far I'd fallen. I don't want to hear
him deny that he minds being stuck with damaged goods. Of
course we are "in love" and therefore go easy on each
other—he puts up with my imperfection—but I *feel* it's true,
at the very least that our dream is in a rut. Because what is
"in love" when it's a habit? Something as unrevealing and
unrelated to your shape as a nun's habit, in fact. I don't feel
choked with anticipation on the bus ride to the Point anymore; I feel a little cynical and know-it-all and patronizing to
the young things with their heads in hopes and curlers. No, it
would be fatal to start talking about any of it.

Also we seem to have an unspoken pact not to mention
politics. We've never gone into it really. As part of my two-
tier life, with Dan I reduced politics to just another inciden-
tal detail, an entry on a form, together with items like Hair
color _____ and Religion _____, something merely
descriptive of human diversity, not substantial—life's very
core, actually—as it is to my father. And to Dan too, I think
more and more. Well that is, after all, what they're up to at
West Point, training not just dopey random killers but
informed, committed killers. His daily menu of enemy
fiendishness has ill-prepared him to digest the smallest miti-
gating circumstance. But living with Daddy has put all my
splits and compartments to the test, one that's harder by the
day to manage. There is a collision on every level. It reaches
a peak when my father, leaving for work one day, is
arrested on the street. He becomes prisoner H-4715 in West
Street Federal House of Detention.

"They've arrested my father again," I tell Dan. "He's in
jail! In solitary confinement!"

"That's not possible." Here we go again.

As always, Dan and I are confident that we know our rights. Unfortunately my family has still been deported and my father is still in the cooler. Visiting days at West Street Jail are Saturdays, so I miss some weekends at the Point. Dan doesn't like that. Explaining why to his friends must take some doing. Sometimes I wish the old man were in for embezzlement or something.

N.Y. Journal-American, May 13, 1955

Cedric H. Belfrage, 50, writer and editor, was picked up at 9:30 a.m. today by immigration officials outside his home, 210 E. 65th St., and taken to the Federal House of Detention to await deportation to his native England early next week.

Belfrage, editor of "The National Guardian," a weekly, was ordered deported last Dec. 9 on a charge of membership and activity in the Communist Party while an alien.

His former wife, Mrs. Mary Belfrage, was deported to England last Oct. 6, on the same charge.

The U.S. Immigration Service in summarizing his case said he had first come here July 6, 1937, and conducted Communist activities in the Hollywood area for several years.

He was at one time research director of the People's Institute of Applied Religion, an organization listed as subversive by the Attorney General.

When proceedings began against him in 1953, he denied ever having been a Communist. The following year, a Hollywood screen writer asserted he knew Belfrage as a Communist back in 1937.

In the course of several trips abroad, he had visited Russia in the 1930s.

Belfrage appealed his deportation order, but a decision handed down yesterday by the Board of Immigration Appeals, highest appellate board in the department, rejected his final appeal.

Following on, after a short line:

Go to church Sunday. For a church of your faith conve-
niently near you, consult the religious page of Saturday's
Journal-American.

How to face his dreadful pain, there in his prison paja-
mas (gray, a shade paler than Dan's uniform, ill-fitting,
torn) on the other side of the glass? With Ellis Island closed
down, most deportees are deposited in some other "special
place," but Daddy and six others are in prison, without the
possibility of bond, because—says Edward Shaughnessy, the
immigration director, to the *New York Times*—they are
"rough tough criminal types and agitators." My Daddy?
Who's he kidding? Visitors have to speak on a telephone
through a pane of glass, unable to touch. We're only
allowed a total of half an hour a week with him, Jo, Jim,
and me together, the three permitted callers; it is arguably
the one place in America with stricter rules than West Point.

Daddy's cell bars are painted a particularly unpleasant
chartreuse, he reports, and nobody's snores keep him awake
this time because he is a "maxie," under maximum security,
which means solitary—on the grounds that as a political
prisoner he might be injured by other prisoners. The fact
that he is on a hunger strike to protest the isolation causes
official anxiety only after some Labour MPs bring the matter up in the House of Commons. The authorities decide to
allow his chartreuse door to remain open during the day
like the others.

After that he is more plausible in his efforts to cheer me
up with anecdotes of "life in the hoosegow," featuring the
amazing characters he meets in exercise periods on the roof.
There is the fake admiral-of-the-fleet who is a fabulist to
nonplus the Baron Munchhausen: having once been a com-
mander in the merchant marine, he decided a naval admiral
might earn more respect, so he promoted himself, made
some campaign ribbons out of old neckties (I cannot quite
believe this part), and started gate-crashing official ceremonies until they got so used to having him around that he
began to be properly invited. He ended up on all kinds of

fancy letterheads as director of various companies, got himself a desk job in London and spent weekends at a ducal estate. By the time they caught him he had so many important chums that the authorities were having to get rid of him quietly. It turned out he wasn't even American but had started out in Belfast and then become some sort of Antipodean. Nobody knew his real name, as he'd gathered so many identities—with matching documentation—from the tombstones of deceased contemporaries; but as soon as they could make one of them stick they were going to ship him out.

Or Harvey Matusow, the FBI's professional canary who had seen the light, come clean, and then got four years for perjury—lying when he said he had lied. Inventor of the stringless yoyo, Matusow had been personally responsible for the total ruin of 244 victims, if he did say so himself. This had been in the period when he—the informer as hero, saving his country—made a living exposing the Communist conspiracy. With his winning boyish grin he had become popular in the best circles. After his recantation he wrote a how-to book, *False Witness,* describing his perfected techniques: how to set up the dramatic courtroom identification, the build-up of suspense leading to . . . "That's him!"; how to "use the names of well-known people in the theatrical world to my advantage as a money-making witness"; and in pre-testimony rehearsals with congressional committees, how to "convince them I could get the headlines for them, not for me, [because] they were the backers of my show." Above all he had learned to "play my cards one at a time—for if I didn't my life as a witness would be short." Harvey had accompanied the committees in their traveling road show all over the country, giving more than a hundred days' worth of testimony, always trying to think of a way to "top yesterday's story." He successfully persuaded the committees and the media that the Communist Party had managed to infiltrate the Boy Scouts, and that there were 126 Communists working for the Sunday *New York Times* when in fact only 96 people worked there at all ("nobody ever questioned it"). Later he said, "I had contempt for people for believing my lies."

Despite his change of heart, his fellow prisoners steer clear of the informer. There are many other stimulating companions—a constantly replenished assortment of gangsters, outcasts, and innocents, whom my father gets to know as typist in the prison hospital: all incoming prisoners pass through to have a physical, and his experienced two middle fingers tap out their notes. Some of the prisoners are illiterate, so he helps them write letters home. His favorite is a sixteen-year-old Puerto Rican who'd been given a dollar to carry a package that turned out to contain marijuana and now is in for two years. Naturally, says Daddy, he was framed.

One of Daddy's preferred dishwashing songs, whenever he's in the mood to mimic an Irish tenor, is "Sonny Boy." He assumes a high fluting voice and lays on the sob stuff. Sometimes, though, when he gets to the part about "Friends may forsake me/Let them all forsake me (I'll still have yooooo, Sonny Boy)," I think about the friends who have forsaken him and us, from the journalists on respectable papers who rarely mention his case and never give his side of things even though they know it, to the refugees from Hitler who once constantly came around, to CP members who won't have any truck with someone so unorthodox. Who does he think he is? In the face of all his ecumenical ambitions for the *Guardian*, it seems sometimes that independence as a leftist becomes a position in itself, by which others measure themselves and then stay aloof. He has hundreds of devotees who would lay down their lives for him, but considering the objective situation you couldn't give them any kind of label; brave to a fault—some might say insanely rash—but with nothing else in common, representing no group or particular tendency, they are the ones who refuse to say they were not party members out of simple opposition to the committees' right to ask.

From one small, sick angle, therefore, I can't help feel-

ing that jail is not such a disaster. Daddy has been so iso-
lated from most American reality in his black-and-white
world that deportation was hardly necessary: he's an internal deportee, almost entirely cut off from influencing or
being influenced. Here he gets to meet a few real live proletarians, even if they are a trifle bent. But since—as he
wrote—they think "of themselves in relation to society pre-
eminently not as those who did wrong, but as those who
got caught," they're right up Daddy's alley. On the other
hand, they are also what he calls sane. To prove it, when
the sirens blow, although there is a bomb shelter in the jail,
nobody moves. "If one of them things falls," a guard con-
fided in him, "you're dead anyway."

Afterwards he wrote that despite their having been
"touched by the wand of 'modern penology,'" the prisoners
of West Street, with its comparatively good food and conditions, were as malcontent as any; "the reason, it seemed to
me, was that the modernizers had thought of everything
except the souls within the bodies. They thought of the
inmates as outsiders do, as a 'criminal class,' whereas in fact
they were nothing more nor less than people: people not of
one kind, but of every kind. The humane regime for the
bodies even deepened the sense of grievance with which
prisoners are filled by the mere fact of being numbered and
caged." And yet "nothing compensates for the loss of freedom; and the most subtle semantics about freedom being
'relative' or 'an illusion' cannot change the reality of bars,
be they of natural steel or painted chartreuse. This is the
elementary thing learned by all who go to prison even
briefly, which makes them in a certain sense forever a
'class.'"

My father has this music problem. For somebody who's
supposed to care about the people, he sure is snotty about
their culture. By him a d.a. haircut is what's on the head of
the district attorney. He's never had the stomach for hot
dogs, and the very word "Coke" makes his stiff upper lip
curl. Installment plans bring out his latent Victorian horror

of being in debt. He can't abide sliced white bread, deodorants, Salvation Army Santa Clauses, Ethel Merman. Talk about the ingredients of the American Way: what's left? Well, they have found it, the precise torture for him—an assault with deadly pop music. Immediately outside his cell is a loudspeaker tuned to the top twenty—interspersed with occasional news flashes and baseball scores—at top volume from before breakfast to after lights-out.

Daddy's idea of a decent soundtrack would combine most of Mozart and Schubert with his favorite spirituals and the old-left standbys (say, "Ballad for Americans," "Joe Hill," "Los Quatro Generales," "There's a Man Going Round Taking Names" sung by Paul Robeson, Pete Seeger, Woody Guthrie, Leadbelly; plus maybe the odd Gracie Fields or his own version of "My Baby Has Gone Down the Drainpipe"). Actually, I'd noticed that his blanket intolerance of popular music had lifted lately when his friends the Weavers made it to the top with "Goodnight, Irene" and "Wimoweh." Unfortunately they're not on the charts just now, so his suffering is total.

But never daunted, he turns it into exactly what he needs: a cause. Since the successful hunger strike he is keeping busy, he reports, organizing a protest to have the loudspeaker turned off, turned down, or switched occasionally to play anything else. Already he knows the hit parade by heart, including every verse of "Davy Crockett, King of the Wild Frontier"—although you can tell he hasn't been really paying attention when he mocks my practically all-time favorite, "Unchained Melody," and can't even get the title right: he thinks it's "I Need Your Love"! One week in the second month he informs me, as if I didn't know, that a "rather rum number" called "Slow Boat to China" is number one. "Out on the o-shun," he croons, "far from all the commo-shun . . . melting your heart of sto-one. . . ." He is drowning in the very melodies I hum all day. I do not tell him that the songs are my hymns. He does not tell me that his cell was Julius Rosenberg's.

For the first time in my life I feel sorry for him. It makes

me feel very lonely and grown up, to pity my big strong
Daddy. Everything he's done has been thrown in his face.
All the big words he fought for—justice, solidarity, equality,
peace: he is the direct victim of a whole society's hypocrisy
about each of them. Just the droop of his shoulders in the
raggedy gray jail shirt. It hasn't worked out.

While I'm waiting for Jo and Jim to finish talking to him I
watch the rows of people telephoning each other across the
terrible distance of that glass. They aren't allowed to kiss
each other, so they kiss the glass between them. There is a
smell of misery. I watch the guards to see if they can feel it
too. They stick their noses up when I try to catch their eye.
I'm used to that.

Once Daddy took me on a May Day parade down Fifth
Avenue. I was six or seven. It was one of the last legal
marches; afterwards they could only get a permit to meet in
Union Square—where, because stationary, they were sitting
ducks for brickbats from the populace (with the *Daily
News* contributing suggestions: "These rats should be
allowed to put themselves on exhibition. If they get pelted
with eggs or wetted down and colored up with squirt guns
by patriotic young Americans that's their tough luck.").

In the parade, most of what we got thrown at us from
the sidelines was a lot of hysterical heckling: "Kill a Commie for Christ!" and the even less comprehensible "Go back
to Russia!" I was riding on a truck with some other little
kids beneath a big red banner. Right behind us was a
mounted policeman. My hobby then was saving lumps of
sugar with the names of different restaurants on the wrap-
pers. At home I had hundreds, and before the parade I got
another from the Schrafft's where we'd had lunch. The
truck stopped for a while—the march had been mobbed up
ahead by a catcalling, tomato-throwing opposition, people
said later—and I struck up a conversation with the cop's
horse. It poked its nose down into my lap, and I remembered the sugar in my pocket. The cop watched me unwrap
a lump, and when I held it out on my palm he suddenly

jerked the reins and the horse reared up, white-eyed, gigan-
tic, like Roy Rogers and Trigger. They seemed to float
above me for a week. There has never been such silence.
Something's happening. A true thing. I scrabbled out of the
way just as the hoofs came down on the back of the truck
exactly where I'd been sitting. Since then I've been allergic
to horses. (It's the wrong allergy. It ought to be to cops.)

We get reports from the folks in England. Mummy could
not possibly be more blissful, she says. She has immediately
found a good job editing a women's magazine—easy, all she
has to do is recycle her old ideas from McCall's. And a
lovely flat in Kensington on a big green garden, absolutely
gorgeous. Social life: best ever—old friends rallying, and
you could tell she was aburst with confidence thanks to her
fantastic new wardrobe and svelte shape (the illness had
cleared up the moment they set sail). Best of all, she reports,
she's managed to get Nicky—who wants to be "Nick" now,
and she has become "Ma"—a place in St. Paul's, a good
public school, provided he passes his exams.

   From him we hear the other side of this one: he has to
learn from scratch English and European history and litera-
ture, French and Latin, algebra and physics and all the
other subjects one isn't taught in America by the age of
fourteen.

   My brother's letters give the impression that he is braving it out in his severed life. I keep remembering a poem
written about him by some counselor when we were at a
family summer camp years ago and he was three or four:

   Nicky everyone's heart beguiles
   With his cheery, dimpled smiles.
   Nick, to you this "A" we give
   Because you know the way to live.

Most Saturdays I board the bus and leave half of me, so to
speak, checked in a locker at Port Authority. The grand
finale is June Week, five whole days at the Point in a row.

The firsties are graduating, tossing their white hats in the air. In September Dan will be one, a first-year man, with extra stripes and powers. President Eisenhower himself comes to give the commencement address, rubbing shoulders with the crowd as he circulates in the sunshine. The bands are playing. The cadets in their snappy starched white summer suits march straight and proud, prepared to defend this best of all countries against the worst of all worlds.

West Point in June Week is like a distillation of the great American experience. Everywhere you look in life is a poorman's version of this: stars-and-stripes and anthems, good men marching in American Legion, VFW uniforms. Well, in their own terms they're good, they think they're good, don't they? Upholding The Land of the Free, Brave, etc.? But what's so free about a land that locks my Daddy up for what he thinks, or used to think fifteen years ago? And talk about enslaved, what better word to describe the life of a U.S.M.A. cadet, or an army officer for that matter?

And yet—I am going to marry mine and live among these people in the next life, and for my darling's sake if no other I must blot out doubt and hold tight to the idea of the good intentions of American patriots: that while they may be misled they are not evil. Though sometimes it appears this witch hunt was tailor-made to achieve such a misled, misguided population—since those with liberal notions to lead or guide have either lost their jobs (the courageous ones) or gone in for self-censorship (the scared). Should I actually be so broad-minded about the superpatriots? Don't they have heads? How come they can't inform themselves? For that matter, see how snarly and snaggle-toothed with hate certain demonstrators are. "Fry the Jews, Burn the Rats." Makes you wonder.

Nobody's frying or burning my dad, but they won't give him bail. At a hearing there is temporary hope when Judge Archie Dawson says, "If I have any power to release this man on bail, my inclination is to do that. I can't see any imminent danger to the community." But the next day he denies bail all the same. People on the left are in an uproar about it, but then they always are about something or other; the point is that nobody "respectable" worries publicly about Cedric Belfrage until the *St. Louis Post-Dispatch* publishes an editorial saying that "we see a threat to our democratic institutions, far worse than any emanating potentially from him, if men can be thrown into prison and held there week after week without bail and not under grand jury charge. Cannot a possible deportee under the McCarran-Walter Act be kept on bond and under FBI vigilance? If not why not?"

The editorial prompts the commissioner of immigration and naturalization to issue a statement to explain why not. Cedric Belfrage, he says, "was jailed in the first place pending deportation because his political beliefs are allied to a world-wide conspiracy to destroy the free world and make him, in our opinion, a threat to the national security."

The same day he loses an appeal before the U.S. Court of Appeals.

"Mr. and Mrs. America and all the ships at sea. Flash. Pinko Cedric Belfrage, who edits a smelly sheet in NYC, will be taken from West Street jail to be deported probably tomorrow. Good riddance!" Thus spake Walter Winchell in one of his rat-a-tat-tat radio bulletins, but he was wrong: it wasn't Daddy leaving yet, it was me, sailing to London right after June Week to visit Mummy and Nicky. Dan had to go practice shooting and bombing in Georgia, and Daddy was still in his cage. He had asked for a good-bye visit with me but the request was returned stamped "DIS-APPROVED." On the way down the Hudson, I was supposed to wave a red kerchief from the railing of the *Liberté* so Daddy could see me from the roof of the jail. But it was raining that day and the prisoners weren't allowed to go out.

EPILOGUE: REPRISE

An autobiography is the most treacherous thing there is. It lets out every secret its author is trying to keep; it lets the truth shine unobstructed through every harmless little deception he tries to play; it pitilessly exposes him as a tin hero worshipping himself as Big Metal every time he tries to do the modest-unconsciousness act before the reader. This is not guessing; I am speaking from autobiographical personal experience; I was never able to refrain from mentioning, with a studied casualness that could deceive none but the most incautious reader, that an ancestor of mine was sent ambassador to Spain by Charles I, nor that in a remote branch of my family there exists a claimant to an earldom, nor that an uncle of mine used to own a dog that was descended from the dog that was in the Ark. . . .
——MARK TWAIN, CHRISTIAN SCIENCE

And now, a third of a century later, Nick and I were on the way to Mexico to visit our father because he was dying. He had been dying for years, although when you got there it always seemed that he had merely diminished to a lesser state, in that dreadful half-of-a-half-of-a-half sort of way that famously never ends. This time it sounded more critical, and I had written to my mother to tell her. As I was packing, she rang from Bermuda to wish me bon voyage and gossiped briefly before reporting, in the same gay little voice, "The doctor says I have six weeks."

"Six weeks what?"

"To live."

Absolutely typical! Who could take her seriously? Upstaging the old man, for god's sake, at a time like this. Knowing her, you could read it: "You want dying? I'll show you dying." *Tasteless.* Anyway, I'd just had a letter from her written a mere week earlier about swimming a daily twenty laps in an Olympic pool. But she was mentioning words that I was looking up in my *Merck Manual* as she spoke: *myeloblastic leukemia.*

Leukemia? Who could fake leukemia?

On the other hand, who could bring it on?

Through the book's jargon the details were pretty convincing. I knew she'd been having mysterious bloody noses for several years. "The average untreated patient survives about 4 to 6 mo from clinical onset." Of course, she was being treated now, but it had been left undiagnosed for too long, despite the doctor in the house—her current husband, Bill, an orthopedic surgeon.

So Nick and I, next thing we knew, had tickets to Bermuda *and* Mexico. I left my daughter and son, Eve and Moby, twenty and eighteen, in charge of our London flat. They were used to it. For two years I'd been leaving them every month to go to Belfast to research a book I was writing—but this time there was no way of knowing how long it would be. Eve said she would probably follow me.

Prosperity had hit both my parents in the end. They landed in different distant places with year-round swimming and blossoms and birdsong, servants and guests. My mother and Dr. Bill, sportsman, bon viveur, went increasingly, and then retired, to his native Bermuda, where she got to entertain visiting cricketers and rugby players, or representatives from conventions of sawbones. She didn't mind, she had the capacity to find almost anything *amusing,* as long as she felt loved and financially secure. Her life back in England had lived up to her hopes; she had calmed down, made a prosperous marriage, and returned to the life she liked and knew, though she had kept on working, on books with titles like *How to Be 30 for 40 Years*, and on magazine articles: whenever British *Vogue* had a health and beauty issue, she wrote most of it.

My father, who landed up back in England a couple of months after I did, spent five years as the *Guardian*'s "Editor-in-Exile" there, hating it as much as ever. "I feel like a ghost," he'd say, drifting around the flat that he and Jo and I shared, which became less a home for any of us than a jumping-off point. I was constantly traveling, he was covering stories all over Europe and Asia, and then Jo had to return to New York to look after two suddenly orphaned nephews. Their marriage seemed unable to withstand the geographical demands being put upon it. He became inspired by the revolution in Cuba and decided to move there when the government invited him to edit an English-language paper. Shutting himself in his study, he learned Spanish in three months and took off for Havana with his usual luggage: a suitcase, a spare pipe, a mackintosh, and his portable Smith-Corona. The newspaper never materialized, as the United States broke diplomatic relations with Cuba at that point and therefore the paper lost its potential readership. He stayed on in Havana for a year and a half, unable to find another way to be useful, and then traveled all over Latin America before settling in Mexico with his fifth wife, Mary, a teacher from Chicago, to write a book about his travels.

Thanks to Mary's hospitality, they received waves of American radicals: "American" in the larger sense, for as well as all his old crew from the United States, joined by representatives of the sixties New Left (radical tendencies having skipped a generation), there were refugees from despotic South American regimes who often came to stay for indefinite periods before finding somewhere to resettle. Among these once was a Brazilian family of six, whose eldest daughter, Candida, age eight then, met my brother and ended up decades later as his wife and the mother of his children.

The refugee philanthropy was mainly funded by streams

of old progressives, so many of them finally prosperous, coming to visit the Belfrages' Cuernavaca paradise and talk on the theme: "Where did we go wrong, Cedric?" This conversation started long before Gorbachev, and it wasn't easy to figure out what they had in mind—guilt? that they had grown too rich for their principles? that their principles got them and the world nowhere finally? Maybe they didn't even know what they meant, or didn't all mean the same thing. But for a while this question was hitting the ears with such regularity it jumbled into Wheredidwegowrongcedric? and was the signal to leap into the pool.

The way people can really get on my nerves is to say I'm like my mother.

But I am like her. I have two children, like she did, a daughter and then a son, like she did. My daughter is not far from the age I was then. I've often wondered if I love my children equally—such a grievance to me as a daughter, Mummy's playing favorites—but it's not really possible to measure: from their births, I identified with Eve and was in love with Moby. Who can say which feeling is stronger? All I know is that having them to love at all is the greatest boon of life, unlike any other love, in its own way more so.

I have no husband anymore, like my mother didn't then. But I don't want another one. In sour moments I think of marriage as an institution between cannibals in which the woman is the meal. That's why men shop around the way they do for the tastiest dish. You can see it in the wives. Some of them look as much like the next meal as doggies look like dog owners.

Mind you, marriage has its uses. It is a definite convenience from the accounting point of view, enabling me, for instance, to say to Mary, my father's last wife (referring to a picture of an actor on the cover of a British TV magazine), "That man is your second husband's second wife's first husband's fourth wife's third husband." But I guess the very number of permutations my parents have wrought upon the institution shows in what esteem it is held around here. The word *wedlock* alone could put you off, with its quaint resemblance to *hammerlock* or *gridlock,* but my begetters locked nothing, or at least took care never to throw away the key. They did it eight times between them, after all.

The sister in the drawer had joined our lives at last. We'd met when she was thirteen and I twenty-three. In 1963 she came to New York to stay with me before Nick joined us for a trip to Mexico to visit our father—all of us together for the first time. She punished us savagely for ignoring her all her life, refusing to eat. Nothing but black coffee passed her lips all summer. She fainted a lot. I took her to Washington for the big civil rights march, and she fainted just as Martin Luther King began his "I Have a Dream" speech. I had to carry her off, murder in my heart. But then you had to think about it: What about *her* civil rights? I never wanted to murder her again. She was a much better sister than any we had a right to, a droll, brilliant, beautiful sister I would not have had the capacity to imagine.

Nick and Anne and I, as happy together as if we were used to it, careered off to visit our father and Mary—Oaxaca, Acapulco, Mexico City. There were only eighty-six pounds of Anne by the time she hit bottom, but she survived. What she didn't understand was that the fun we were having as a family was as novel to Nick and to me as to her.

At a certain point in the mid-sixties, when I was in New York, all my contemporaries seemed, almost Titania-like, to marry the next one who came along: "What thou seest when thou dost wake, do it for thy true-love take." Mine was Bernardo. A moody word sculptor: playwright, poet, novelist. And a wild card, amateur pasta chef, comedian. Of all triumphs, my parents both liked him. To truly please my father I'd have had to choose a black Chinese Russian Marxist-Leninist guerrilla who spoke nine languages and composed witty songs, but Bernardo would do: he came from a liberal family and was personally anarchic enough to pass. The liberal family was also well off, so my mother was happy. And I was, too. He was not only handsome and brainy, and of course Jewish, but wickedly funny: for years our laughter kept us rolling. Then, two children later, it stopped. I don't know why. But even now, a decade and a half after he left (did he leave or was he pushed?), whenever I turn toward where he used to lie, my knee automatically juts out to ward him off. Even in my sleep. *Any bed*.

The fact is, I wasn't designed for the role of wife. Maybe my mother was more typical there. She was always half of something. I don't feel like a whole of anything, but it seems the one goal worth trying for.

Once upon a time you could fly from Bermuda to Mexico direct, but no longer, and the weeks following my mother's phone call passed on a seesaw with JFK airport the fulcrum: London-NY-Bermuda-NY-Mexico-NY-Bermuda-NY-London. He hung on; she got worse. But her state of mind could hardly have been more blithe. She seemed to treat her death as some kind of giant moving day. Her bemused husband, who hadn't a tenth her energy, sat blinking at the television as she merrily organized everyone from her spot on the couch, dressed in an assortment of bright, well-cut trouser suits and lots of beads: "Put this here, take that for yourself, I want those earrings to go to Eve, can you hear the kiskidee? *Qu'est-ce qu'il dit?* I'm sure that dratted maid stole my ring. Do you think Moby could use this? Did I tell you the bishop's coming to tea on Saturday? Bill's sure to need that, put it on his highboy where he can see it. Try on my purple suit—I want you to wear it to my funeral, with that top, no that one's better, isn't it gorgeous? I don't mind dying but I hate to leave Bermuda."

When the golf came on she'd join Bill at the TV to hex the players she disliked with hissing and witchy fingers. Eve arrived from London and interviewed her about her whole life on a cassette recorder. Nick was sent shopping, I was told what to cook, everyone got dispatched regularly to the beach or the pool. When the work load increased we hired a full-time housekeeper. The main thing from her point of view was that we all should have a lovely time.

It was a curious disease, leaving her as merry and fine-looking as ever, and with every faculty but strength until the very end—which was precisely predictable from the blood count. As for what was to happen after the end, she was taking no chances. My brother, who had studied Eastern religion, had helped her get a mantra and she was meditating regularly; she had been reading widely about reincarnation, past and future lives ("How come nobody was ever a Chinese peasant, Ma?"); and in case none of that worked out the vicar cycled over every day in his Bermuda shorts to administer communion. Her preferred vision of death was "a long tunnel with all your old chums in it. And Wol." Wol was her father. All my life she'd seldom mentioned him. Yet while her Bermuda house was littered with photographs, only his hung in her room.

She never cried.

My father, in his bed in Cuernavaca, cried frequently. There was plenty to cry about, from his point of view; the socialist bloc was crumbling: the great experiment, which had begun the year he reached puberty, was dying with him. But that wasn't it: he'd had a stroke, and his personality was out of kilter. Intelligence and sense remained, and old memories, never before revealed, were summoned up by Eve and her tape recorder. Mornings, he kept on working—translating a trilogy by the Uruguayan writer Eduardo Galeano. The words always came, slowly. And as if an earthquake had upturned his mind, he'd burst out with songs and stories unheard for years, waking early with a Gracie Fields number or, one day, his version of a Louis Armstrong song I could have sworn he never knew:

> *You made the mountains high*
> *You made the birds to fly*
> *And who am I to say you're wro-o-ong?*
> *But Lord, you made the nights too long.*

But his pure voice had trouble hitting the notes, and he said he didn't hear music as he once had. Other aspects of his character had changed indefinably; when I later heard someone on the BBC say, "The right hemisphere is all about *awe*," it made perfect sense. Above all, his emotions were now on the surface, ruling him, choking him, defying him to cope and be British.

But he wasn't dying yet; he just seemed to need to get us to come—though all of us year after year were still not enough to appease his need for all of us year after year.

And he could still write letters. I delivered one to him from my mother, and his answer was in her pocket when she died.

Dear Moulie,

I really didn't deserve the effort that your long, kind, gallant letter must have cost you. It has touched me very much. I have been extremely distressed by the recent news about you from the kids. When I count my blessings through the big holes I've had in my head recently, you are high, high on the list, as a real wife whom I didn't properly appreciate and as the great mother you've always been to our splendid children. We anxiously await the latest news of your condition from Nicolas or Sally who I suppose are now both with you. Your cheerfulness with that heavy sword hanging over your head would be quite amazing to anyone not knowing you well—a model for me who am so much more vulnerable to depression.

We are looking forward to finally getting to know Eve a bit more intimately when she and Sal and the others are here in April. Geography and politics have worked together to keep us from knowing her and Moby more than casually up to now—the biggest part of the personal fall-out from all that nonsense I brought upon myself in the 50s.

Thank you again for being and for that beautiful letter.

Love
Cedric

He wasn't dying yet, any more than to him socialism was dying with the collapse of the Soviet bloc. He had done what he could, and he refused to give up. Of him, I thought when I read them later, you could use the words of the Soviet writer Nikolai Ostrovsky: "Man's dearest possession is life. And since it is given him to live but once, he must live so as not to

be seared by the shame of a cowardly and trivial life; live so
that dying, he may say: All my life and strength were given to
the finest cause in the world—the liberation of mankind."

Through the years I had often tried to impress my father
with some political deed of mine—a demo I'd gone on, a
petition signed or article written or sit-in sat—like a pet cat
offering its beloved owner a bedraggled, half-dead bird. He
initially approved of the fact that two years after we left the
United States, I was living in Moscow, in my own place,
editing a new translation of *Quiet Flows the Don*. (Such a
case of political symmetry suggested to the cursory onlooker
a Serious Student of Affairs—though in reality, after two
years of working in poky little publishing jobs in London, I
had simply failed to save enough money to go where I
wanted: Paris.) But the book I wrote about it in 1958, *A
Room in Moscow,* caused him all kinds of difficulties,
because I'd come home believing in nothing but the fallibility
of absolutely everyone. On the proceeds of the book, I spent
a year in the Middle East researching the Arab-Israeli con-
flict and developed a lifelong commitment to the Palestinian
cause, which at least helped my father and me communicate
better, even though he didn't share it. Perhaps he was most
pleased about my going to Mississippi in 1964 to work in
the civil rights movement, and the subsequent book I wrote
about that. He didn't know I'd gone in much the same spirit
with which I'd once collected names of the Worst Man in the
World: I had a broken heart and was interested in ending it
all. My sacrifice to a lynch mob, I thought, wouldn't hurt
him too much.

My father passed on to me his obsessions about justice
and truth. It was just that with me they remained abstract for
lack of a place or power to believe in the way he had. There
seemed to be no country with any special purchase on
virtue—except China and Cuba when their revolutions were
new and untainted and the people worked as one, with
uncommon energy and joy, for the common good. Having
been lucky enough to see them early enough, I know it's possi-

ble for people to live together in a spirit of mutual generosity and harmony. If almost impossibly rare.

On the whole I think my father was right about the way the world works. The leaders are corrupt and hypocritical, the poor and dark-skinned always lose, no one is even interested in the altruistic, humanitarian mottoes they mouth, and it's SITUATION HOPELESS, never mind WORSE. I might even go further than he did, and agree with a version of my father's beloved Sermon on the Mount by Roger Woddis, a *New Statesman* writer:

> Blessed are the poor in spirit, for theirs is the quick way to heaven. Blessed are they that live in luxury, for they shall be comforted. Blessed are the meek, for they shall see where it gets them. Blessed are they that hunger, for they shall be fed with words. Blessed are the powerful, for they shall keep their power. Blessed are the pure in heart, for they shall believe anything. Blessed are the speechmakers, for they shall be called wonderful. Blessed are they that are tortured, for they shall gain humility. Blessed is the Church of the Poor, for it shall say nothing of the violence of the rich.

Yet finally my father lived on hope, and made hope his chief bequest to me: a lifetime's basic faith in people, which must be disabused daily, when every morning's newspaper comes as a blow to the naive optimism that somehow grew again in the night as you lay helpless to defend yourself. What's needed is what Gramsci called "pessimism of the intellect; optimism of the will."

One thing I got from my father for sure: I'm an un-American.

I never joined anything except the Cancer Club, and I don't like groups because of how they act to people they won't let in. I haven't even got a country, really, since having one turns out to be not a given after all, but conditional on good behavior ("Go back to Russia!" Who can get a passport?), and while it would feel good to consider this a matter of principle, since nationalism implies xenophobia, the fact is if you have two countries they tend to cancel each other out. Ditto religion, ever since I took up Judaism and rejected, or was rejected by, both it and the Holy Ghost. If there is no group of people like you, no one can claim you. Being inside nothing, you're nobody's insider. Being outside everything, you are free.

And there is even a way, if you need it, that you can get inside being an outsider. You can really move into it, learn to inhabit it as if it were a warm, fully furnished room. One great advantage of belonging nowhere is never having to gang up in the business of killing others. For what? For being others. For being *named* as others.

You can damn people just like that by calling them a name. The British have historically repudiated outlanders with "The wogs begin at Calais"—gentler if no less dismissive than the kike/nigger/wop school of paranoid jingoism. Then there is the gringo/honky/big-nose approach; I've been called those, and also shiksa/goy/gentile. These names are not *necessarily* hostile, though they sure put you in your place. Sometimes the word for outsider becomes official. The Americans have this special word: un-American. (Who could imagine a House of Commons Un-British Activities Committee?) At least fifty thousand people lost their jobs in the decade after World War II because they were called un-American. The FBI still has files on more than a million "un-Americans" that they compiled for J. Edgar Hoover. I'm not an American, I'm an un-American. That's what I got from my father. Though what a terrible long time it took for me to be glad of it.

Dan was the first enemy within. I thought I was torn between what he stood for and what my father stood for; it wasn't so. But being with Dan taught me to consolidate the enemy so that it became me too, part of a composite identity. The first step in *How to be a foreigner everywhere*.

And now look, just before my mother phoned about having six weeks—after a third of a century, Dan was on the phone inviting me to dinner. It was the last thing I expected. He happened to be in London, he said, and was staying at a hotel down the street from my place. I said I'd meet him there.

I had hardly thought about Dan. The decision not to return to him after that London summer seemed even then to go back further, to the abortion, maybe. Later it got mixed up with other things, or a dream had intervened, but I began to think of the abortion as when they ripped the American out of me.

The first shock was how unchanged, how absurdly *familiar* he was, but smaller. "You're smaller than I remembered," he said.

The second shock was that seeing him felt like encountering an amputated limb I hadn't known was missing.

The third shock emerged in the dialogue. He was a general officer, he said. (He didn't say "general.") Two stars. Engineering.

Oh, hm, I thought. Boring old bridges and tunnels.

No, missiles, as a matter of fact. Rockets. SDI. (He didn't say "star wars.") A remote-control death man. "I'm a concept person, not a detail person." He was up there planning it all in the Pentagon, with personal responsibility for an annual budget of $1,300,000,000. The guy in charge of Armageddon.

Not, of course, that he saw it that way. He looked at it *quite* another way. He was winning the Cold War, more or less, was how he saw it.

Funnily enough, I thought it had something to do with the inherent contradictions in the Soviet system. With their bureaucracy, inefficiency, and corruption, maybe egged along by the policies of Gorbachev? Ryszard Kapuscinski said it was the logical outcome of the system's political repression of the people, lying to the people, contempt for the people. Chomsky attributed it to "economic stagnation and increasing pressures for an end to tyrannical rule."

Forget all that. Just shows how wrong you can be. A certain missile experiment, that's what did it: and it was Dan's baby, that test. He'd sent one missile up to catch another missile in this world-shattering piece of target practice with everybody watching. And bam! Direct hit. Worked like a charm. See what it means? Means there's nothing they can throw at us that we can't hit. We're invincible. Invulnerable, impregnable. Scared the shit out of the Russians. (He didn't say "shit.")

So what could they do? They cried uncle.

Was I really listening? My other half. His lips had beautiful sculptured edges like an Egyptian pharaoh's. That tiny cleft at the end of his nose. Olive eyes, hair dark as night (thinning on top). Still a bit of a gangster. Terrible as an army with banners. He sank into me again. He came in past my guard, involuntarily, somewhere I wasn't looking, somewhere unprotected. (It just swam in.) We didn't touch.

He came back to London though. I had finished commuting to Belfast and was home finishing a book about it. It was the fall after my mother's death, and he happened by that hotel again. He'd been faithful all those years to his wife, the next woman after me, a good woman, Jewish. He really wanted to keep it that way. I really wanted it kept that way too, because to break such a spell was far too big a responsibility. But just speaking all this seemed enough to acknowledge it, bypass and negate it.

I had no memory to match the perfection of his body. It was somehow like being home. Once, we'd been grafted together like two growing trees, and the joins still met in a tight fit.

Ambiguity had no place in a life like Dan's. When we talked about what had happened long ago, *you broke my heart,* he said, and I told him how much I'd hated as well as loved him, and for the same reasons. "Did you know that then?" "No, probably not." He was upset: he didn't understand. But then, he confessed, he had "no sensitivity." Never had. He recognized this fault, among others. The recognition was important because he could compensate by having men under him who possessed the qualities he lacked. For example, he said, if he made the wrong decision—and his decisions were taken without looking back—he needed people who would tell him "when it might be necessary to review them."

A stranger. Verging on the extraterrestrial. My other

half? "I'd be far less interested in you without those stars," I said, to bring this back to earth. "How did you get them? What did you have that the others lacked?"

He'd worked hard, he said, and he was smart. He wasn't a rebel, and he didn't get into trouble. Very quickly he figured out that the men who earned the others' respect were those who kept quiet. Above all, he *had power and knew it from the beginning*. That's it—the power, stars or no stars.

My masculine other half, a stranger. Is blind passion only possible between strangers? Can the familiar remain strange? It can when it's the enemy. The Greeks had the same word for "stranger" and "enemy": *barbaros*.

We made plans to meet again.

I thought: Oh, no. After all this time, all these layers and accretions of what passed for civilization and sophistication and sense, there she sits, alive and bubbling away inside the person I thought I was: this despicable tiny-minded conformist of the fifties, a regular Girl Scout cookie (who knows, still desperate for the ranch house in suburbia, split-level two-car garage, rotating sprinkler), impressed out of her mind by some tough-guy Rocketman. What can I do about it? I'm as much its plaything as in giving birth, unable to halt the process or control it in any but the most superficial way. How to explain this lunacy, fix up a pose for the outside world, or harder, for myself?

You'd think he might have the same problem, or at least feel guilty. But guilt wasn't something he was used to, having never done anything to feel guilty for. He worked twelve hours a day, he'd done his duty in Vietnam, his duty by his religion, by his kids, by his wife, by his mother (still alive, living with them). And all of it wholehearted. Himself: he ran or jogged for half an hour every day, five miles, wherever he was; hardly drank; of course no smoking, swearing, sugar, salt, those wicked things that start with *s*. Such a proud, immaculate life he'd led that his children desired only to emulate it, even to go to West Point. His children were well and wonderful.

Mine too.

We did not knock on wood. We're still the only ones we know who don't, we said.

Eve, who had just moved out from home, called me during a break at the film college where she was studying, to report that she'd been approached in the street and asked to be a "Page 3 girl," to display her upper half naked in the *Sun*.

"What did you do?" I asked, unable to think of anything ferocious enough for what *I'd* do. But then, who'd ask me?

"Oh, I just said, 'You're going to be *so* disappointed! Can I have the money first?'" What a wonderful girl.

When I told her my news about Dan she commented: "I should really make a Buñuel movie about you. You are getting to be so bourgeois."

Apart, Dan and I got back to writing letters every day. The next time he came he brought me an A-pin, class of '56, acquired with some difficulty, to replace my old one that had been stolen. "Does it mean what it once did?" I asked. "OAO," he said. "Do you remember OAO?" We were walking to my house in the pewtery London twilight, hand in hand: he was twenty, I was eighteen. Nothing had ever happened. We were in step, as always. "I am happy with you," he said. "I have a right to be happy." I thought: the neighbors will see me holding hands with the enemy. At that moment, he let go.

Growing old: that's what he dreaded. He looked the same, felt the same, had never taken a pill in his life but aspirin and vitamins. Every morning he took off running somewhere and returned more dead than alive. Was it fun? Would it make him live forever?

The worst thing about Vietnam—where he'd been a major, an "adviser"—was coming home. Straight from the jungle to Guam to San Francisco in '68 they flew, landing at three in the morning at a far-off end of the airport where the incomers were segregated from the troops going out—and "*Nobody thanked us, nobody even offered us a doughnut and*

a cup of coffee." He referred frequently, bitterly, to the doughnut and the cup of coffee. Otherwise he had never been happier than in Vietnam. He learned he was brave because he
always did what he had to, no matter what.

"How many people did you kill?"

"I shot a lot of bullets." Anyway, "I've never lost any
sleep over it. I've never had a single nightmare about it."

I thought: he's not like other men I've known. Even
though they all in some way reminded me of him, I shared
some identity with them, they never went so far to deny the
feminine in themselves. Besides, the ones who really mattered
made me laugh. But they competed, too: counting, scoring,
mean with their credit. This man's generous. The enemy need
not compete. He's running on a different track.

Dan and I had honeymoons in San Francisco, Boston, Belfast.
On the way to meet him, I'd feel the same explosive fullness I
could only remember before from the West Point bus:
impending, ludicrous happiness on a scale I couldn't imagine.
The intake of breath—catching sight of him each time. First
love again. A healing of this yin and yang I'd ripped apart.
Something you somehow haven't to deserve. And every
minute, I felt like a madwoman.

I told him who I really was, not sure if he was getting it,
but what he didn't understand, he made no move to change.
Somehow he had to assimilate that my friend and hero was
Alger Hiss. That I still thought socialism was a good idea
whatever corruptions the Russians et al. had visited on it; and
that in fact all casual, unfeeling evil resided in the building
where he worked. Even my most disrespectful antisocial attitudes, all quite novel to him, met with a kind of acceptance. I
bludgeoned him with politics, a mixture of anarchic bloody-
mindedness and National Health Service socialism stirred into
what I'd chosen to inherit of my father's Communo-Christian
heritage. He took it. "You are the only woman I've known
with underarm hair," he said. It was an observation. He didn't
realize there was a world of underarm hair out there. He was
due to retire soon. "Why don't we get a camper and wander

around the States for three months?" he said. (This is not a detail person? Camper? Three months? I'd have said "Let's go!") We made love whenever we couldn't think of anything better to do. That was a lot of the time.

My friend Tim sighs: "This saga of the general. Really, it's a cheap novel, a penny-dreadful. All that lust, all that power, all that lust for power."

I don't think it's a cheap novel. I think it's a Nabokovian novel. It's *Laughter in the Dark,* it's *Lolita.* The condition is called "limerance": "a consuming, obsessive love." The love's object is probably always unsuitable, often too young. In our case, we are both pretending to be who we once were all over again. *Much too young.*

The next time Dan came to London, after honeymoons everywhere, he had to speak at a meeting. Something about electromagnetic launcher technology. Say what? He was annoyed to find his audience had not been cleared for secret, which meant he had to skirt around a lot he'd intended to say—particularly hard when answering questions. "How on earth do you remember what you can say and what you can't?" "I'm paid to." He could not, however, remember my address.

This time, he encountered my children. Eve, curious, met us for a meal. She gave him quite a grilling. It came to a head over Dan maintaining that his army training had helped him to overcome his fear of death; he was now immune. Then why, Eve asked, do you jog five miles every day?

Moby was about to leave home too, on a cheap ticket around the world. But he was still there to encounter Dan at breakfast.

There was something peculiar about this one. It so happened that Moby looked like no one else in the family. Who does he take after? people had long since given up asking. Not his father; certainly not me; nobody's ancestors. *He looked like Dan.*

Moby noticed it too. It so happened he was having trouble getting along with Bernardo, and he observed, "Since I have no relationship with my own father, I might as well try Dan." That said, he immediately picked a fight. The subject (although it didn't seem to matter) was an atoll in the Pacific that Dan was using to test his missiles. It so happened that Moby had read about it; he thought Dan had no right to interfere with the lives of the people there. Dan said his men were very good to the people. Moby said he didn't believe it.

"'Once the rocket goes up, who cares where it comes down?'" I said to Dan, but he had never heard of Tom Lehrer. It was surprising what he had never heard of—L.L. Bean, the *New York Review of Books*. You'd think a basic course in American civilization would be useful in the army. But "'It's not my department,' says Werner von Braun."

One day I told Dan that I and people like me in the United States had been allocated places in concentration camps, in case of active East-West hostilities. (I suppose I had earned this honor by going to China when it was against U.S. passport regulations, and presumably because of living in Russia.) I told him that someone I knew had actually wangled, through a pal of his in Washington, a transfer of his name and mine from the list of those headed for the camp in Pennsylvania to the one in Arizona. The sunshine would be nice, my friend reckoned, and we'd be farther from the fighting.

"That's impossible," I expected him to say, but Dan took it in.

By now, about half a year after it had all begun again, his wife knew: she found out I was in Ireland at the same time he was. There were scenes when he went home. "You can't communicate with someone who's yelling," he said later, "because they're on transmit, not receive." Radios in battle had only one antenna, he explained, and couldn't do both. It was time for choices. "I could live in Yurp," said he. As for me, my favorite stance in a triangle is up toward the high moral ground. Here there was no ground, not even a foothold, never mind high, low. It was all another element, another kind of place. But I knew one thing, which hit me one day and wouldn't let go: this man didn't know what freedom was. He'd been so sheltered and structured, his every move and moment spoken for, that in spite of a life spent "defending freedom," he wouldn't recognize the stuff if it was dancing on his eyeballs. He'd never spent a single day outside institutions. For all those decisions he'd made, putting countless lives on the line and costing billions, never once had he got up in the morning wondering how to make his life today. Most people I know have to do that every day. Who was he anyway? How could he know? He might think he wanted me, but he didn't comprehend the choices. I had this idée fixe for him: that he must go off by himself.

What this plan failed to take into account was Dan's greatest fear and horror in life, his equivalent to Winston Smith's rat problem, only now revealed: *living alone.*

Terrible as an army with banners.

Maybe I'm being too hard on him. Considering this short sharp shock of an existence, the people before us and after, the life all over the universe, the hugeness and scariness of Out There, the past (in a place like Yurp) and the future, if any (in a place like the Pentagon), maybe it's all we can do to huddle together fearfully for comfort, conform to the customs of whatever group will give us that, and hope for the best.

It's only natural, after all. Nature's sounds seem mostly to be of groups. The crows cawing at each other in the tree-tops, the mothers bunched together in the garden out my window sharing tales of nappy rash, teaching their babies to flock. A church bell calling another crowd together. All the rituals of "belonging." Who do I think I am? What kind of impossible positions do I require of others? Learning to be alone without being lonely is not that easy. Probably not too many people would do it if they didn't have to. It's like learning to be a foreigner.

On our sixth honeymoon, back in London, I insulted him. It so happened he was humming along off-key with Nat

King Cole. "You're like my father after his stroke. You have
no right hemisphere!"

He didn't care for that. Seriously did not care for it. There
was none of the burlesque that greeted my saucier calumnies:
"Have you no respect for the general?" But the fact was that
we were having trouble filling the gaps between getting out of
bed and going back to bed. Crossword puzzles, walking in all
directions, dining out. Museums. Groping in public. An unde-
niable attraction of the flesh, mine to come together with his:
his texture, a certain tough softness to it. But in between,
some relentlessly humdrum time was going by. And if it
seemed that way to me now, wouldn't it to him soon?

What would I like, ideally? To be curator of the General
Dan Museum? Three months in a camper, then out?
Another Dan entirely? But I am stuck with this Dan, as in
death or taxes. Have you no respect for the general? No.
Yes. I have spent a lifetime denying him in me, but it seems
it doesn't wash, and the tick of a tock a year ago established
that. I think he saw before I did, and that's why he won't or
can't rise to my provocations—why bother? Why add to
whatever ill will there is when nothing can be done about
it? Is this the reason we don't knock on wood—far from
some superior rationality, just a case of terminal fatalism?
His body next to me: it feels right. That's all.

Once upon a time Dan's mother had threatened to inform on
her son as her only remaining way to shake me loose. She
never did it, obviously. Now, however, someone has done it.
Army intelligence has been apprised of the situation. What
they are to make of it is their affair. This Graham Greene-ish
outfit apparently comes out of—and is referred to as—the
"third floor." So squat and low does the Pentagon appear that
you wouldn't imagine it had a third floor. Maybe, as I wrote
to Dan, it's the third from the bottom, which starts a hundred
stories underground, just above hell. Circumspectly and as
usual, he did not reply to this. He never reacted to anything
that might have compromised him—revealing how many
floors underground the Pentagon goes, say. That's all right; in

Moscow, even after Gorbachev, a high official would not tell me how deep the Lubyanka secret police HQ went either. But the very fact that Dan never told me anything (what else could have disturbed them anyway but that I was a security risk?) made the ensuing investigation even sillier. They read our letters, so they knew.

Coming up next was the fiftieth anniversary celebration of the Bronx High School of Science: a dinner dance in Manhattan. For months I'd thought of meeting him there. It would make up for the senior prom. But all this third-floor investigation stuff meant "the lawyers" (his) said we shouldn't see each other.

It was all very last-minute. I was going to New York anyway in the meantime, en route to Mexico again. I called on arrival to say I didn't expect to see him, I accepted that we couldn't meet this time.

"Come to Washington," he said.

"Don't be crazy. It's your life!"

"As I see it, my life is with you."

Long silence. For a moment it crossed my mind that it was all because his wife was out of town and he didn't want to be alone. Oh, for god's sake. "Dan, why not wait until you know where you are?"

"I'm afraid of losing you."

"What are you talking about? This is madness. I'm here." Why is he so insecure? Is he drowning and I'm the raft?

"If they're bugging us, they know everything already. If not, they won't know you came here because I won't tell anybody."

"You think they're so simple-minded? Their resources don't stretch further than that? Do you want to risk everything?"

"Yes."

When I arrived in Washington, the unlikely proposition that Dan really had been faithful to his wife for thirty-three years was nailed down. Here in his home town he hadn't any notion where to go. If you spent your whole time in the Pen-

tagon—or twelve hours out of every twenty-four—sites for
sinning didn't come up. We traipsed around a dozen seedy
motels before finding a room. Then he couldn't think where
to eat, and we ended up near his neighborhood, the only area
he knew, in a place where revolting food came served with
such a blast of noise we couldn't talk. In his dashing little
sports car we drove around next day; he knew one route.
Veering off it, we got lost. If something of a person's character
can be said to come out at the wheel, Dan's was unexpected.
Not the type who snarls or swipes at drivers in his way, he
was fretful, anxious, and given to making mistakes, taking
what even *I* knew to be the wrong road time and again and
unable to undo the consequences for miles, during which he
mumbled and moaned to himself. At least it created rather a
Tour de France for our pursuers, if any.

We finally and accidentally encountered a wonderful har-
bor restaurant serving more exotic fresh fish than I thought
existed. Dan ordered a tuna melt.

We went to his house to pick up his mail. It was the
anonymous house of my dreams, all right: cozy with its
neighbors on a neat pretty middle-class street, each "home"
with its lawn and fruit trees. The perfect setting for Eve's
Buñuel movie. You could say this for the U.S. Army: they
did not corrupt their brass. My reprobate parents lived better than he did.

I waited while he talked on the phone to one of his sons.
We were in a huge family room, full of leisure equipment,
exercise machines, photographs, and accumulations of silly
souvenirs from all their lives. "Take care," I heard Dan sign
off. "Love you."

There is a bonus to growing older that they don't tell you
about, I was thinking: the bonds you make with people after
years together, a certain density to a relationship that gives it
an almost independent life, one that cannot be betrayed or
sloughed off no matter what. This is his. He has a world here.
A family has made this. You could hear them, feel the chaos of
them all together, loving, growing, kids doing homework,
watching TV, being like their father, he and his wife making

something here. I know he once found another dimension to his life in me, but it stayed flat, that one, we never breathed life into it. Nothing to match that simple "Love you" to his son. This is his. It's what he's got.

Back in London weeks later, the third floor called. Two men, very polite, "on the authority of a directive of the Vice Chief of the Army," wanting to know if I could help them; and "do you mind if we record the conversation?"

They had some questions to ask me, they said.

"What are the questions? I'd like to know all the questions first, please." (Too bad I didn't have my own phone bug; I'd have to write quick. The Vice Chief?)

"Well, we can read them to you first."

"Why don't you do that."

The questions ranged from one to six. The first was: Do you know Daniel King? They built up from there.

2. How did you come to know him?

3. How would you characterize your relationship with him?

4. How often do you see him and where?

5. Have you and Daniel King ever been lovers?

6. Have you ever engaged in sexual intercourse with Daniel King?—where, how often, and is the relationship still ongoing?

Whoever had framed this bunch must have meant them to be asked (and answered) in sequence, with number six the one that counted. Number six would never now apply again, either, it seemed certain. I asked if they would send me the questions in writing so that I could get advice. I thought they'd look really terrific on U.S. Army stationery.

They agreed to send them. But in a week they called back. "It has been determined," one of them said (in their unique lingo, never using one word—as in "no"—where seventeen would do), "that it would be inappropriate to offer a written copy of our interrogatory." They wondered, however, whether they could fly over a couple of investigators from Germany to talk to me face to face; would I cooperate? They admitted they had no authority over me, but it would cost something like $2,000 "to conduct this part of the investigation," so they really wanted to make sure I'd cooperate. I said I still wanted something in writing. Well, surely you wrote the questions down, they said, and if not shall we read them to you again? No thank you. I held out for something in writing.

This all felt very unsatisfactory after we'd hung up. I hadn't been ready for them and was standing on one foot, so to speak. After a few minutes I realized it was pointless to beat around bushes, what for? J. Edgar Hoover was dead. And so I called Dan to get their number and then called them back. I said I didn't want to waste their time and money (why not?); with some thought I felt I didn't need a lawyer. As they'd admitted, they had no authority over me, and I just wasn't willing to address those questions. I found them prurient and voyeuristic and revolting. "In fact, I don't actually see how you could even ask them. I can't understand how you can lend yourselves to this business, as people. But I'm not having anything to do with it."

"I respect that, I respect that," one of the men said, sounding nervous. "I just have a job to do."

That was the end of that.

I went without Dan to the Science Gala Dinner Dance. Bonhomie, squeals of recognition, drinks and speeches. All alumni over a certain age whipping their glasses on and off to read each other's badges. Fran wasn't there, but other old friends were; they had made distinguished lives. The band played: *I should care, I should let it upset me. . . .*

I sat gazing at my plate, eyes stinging. Beside me and observing my state was a gray old woman (according to her badge, one class ahead of me). She leaned over and touched my arm. "I understand," she said. "You got certain kindsa memories, right?"

I never told my father that I'd met Dan again. He would have seen it politically, as he saw everything—though with his socialist world disintegrating, nothing political astonished him now. He was too busy hurting. "I'm just the same bit of wreckage I was before," he said when I next came—even then, not yet his time to die—but there was perceptibly less of him. Searching for his old self in who was there now, wrapped in its loose whitish skin barely distinguishable from the sheets, I was reminded of trying to find my cuddly curly-headed baby boy in the great grand man my son has grown to be. The past person, buried in the present one, can be harder to perceive than the carving in the block of marble. My pa was papery, almost transparent, with nothing working but his brain, and even that part-time. "There is something very inefficient about the planning of my interior," he fretted. Too true.

He was lovely in the morning after a night's rest, silly and still singing. "There's life in the old dog yet," he'd say. "Not much, but some." We got "He Is an Englishman" one day, "Brighten the Corner Where You Are" the next. Inspired by the chill of a cucumber the gardener plucked straight from the earth, he burst out with:

> *Down in the cornfield*
> *Hear the mournful sound*
> *All the darkies am a'weepin*
> *Massa's in de col' col' ground.*

Then he laughed and laughed and laughed. Alone.

We never got the same song twice. Once he came up with one I thought I'd never heard, but he said he'd made it up a half century ago to sing when urging upon me an infant formula known as Dextrimaltose Number One—all about if I'm a very good girl and eat this goo, I'd soon rate Dextrimaltose Number *Two*. He sighed. "It was terribly disappointing."

"What was?"

"There *was* no Dextrimaltose Number Two."

Except for physically turning and collating pages, he could work, and spent the mornings on his newest Galeano translation; finding the mot juste for this phrase or that was a great occupier. Life went on around his bed and he heeded it not.

Consulted about anything that didn't directly affect him, "It's not my department," he'd say.

But as the day wore on he'd get increasingly testy and make nonstop demands on Mary, or anyone in earshot. If they were not met he ran to fits of self-pity and tears. He seemed to want to make us all complicit in the self-pity, impossible even if it weren't battling with our opposite need: to honor him. There was no dignity in it. When my mother was dying, up to the minute she lost consciousness she maintained her curious decorum, concerned above all about not imposing, still anxious that we be enjoying ourselves and not too put out by the inconvenience of her illness and death. Also dying, my father couldn't care less who had to do what for him: he was the center of the universe, and that was the end of it. He never used to be like that. Stripped of their complications and contradictions, they had each become their opposites and finally were only what they were—a man, a woman.

"Don't step on me!" he yelled as Mary and I cleaned the repugnant folds of the skin of his bottom.

"I promise I won't step on you," Mary said.

"That's what it feels like. I need freedom. I can't sleep and I can't scratch."

We heaved him back to bed. He was heavy as a piano. "Are those the only options?" I asked.

He nodded.

"Go to sleep," said Mary.

"They won't let me sleep."

"Who won't?"

"They won't."

I sat and read Jane Austen to him; he dozed off. One day, I thought, my father who now sleeps there will be absent from the world. How can I believe it? Gone will be the mind containing everything from insurrectionary fantasies against *his* father (i.e., the government) to the tune of "Dextrimaltose Number One." It's his mind I can't bear to lose. It's not my mother's mind I miss, it's something intangibly there about her which, god knows, is not now.

Unlike her, he was so scared of death. Why? as Nick asked—since he believed it meant "nothing." Unless he feared he was wrong.

But his fear did mean he wanted company, constant mobilizations of family to keep the show on the road. He liked to see us all gathered in from around the globe, his three children (including the wonderful Anne, now a professor of linguistics at the University of Paris) and our children, everyone together singing our favorite calypso, "Linstead Market," while Nick played the guitar. We all knew that nobody would ever care for us the way we cared for him, or keep us going so long past our expiration date. *It isn't death I fear,* I wanted to tell him, *it's this awful kind of half-life of yours: that's why*—I was thinking of the general—*I've been so reckless lately.* If the genetics of the situation were anything to bank on, we had years to go before we died. His mother, my beloved Granny, had lived to eighty-six, when she was burnt to death by an electric blanket. He was now eighty-five.

He stirred and woke. Lying beside him and holding his hand, I observed that his skin now had the same mottled pigmentation as Dr. Du Bois's in his old age.

"How I loved that man," he said. "What a lovely man he was."

"I love you," I said.

"Don't say that!"

"Why not?"

"I can't stand it!"

"But you always taught me to tell the truth."

Mary was digging out a special Robeson record so that Daddy could sort out the verses: "No more auction block. . . no more driver's lash. . . ." Then he said he wanted some ice cream with Kahlua; I fetched some and spooned it in. "I just don't know what I will do without you, baby," he said.

"Oh—something will come along."

"Like what?" He was going back to sleep. I kissed him and he said, "That's perfect."

ACKNOWLEDGMENTS

All of the following played in one way or another an essential role in making this book possible: Eve Arnold, Francis Arnold, Aaron Asher, Harriet Barlow and the Blue Mountain Center, Chana Bloch, Tessa Coombs, Ernie Eban, Nan Fromer, Joanne Grant, Matt Hoffman, Brian Inglis, Joy Johannessen, Richard Kershaw, the MacDowell Colony, Jo Martin, Marshall Perlin, Bernard Pomerance, Eve Pomerance, Moby Pomerance, Victor Rabinowitz, David Rakoff, Andrew Roberts, Cordelia Rowlatt, Rae Shirvington, John J. Simon, Irene Skolnick, Bob and Decca Treuhaft.